Capital Structure in the Modern World

Anton Miglo

Capital Structure in the Modern World

The Fundamentals of Capital Structure Management and Financing Decisions

Second Edition

palgrave
macmillan

Anton Miglo
Toronto School of Finance
Toronto, ON, Canada

ISBN 978-3-031-85458-3 ISBN 978-3-031-85459-0 (eBook)
https://doi.org/10.1007/978-3-031-85459-0

This Palgrave Macmillan imprint is published by the registered company Springer Nature Switzerland AG
The registered company address is: Gewerbestrasse 11, 6330 Cham, Switzerland

To my parents Alla and Viktor, to my son Victor and to my wife Djoulietta.

Preface to Second Edition

The second edition continues the tradition of the first edition and covers both the basic ideas of capital structure management (Part I) and more advanced topics (Part II). The main additions/changes include materials related to some major developments in the finance industry in recent years e.g., FinTech development and to some extent COVID-19 crisis that are associated with major shifts to online technologies and had a profound impact on firm financing opportunities including e.g., crowdfunding and token issues (this will be covered in new Chapter 12). Also the second edition will cover some important recent developments in capital structure theory incl. for example the debates about zero-leverage puzzle and the role of behavioral finance and incomplete contracts (these will be covered in new Chapter 6 and also in some parts of Chapter 5). Further in recent years one can observe a usage of traditional capital structure theory in non-traditional areas incl. for example government financing choices (covered in new Chapter 14). The second edition also has chapter dedicated to security design problem and financing innovations (Chapter 11).

Similarly to the first edition, the book can be used by readers of different levels. It combines theoretical results with a large number of examples, exercises and applications. These have been updated and improved in the second edition. Further note that capital structure theories continue to gain recognition at universities and in the real world. Such professions as investment bankers or corporate treasurers, which require fundamental capital structure education, remain very popular.

I would also like to thank the readers of the first edition of the book. The book has had a good amount of success including a good amount of citations in academic literature. Further, an independent review was published by the Journal of Economics in 2017.[1]

In the preface to the first edition I said that capital structure is a very interesting and probably one of the most controversial areas of finance and that it is the area of permanent "battles" between managers defending their favorite approaches, between theorists and practitioners looking at the same problems under different angles, and between professors and students since the area is very complicated and requires a superior knowledge of econometrics, microeconomics, accounting, mathematics, game theory, etc., and that among the researchers who contributed significantly to capital structure theory, note Nobel Prize Award winners Franco Modigliani, Merton Miller, Joseph Stiglitz, and Jean Tirole. All of the above certainly remains my viewpoint when I'm writing the second edition of the book. Further note that capital structure researchers continue to be among very best—one of the proofs is that Oliver Hart whose works will be particularly discussed in new Chapter 6 (related to capital structure and incomplete contracts) received a Nobel prize in Economics in 2016 as well as Douglas Diamond (contributed to debt overhang as well as debt flexibility ideas and theory) and Philip Dybvig (contributed to capital structure and asymmetric information research) who both received a Nobel prize in 2022. Also note Myron Scholes (received it in 1997) and Ben Bernanke (received it in 2022). Although primarily they are known for other works they both also had some quite influential research in the capital structure area as we discuss in this edition. Further, some of the most important corporate events in the world in the last 10 years (e.g., Trump's legal battles) that are related to firms debt policies/debt valuations problems or to stock evaluations and reorganizations problems (e.g., Microsoft, Facebook, Tesla, etc.) usually are a part of capital structure management and policies or are closely related or depend on them.

[1] Menichini (2017).

The second edition will keep other important ideas of the first edition. For example, the main focus remains on the microeconomic foundations of capital structure theory. Some areas are based on traditional cost-benefit analyses, but most include analyses of different market imperfections, primarily asymmetric information, moral hazard problems and, more recently developed, market imperfections related to incomplete contracts and behavioral finance. Knowledge of game theory and contract theory prior to reading this book is beneficial but we tried to present the material in the most accessible way possible, with lots of examples for readers with different levels of preparation.

Many advanced theories of capital structure discussed in Part 2 are still growing areas of research. At the same time, the objective of the book is not to cover as many topics of capital structure as possible but rather to review the major theoretical concepts and provide basic tools to understand the complicated area of capital structure. As before, for additional readings in the field of capital structure, I recommend "Capital Structure and Corporate Financing Decisions" (Ed. Baker and Martin, 2011) and "Financing Growth in Canada" (Ed. Halpern, 1997) and a review article by Rao, Kumar, Chavan, and Lim (2021). The first two works have a more applied approach to capital structure, including empirical research and econometrics, and cover a lot of interesting topics related to capital structure and financing decisions; the last one provides an excellent review of literature related to small-medium-sized enterprise financing and capital structure problems.

Many of the existing ideas of capital structure were created by "injecting" a new type of market imperfection into different capital structure analyses. From my experience, the comprehension of this fact is crucial to understanding the theory of capital structure. At the beginning of my PhD studies I was spending a lot of time explaining to my advisor why debt financing and equity financing create different degrees of risk for a company. At the time, I was surprised to not see an extremely enthusiastic reaction to my "discoveries" from my PhD advisor who was mostly pointing to the importance of market imperfections in my research. When teaching capital structure in my classes, I am always primarily concerned with how well students understand the difference between perfect and imperfect markets. The challenge for me was to explain the importance of the marginal differences in my model's assumptions. These differences are often responsible for large variations in models' predictions and their capacities to explain existing empirical evidence. It has been a fascinating experience for me to see how much progress students demonstrate in understanding different financial concepts.

This book was inspired by over twenty years of my experience in capital structure research. I was also inspired by my experience with teaching finance courses at different universities in Europe and North America including courses directly related to capital structure such as Financing Strategies and Corporate Governance, Advanced Corporate Finance, Financial Management II, Entrepreneurial Finance and more recently Fundamentals of Crowdfunding and Crowdfunding and Token Issues that I taught at University of Glasgow. It was also inspired by my working experiences in areas of capital structure management including issuing stocks and bonds in commercial banks. The new developments in FinTech which is considered as a major developments in the finance industry in the twenty-first century has also brought a lot of inspiration for people working in capital structure area by creating totally new ways for firms to raise funds.

Toronto, Canada Anton Miglo

Acknowledgments Many thanks to Anna Menichini who wrote a review of the first edition of the book that was published in the Journal of Economics that was greatly inspiring for me in terms of future improvements to the book. I should say that in last couple of years I had a good number of conversations with Anna that were also very helpful and inspiring especially conversation we had regarding crowdfunding. I have also benefited a lot from my conversations with Paul Belleflamme, Jamie Zender, Gilles Chemla, Thomas Hellmann, David de Meza, Thomas Chemmanur, and Armin Schwienbacher regarding many ideas that are part of the second edition. I would also like to thank Tula Weis, the editor from Springer/Macmillan who provided a very high-quality support throughout the initial stages of application, approval and work on the second edition. Also many thanks to anonymous referees.

References

Baker, H., and G. Martin, (Eds.), (2011), *Capital Structure and Corporate Financing Decisions*, Robert W. Kolb Series in Finance. John Wiley and Sons, Inc.

Halpern, P. (Ed.), (1997), *Financing Growth in Canada*, University of Calgary Press.

Menichini, A.M., (2017), Miglo, Anton: Capital structure in the modern world, *Journal of Economics*, Springer, *122*(3), 303–306, November.

Rao, P., Kumar, S., Chavan, M., and W. M. Lim, (2021), A systematic literature review on SME financing: Trends and future directions, *Journal of Small Business Management*, *61*(3), 1247–1277.

Preface to First Edition

Capital structure is a very interesting and probably one of the most controversial areas of finance. It is the area of permanent "battles" between managers defending their favorite approaches, between theorists and practitioners looking at the same problems under different angles, and between professors and students since the area is very complicated and requires a superior knowledge of econometrics, microeconomics, accounting, mathematics, game theory, etc. Many of the results obtained in capital structure theory over the last 50–60 years have been very influential and led their authors to great international recognition. Among the researchers who contributed significantly to capital structure theory, note Nobel Prize Award winners Franco Modigliani, Merton Miller, Joseph Stiglitz, and most recently Jean Tirole. Although not long ago, capital structure theories did not have strong support from practitioners and were too complicated to teach at colleges and business schools, they are quickly gaining recognition at universities and in the real world. This field has become extremely intriguing to potential employees and students. The words investment banker and corporate treasurer, which require fundamental capital structure education, are very popular.

This book focuses on the microeconomic foundations of capital structure theory. Some areas are based on traditional cost-benefit analyses, but most include analyses of different market imperfections, primarily asymmetric information, moral hazard problems and, more recently developed, imperfections involving incomplete contracts. Knowledge of game theory and contract theory prior to reading this book is beneficial but we tried to present the material in the most accessible way possible, with lots of examples for readers with different levels of preparation. For additional readings in the field of capital structure, I recommend "Capital Structure and Corporate Financing Decisions" (Ed. Baker and Martin, 2011) and "Financing Growth in Canada" (Ed. Halpern, 1997). Both of these editions have a more applied approach to capital structure, including empirical research and econometrics, and cover a lot of interesting topics related to capital structure and financing decisions.

This book attempts to explain the basic concepts of capital structure as well as more advanced topics in a consistent fashion. The first part is focused on providing an introduction to the major theories of capital structure: Modigliani and Miller's irrelevance result, trade-off theory, pecking-order theory, asset substitution, credit rationing and debt overhang. I think that the majority of the basic ideas in capital structure complement each other quite logically although significant disagreement between researchers still exists about which theory is more important in practice. Part 2 discusses topics such as capital structure and a firm's performance, capital structure and corporate governance, capital structure of small and start-up companies, corporate financing versus project financing and examples of optimal capital structure analyses for some companies. Many advanced theories of capital structure discussed in part 2 are still growing areas of research. At the same time, the objective of the book is not to cover as many topics of capital structure as possible but rather to review the major theoretical concepts and provide basic tools to understand the complicated area of capital structure.

Many of the existing ideas of capital structure were created by "injecting" a new type of market imperfection into different capital structure analyses. From my experience, the comprehension of this fact is crucial to understanding the theory of capital structure. At the beginning of my PhD studies I was spending a lot of time explaining to my advisor why debt financing and equity financing create different degrees of risk for a company. At the time, I was surprised to not see an extremely enthusiastic reaction to my "discoveries" from my PhD advisor who was mostly pointing to the importance of market imperfections in my research. When teaching capital structure in my classes, I am always primarily concerned with how well students understand the difference between perfect and imperfect markets. The challenge for me was to explain the importance of the marginal differences in my model's assumptions. These differences are often responsible for large variations in models' predictions and their capacities to explain existing empirical evidence. It has been a fascinating experience for me to see how much progress students demonstrate in understanding different financial concepts.

This book was inspired by over twenty years of my experience in capital structure research. I was also inspired by my experience with teaching finance courses at different universities in Europe and North America including courses directly related to capital structure such as Financing Strategies and Corporate Governance, Advanced Corporate Finance, Financial Management II and Entrepreneurial Finance. It was also inspired by my working experiences in areas of capital structure management including issuing stocks and bonds in commercial banks. The financial crisis of 2008 and 2009 provided extra motivation as well. It seemed that many companies faced problems that stemmed from their financing policies. Some discussions in this book are devoted to this topic.

North Bay, Ontoria, Canada Anton Miglo

Acknowledgments For very helpful comments and suggestions regarding some topics I would like to thank Rodrigo González, Finance professor in Pontifi-cia Universidad Católica de Chile. I would also like to thank Di An, Victor Bruzon, Sean Coughlin, Benjamin Dilq, Fei Dio, Julian Dove, Sajal Dutta, Athanasios Gouliaras, Shun Jiang, Jianfeng Lin, Ivana Nesterovic, Sabilla Rafique Le Sheng, Milos Suljagic, Xumei Tan, Shuai Wang, Heran Xing, and Joel Wood, for editorial assistance and comments. Last but not least, I would like to thank Aimee Dibbens, Alexandra Morton and the designer team from Palgrave for their work on the cover design as well as the overall support with the manuscript preparation.

References

Baker, H., and G. Martin, (Eds.), (2011), *Capital Structure and Corporate Financing Decisions*, Robert W. Kolb Series in Finance. John Wiley and Sons, Inc.

Halpern, P. (Ed.), (1997), *Financing Growth in Canada*, University of Calgary Press.

Contents

Part II Advanced Topics

List of Figures

List of Tables

PART I

Basic Capital Structure Ideas

This part covers such topics as Modigliani–Miller proposition, the role of bankruptcy costs and taxes, trade-off theory, the role of asymmetric information, the role of moral hazard as well as the role of behavioral finance and incomplete contracts for capital structure policy. The latter two topics would probably have been considered very advanced even a few years ago but now they are already used in a very significant number of discussions related to capital structure and a very significant number of explanations of the capital structure phenomena.

CHAPTER 1

Introduction

1.1 Capital Structure Problem

Capital structure is a firm's mix of debt and equity. For a long period of time, capital structure was considered a very "technical" area that concerned at most 1–2 employees in an average company. To a traditional businessman, this area was unlikely to generate significant revenue compared to other areas of finance like, for example, correctly chosen investment projects. In recent years, the situation has changed significantly. Capital structure has become an incredibly important and intriguing area of theoretical and practical finance. Here are some examples.

In 2009, former Google CFO Patrick Pichette was asked by James Manyika from McKinsey consulting firm: "On that point, to what extent do considerations about capital structure factor into your thinking?" Mr. Pichette said that capital structure matters a lot. He also connected the problem of capital structure to the degree of business freedom: "If we could predict the strategic flexibility we'll need in such an uncertain environment, we could optimize the balance sheet perfectly. But consider

Supplementary Information The online version contains supplementary material available at https://doi.org/10.1007/978-3-031-85459-0_1.

A. Miglo, *Capital Structure in the Modern World*,
https://doi.org/10.1007/978-3-031-85459-0_1

the constraints: leverage (capital structure!-A. Miglo), dividends, and so on. Then call me the next day and say, "Hey, I need something. I'm inventing *X*." But I can't help—I don't have the flexibility—and end up giving up what could be the most important asset the company needs in order to change over the next ten years. We believe there's an opportunity cost of not having that flexibility…"[1] As we will later learn, Mr. Pichette is talking about the relatively recent flexibility theory of capital structure. Usually it means keeping the amount of debt low.

Conversely, famous fast-food chain McDonald's does not mind using more debt. In July 2007, according to the article entitled "McDonald's reviews capital structure, CFO retiring," McDonald's announced the retirement of CFO Mr. Paull and at the same time announced that they were issuing more debt. They argued that it will help increase the return to shareholders.[2] Just recently, in 2015, McDonald's used a similar strategy.[3] Unlike Google, McDonald's assets structure has a much higher fraction of tangible assets, which, as we will later learn, usually makes debt financing more affordable and meaningful. McDonald's business relies significantly on franchising and a lot of their investments depend on their franchisees. They have a limited ability to raise equity capital and therefore debt financing is a logical choice. Using debt may also be related to the problem of providing additional financial discipline. As we will later learn, this idea is called "debt and discipline" theory.

Recently there has been a growing interest in capital structure of start-up and small companies. Traditionally, it was assumed that most financing comes from entrepreneurs' friends and relatives and the rest possibly from venture capitalists and angel investors. The role of banks and external debt financing was not important. In the last 10–15 years some research argues however that small firms that use external debt perform better than those who do not. Kauffman Foundation, dedicated to entrepreneurial research and support, in a publication entitled "The Capital Structure Decisions of New Firms," suggests that contrary to widely held beliefs that startup companies rely heavily on funding from family and friends, outside debt (financing through credit cards, credit lines, bank loans, etc.) is the most

[1] Manyika (August, 2011).

[2] Groom (July 24, 2007).

[3] Gandel (December 4, 2015).

important type of financing for new firms, followed closely by the owner's equity. These two sources accounted for about 75% of startup capital.[4]

What are other reasons that capital structure is a "hot" area in finance? First, a series of surveys conducted among financial executives revealed that a very significant gap exists between the theory and practice of capital structure. In one of the most notable works in corporate finance Graham and Harvey (2001) wrote:

> In summary, executives use the mainline techniques that business schools have taught for years, NPV and CAPM,[5] to value projects and to estimate the cost of equity. Interestingly, financial executives are much less likely to follow the academically proscribed factors and theories when determining capital structure. This last finding raises possibilities that require additional thought and research. Perhaps the relatively weak support for many capital structure theories indicates that it is time to critically reevaluate the assumptions and implications of these mainline theories. Alternatively, perhaps the theories are valid descriptions of what firms should do - but many corporations ignore the theoretical advice. One explanation for this last possibility is that business schools might be better at teaching capital budgeting and the cost of capital than teaching capital structure. Moreover, perhaps the NPV and CAPM are more widely understood than capital structure theories because they make more precise predictions and have been accepted as mainstream views for longer. Additional research is needed to investigate these issues.[6]

Second, researchers have very different opinions.[7] For example, Frank and Goyal (2008, 2009) and Singh and Kumar (2008) lean toward the trade-off theory as being the driving force of capital structure decisions while Shyam-Sunder and Myers (1999), Bulan and Yan (2009, 2011), Lemmon and Zender (2010) and Jarallah et al. (2019) lean towards the pecking-order theory. Graham and Leary (2011) discuss whether the

[4] The Capital Structure Decisions of New Firms, Kauffman Foundation (2009). http://www.kauffman.org/what-we-do/research/kauffman-firm-survey-series/the-capital-structure-decisions-of-new-firms

[5] Net-present value and capital-asset pricing model.

[6] For other surveys see Graham and Harvey (2002), Bancel and Mittoo (2004, 2011) and Brounen et al. (2006).

[7] For a review of capital structure theory see, for example, Harris and Raviv (1991), Klein (2002), Miglo (2011) and Khanna Srivastava and Medury (2014).

main problem in the field is the lack of compelling theories or difficulties with empirical estimations of facts related to capital structure including problems with exact measurements of capital structure! They also suggest that the areas where interesting results are expected include, among others, the supply side of capital, connections between capital structure and labour contracts, financial contracting, dynamic trade-off theory and capital structure speed of adjustments.

Third, asymmetric information and moral hazard problems between investors and issuers of various securities played an important role in the financial crisis of 2008 and 2009. As we will discuss in the book, some researchers link this fact to capital structure problems. Hence, works like Hennessy et al. (2010) and Acharya and Viswanathan (2011) perhaps represent examples of new research related to asymmetric information and moral hazard aspects of capital structure required in this field.

1.2 The Concept of Perfect Market and Some Stylized Facts

The perfect market is a theoretical concept that assumes a world with no asymmetric information, no moral hazard, no bankruptcy costs, etc. This concept predicts the following outcomes:

1. Capital structure does not matter (Modigliani & Miller, 1958).
2. Prices of securities are equal to the expected value of future earnings.
3. Investment and capital structure decisions are independent (Fisher separation theorem, 1930) and all investment projects with positive NPV should be undertaken.

In the real world, we find empirical evidence that contradicts the predictions of a perfect market. For example, empirical evidence supports the following:

1. Capital structure does matter.
2. Newly issued shares are underpriced.
3. Firms with positive NPV projects may have different levels of access to credit.

Table 1.1 shows the average capital structure (debt to assets ratio) of firms in different industries in the United States. One can observe that capital structure does matter as firms with large amounts of tangible assets (Trucking, Automotive, Air Transport, Water Utility) tend to be financed with more debt than firms with large amount of intangible assets (Computer Software, Internet, Educational Services, and Drugs). The reasons behind this will be further covered in Chapter 2 in the trade-off theory.

Table 1.2 shows that prices of newly issued shares during IPOs (initial public offerings) are below their market values. This creates a puzzle. If the market prices correctly reflect the expected value of future earnings why do firms leave money on the table? The latter is not consistent with firm value-maximizing behavior. Also, prices that do not correctly reflect the expected values of their earnings is not consistent with the price efficiency prediction of the perfect market. There are many reasons for this observation, which will be covered later in the book.

The pattern presented in Table 1.2 holds not only for US firms but international firms as well (Table 1.3).

Table 1.1 Debt ratios for selected industries

Industry	*Market value based debt ratio (%)*	*Book value based debt ratio (%)*
Air Transport	37.14	68.51
Automotive	50.84	56.57
Computer Software	6.15	20.51
Drug	12.89	31.03
Educational Services	19.83	29.27
Electronics	18.34	29.89
Internet	2.24	10.73
Power	62.04	57.29
Steel	35.98	33.21
Trucking	29.74	56.51
Water Utility	42.26	59.35

Source of data Damodaran Online, http://people.stern.nyu.edu/ADAMODAR/New_Home_Page/datafile/dbtfund.htm[8]

[8] Many other sources of data usually confirm the link between the degree of asset tangibility and capital structure. See Chapter 2 for more details.

Table 1.2 Average initial IPO returns

Aggregate year	*Aggregate number of IPO's*	*Gross proceeds (millions)*	*Average first day return*
1960–1969	2661	$7988	21.2
1970–1979	1536	$6663	7.1
1980–1989	2375	$60,380	6.9
1990–1999	4205	$296,693	21.0
2000–2013	1790	$402,306	22.3

Sources of data Ritter (2014), https://site.warrington.ufl.edu/ritter/files/2015/04/IPOs2013Underpricing.pdf[9]

Table 1.3 Average initial IPO returns in selected countries

Country	*Time period*	*Average first day return (%)*
Australia	1976–2011	21.8
Brazil	1979–2011	33.1
Canada	1971–2013	6.5
China	1990–2014	113.5
France	1983–2010	10.5
Germany	1978–2014	23.0
India	1990–2014	88.0
United Kingdom	1959–2012	16.0

Sources of data Loughran et al. (1994, updated 2015) https://site.warrington.ufl.edu/ritter/files/2015/12/Int.pdf

Table 1.4 demonstrates that firms that issue equity underperform, *ceteris paribus* (same risk, size, etc.), comparable firms in their industries in the long term. If, as the perfect market concept predicts, capital structure does not matter, a systematic relationship between firms' capital structures and their operating performances should not exist.

From Table 1.5, one can observe that smaller firms do not have the same access to debt as larger firms. This is another piece of evidence that cannot be easily explained using the perfect market concept.

[9] Other sources of data also confirm that there are systematic differences between prices of newly issued securities and their market prices. It includes among others seasoned equity offerings. More discussions will be provided in Chapters 3 and 7.

Table 1.4 Average long run operating underperformance of firms that issue equity

Sample	*Time period*	*Median industry-adjusted operating return on assets change from year before IPO to 3 years after IPO (%)*	*Median Industry-adjusted cash flow to assets ratio from year before IPO to 3 years after IPO (%)*
682 US IPOs	1976–1988	–6.8	–4.72
555 IPOs by European firms	1995–2006	–3.44	–2.87

Sources of data Jain and Kini (1994) and Pereira and Sousa (2017)

Table 1.5 Firms' access to debt

Size	*Percentage of firms that never had access to long-term debt (%)*
Smallest	50
Small	43.5
Large	26.5
Largest	9.1

Source Schiantarelli and Jaramillo (2002, Table 7, SC1 sample)

The perfect market model is an interesting starting point for capital structure analysis. Realistically, however, only imperfect markets exist. This book will investigate in depth the difference between perfect and imperfect market models and the difference between the predictions of perfect market and imperfect market models.

1.3 Capital Structure Choice Analysis: The Beginnings…

This section considers a hypothetical start-up firm that is about to make its first capital structure decision. Some relevant concepts from other disciplines will also be considered such as law, accounting, and microeconomics.

A firm's initial capital consists of $10 cash that was invested by the firm's founder who owns 1 share of stock, which currently means 100%

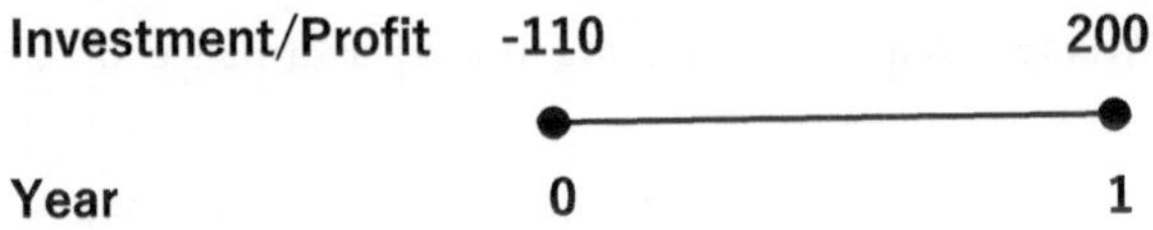

Fig. 1.1 A project's timeline

of the company's ownership. The firm has a project available. The project is an expenditure that will generate future cash flows. It can be illustrated using a timeline that indicates investments and revenues at different points in time (Fig. 1.1).

The project costs \$110. This amount represents investments in fixed assets that will fully depreciate during the project. Aside from depreciation there are no other costs involved. The project will generate sales in the amount of \$200 at the end of the year (throughout the text, if a currency is not indicated then it is irrelevant). The firm has to find \$100 to finance the difference between the total cost of the investment and the amount of cash currently available. It has a choice of two strategies: borrowing at an interest rate of 10% or issuing shares (10 shares of \$10 each).[10]

1. Under the first strategy, the following sequence of events occurs: borrowing, investment, sales, payment to debtholders, and distribution to shareholders. These events will be recorded using balance sheets and income statements (recall that a balance sheet shows a firm's assets (A) and liabilities/capital (LC) at a given moment in time and an income statement shows earnings/expenses for a given period of time).[11] It is illustrated in Fig. 1.2.

The above income statement shows the firm's earnings between the initial issue of shares (prior to undertaking the project) and the project's completion. Subtracting Amortization from the Sales, we get the earnings, which are \$90. Then we subtract interest, which equals \$10, and we are left with \$80 net earnings that are distributed as dividends to shareholders.

[10] These two strategies (also called debt and equity) are two most important types of financing strategies for a firm. In fact, for long period of time, all other strategies could be seen as a type of either debt or equity. Only in the twenty-first century, new forms of financing were created that can not be classified as either one of these (e.g., reward-based crowdfunding). These will be discussed later.

[11] For a review of accounting principles see, for example, Wild et al. (2014).

Initial situation

A	LC
Cash 10	Capital 10

Borrowing

A	LC
Cash 110	Loan 100
	Capital 10

Investment

A	LC
Fixed Assets 110	Loan 100
	Capital 10

Sales

A	LC
Cash 200	Loan 100
	Capital (initial 10 plus earnings 90) 100

Payment to debtholders

A	LC
Cash 90	Loan 0
	Capital 90

Distribution to shareholders

A	LC
0	0

Income statement

Sales	200
Amortization	110
Earnings	90
Interest	10
Net Earnings	80
Dividends	80
Retained Earnings	0

Fig. 1.2 Balance sheet changes and final income statement under debt financing

2. When firms use equity to finance projects, the following sequence of events occurs: issuing shares, investment, sales, and distribution to shareholders (Fig. 1.3).

Initial situation

A	LC
Cash 10	Capital 10

Issuing shares

A	LC
Cash 110	Capital 110

Investments

A	LC
Fixed Assets 110	Capital 110

Sales

A	LC
Cash 200	Capital 200 (initial 10 plus issue 100 plus earnings 90)

Distribution to shareholders

A	LC
0	0

Income statement

Sales	200
Amortization	110
Earnings	90
Net earnings	90
Dividends	90
Retained Earnings	0

Fig. 1.3 Balance sheet changes and final income statement under equity financing

The new income statement looks similar to the previous one—the only difference being the absence of interest payments since the firm used equity instead of debt to finance the project. The new amount of shares outstanding (often shown under the balance sheet) equals $1 + 10 = 11$. One can also calculate the fraction of shares belonging to the firm's founder after the issue of new shares: it equals $1/11$.

Looking at the results of the two strategies described above, which one should be chosen? Under strategy 1, the shareholders will receive 100. Under strategy 2, the shareholders will receive 200 but it must be split between the founders and new shareholders. This is an example of a capital structure choice problem that will be analyzed in this book. In reality, the problems are more complicated. For example, how does the uncertainty about sales affect the decision? If there aren't enough sales to cover the loan under strategy 1, what is going to happen? What is the value of the founder's shares under strategy 1, etc....?

The spectrum of potential capital structure strategies depends on the organizational structure of the firm. Consider the different organizational structures: sole proprietorship, partnership, and corporation. Sole proprietorships and partnerships cannot issue shares publicly so their choices are limited to the founder's own resources and raised debt, which is a challenge in many cases. Corporations typically have a larger spectrum of potential strategies including public issues of stocks and bonds.

The issue of potential bankruptcy, a situation when sales are not sufficient to cover the firm's debt, is directly related to a firm's capital structure. Let D denote the face value of debt that has to be paid by the firm and let V denote the firm's value. If $V \geq D$, the firm will use the available cash, or sell its assets, to pay the debt and avoid bankruptcy. What happens when $V < D$? Firms can be divided into two large groups depending on the scenario at hand: firms with unlimited liability (usually includes sole proprietorship and partnerships), where owners are not protected, and may have to resort to selling their own assets to repay a debt, and firms with limited liability (includes corporations and some types of partnerships) where owners' assets are protected.

There also exists literature about the advantages and disadvantages of different organizational structures, about corporations being subject to "double taxation," and how it is related to limited liability (see, for example, Ewert and Niemann (2012), Horvath and Woywode (2005), Miglo (2007) and Lindhe et al. (2004)).

Recall that one of the major features of corporations is that shareholders have limited liability. This feature will frequently be used in the book to demonstrate the patterns of payments of different claimholders in different scenarios.

In Fig. 1.4, the solid line represents the creditors' payoffs and the dotted line is the firm's managers' payoffs. The x-axis represents the amount of available resources[12] and the y-axis represents debt payments. The original creditors have seniority and are entitled to payment up to the value of the principal and interest (equal to 5 in Figs. 1.4 and 1.5). So if the amount of available resources is less than5, they belong to creditors. However, if the firm's revenue is greater than5, the creditors will receive 5 and the firm's shareholders will receive the rest. In the case of unlimited liability, the firm's owners are mandated to pay creditors out of their own pockets. This is illustrated in Fig. 1.5.

Assuming that the owners' personal assets are sufficiently large, then under unlimited liability the creditors will still be repaid fully regardless of the firm's resources. Net profit of the owners will be negative in case the firm's resources are less than 5 and they will have to sell a part of their own assets in order to repay the debt.

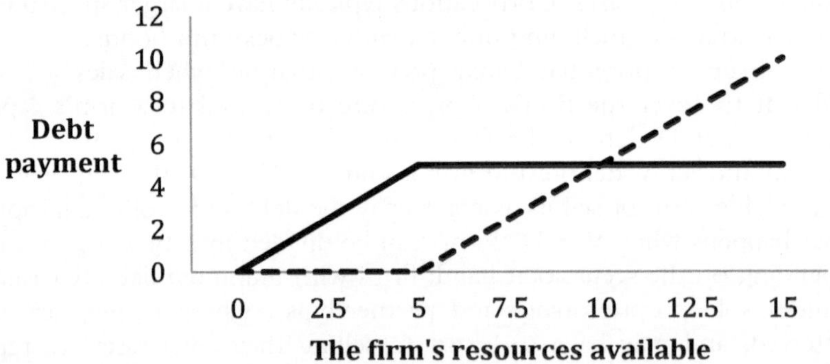

Fig. 1.4 Debt payments under limited liability

[12] The amount of available resources depends on specific debt contract. In most cases the payment of debt requires cash. However, the firm always has an opportunity to sell its assets. So in most cases the amount of available resources is equal to the firm value as long it is expressed in market values.

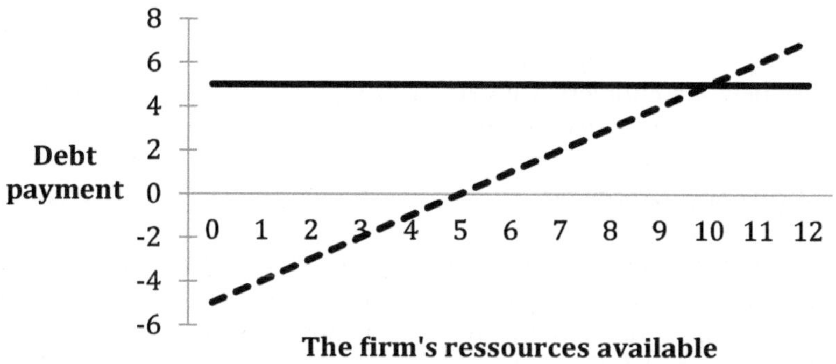

Fig. 1.5 Debt payments under unlimited liability

As we have seen, interest on debt is paid prior to dividends on shares. There are other differences between debt and equity that further complicate capital structure decisions. They are summarized below:

Debt

- No ownership interest
- Creditors do not have voting rights
- Interest is considered a cost of doing business and is tax deductible
- Creditors have legal recourse if interest or principal payments are missed
- Excess debt can lead to financial distress and bankruptcy

Equity

- Ownership interest
- Common stockholders vote for the board of directors and other issues
- Dividends are not considered a cost of doing business and are not tax deductible
- Dividends are not a liability of the firm and stockholders have no legal recourse if dividends are not paid
- An all-equity firm cannot go bankrupt

In our example above, the founders may take into account that in case of equity financing their control over the company will be reduced because new shareholders will get voting rights. Financing with debt may bring tax advantage since interests are tax-deductible, etc.

Questions and Exercises

Throughout the book we have four types of questions: "multiple choice," "true–false," "problems," or "mix." For multiple choice questions, choose a letter corresponding to your answer. For true–false questions, the answer is "TRUE" if you agree with the sentence and "FALSE" otherwise. A sentence without options for answers usually represents a true–false question like question 1 below. Problems usually require a complete solution.

1. A project is a firm's obligation to pay a fixed amount of money to its creditors.
2. Payments are usually promised and fixed for:

    a) Stocks
    b) Bonds

3. The following is not considered one of the differences between a corporation and a general partnership:

    a) Limited liability rule
    b) Taxation
    c) Collective form of business
    d) Lifetime

4. All participants in large business organizations have limited liability.
5. Unlimited liability and small opportunities for external financing are the disadvantages of a sole proprietorship.
6. X-tutoring is a sole proprietorship owned by Bill. What would likely happen if the firm's value was $20,000, the firm's current debt $50,000 and Bill's personal wealh $100,000?
7. A corporation's inability to pay off its creditors will usually result in the sale of personal assets by a major shareholder.
8. The following is not one of the differences between debt and equity.

a) Debtholders have legal recourse if interest or principal payments are missed
b) Debtholders do not have voting rights
c) Equity is publicly traded
d) Interest on debt is considered a cost of doing business and is tax deductible

9. List out facts that seem to contradict a perfect market concept of capital structure. Explain.
10. Financial flexibility is an important factor for Google when choosing its capital structure.
11. McDonalds does not rely on debt financing.
12. Suppose that currently ABC has $600,000,000 debt and $200,000,000 own capital. The estimated construction cost of a new plant is $100,000,000 and ABC will have to take a bank loan to cover the construction cost. How does the balance sheet of ABC look like initially? What is its debt/equity ratio? Show the company balance sheet after opening the new plant. What can change in ABC profit calculations compared to previous questions?
13. A newly created firm created by an entrepreneur (who owns 5 shares of stock, which currently means 100% of the company's ownership) has no initial capital and plans to raise external funds to finance its project. The project costs $100. This amount represents investments in assets that will fully depreciate during the project. The project will generate sales in the amount of $150 at the end of the year. The firm has a choice of two strategies: a loan at an interest rate of 5% or equity (20 shares of $5).

a) Under the first strategy, the following sequence of events occurs: borrowing, investment, sales, payment to debtholders, and distribution to shareholders. These events will be recorded using balance sheets and income statements. Provide these recordings.
b) When the firms uses equity, the following sequence of events occurs: issuing shares, investment, sales, distribution to shareholders. Again describe the firm balance sheet and income statement and also the fraction of shares belonging to the firm's founder after the issue of new shares.

c) Looking at the results of the two strategies described above, which one should be chosen? Assume that the firm maximizes its founder's expected earnings.

14. Project.

Choose a firm on Yahoo!Finance. You can find financial statement information on the company on Yahoo! Finance (usually by finding the item "Financials" in the menu on the company Yahoo!Finance webpage). In addition, if you choose to, you can obtain additional information, either from the company itself or from other websites.

The report should answer the following questions:

What is the total amount of the firm's capital (book value)? What is the market value of the shareholders' capital? Hint: find the number of shares outstanding and multiply it by the current share price.

What is the total amount of the firm's liabilities? What is the total amount of liabilities excluding current liabilities? How (if at all) does the firm borrow money? What are the characteristics of the debt? (maturity, coupon, or stated interest rate, etc.)

A bonus question. Find information about any derivative securities issued by the firm including warrants, convertible bonds, etc.

References

Acharya, V., & Viswanathan, S. (2011). Leverage, Moral Hazard and Liquidity. *Journal of Finance, 66*, 99–138.

Bancel, F., & Mittoo, U. (2004). Cross-Country Determinants of Capital Structure Choice: A Survey of European Firms. *Financial Management, 33*, 103–132.

Bancel, F., & Mittoo, U. (2011). Survey Evidence on Financing Decisions and Cost of Capital. In H. K. Baker & G. Martin (Eds.), *Capital Structure and Corporate Financing Decisions—Theory, Evidence, and Practice* (pp. 229–248). John Wiley.

Brounen, D., De Jong, A., & Koedijk, K. (2006). Capital Structure Policies in Europe: Survey Evidence. *Journal of Banking & Finance, 30*(5), 1409–1442.

Bulan, L., & Yan, Z. (2009). The Pecking Order Theory and the Firm's Life Cycle. *Banking and Finance Letters, 1*(3), 129–140.

Bulan, L., & Yan, Z. (2011). Firm Maturity and the Pecking Order Theory. *International Journal of Business and Economics, 9*(3), 179–200.

Ewert, R., & Niemann, R. (2012). Limited Liability, Asymmetric Taxation, and Risk Taking—Why Partial Tax Neutralities can be Harmful. *Finanzarchiv/public Finance Analysis, 68*, 83–120.

Fisher, I. (1930). *The Theory of Interest* (1st ed.). The Macmillan Co.

Frank, M., & Goyal, V. (2008). Profits and Capital Structure, AFA 2009 San Francisco Meetings Paper. http://ssrn.com/abstract=1104886.

Frank, M., & Goyal, V. (2009). Capital Structure Decisions: Which Factors Are Reliably Important? *Financial Management, 38*, 1–37.

Gandel, S. (2015, December 4). McDonald's Jumbo Bond Deal Finds Hungry Investors. *Fortune*. http://fortune.com/2015/12/04/mcdonalds-bond-deal/

Graham, J., & Harvey, C. (2001). The Theory and Practice of Corporate Finance: Evidence from the Field. *Journal of Financial Economics, 60*(2–3), 187–243.

Graham, J., & Harvey, C. (2002). How Do CFOs Make Capital Budgeting and Capital Structure Decisions? *Journal of Applied Corporate Finance, 15*(1), 8–23.

Graham, J., & Leary, M. (2011). A Review of Empirical Capital Structure Research and Directions for the Future. *Annual Review of Financial Economics, 3*, 309–345.

Groom, N. (2007, July 24). McDonald's Reviews Capital Structure, CFO retiring. *Reuters/Markets*. http://www.reuters.com/article/2007/07/24/us-mcdonalds-results-idUSN2442330320070724

Harris, M., & Raviv, A. (1991). The Theory of Capital Structure. *The Journal of Finance, 46*(1), 297–355.

Hennessy, C., Livdan, D., & Miranda, B. (2010). Repeated Signaling and Firm Dynamics. *Review of Financial Studies, 23*(5), 1981–2023.

Horvath, M., & Woywode, M. (2005). Entrepreneurs and the Choice of Limited Liability. *Journal of Institutional and Theoretical Economics (JITE)/Zeitschrift für die gesamte Staatswissenschaft, 161*(4), 681–707.

Jain, B., & Kini, O. (1994). The Post-Issue Operating Performance of IPO Firms. *Journal of Finance, 49*(5), 1699–1726.

Jarallah, S., Saleh, A., & Salim, R. (2019). Examining Pecking Order versus Trade-off Theories of Capital Structure: New Evidence from Japanese Firms. *International Journal of Finance and Economics, 24*(1), 204–211.

Khanna, S., Srivastava, A., & Medury, Y. (2014). Revisiting the Capital Structure Theories with Special Reference to India. *The International Journal of Business and Management, 8*, 132–138.

Klein, L., O'Brien, T., & Peters, S. (2002). Debt. *The Financial Review, 37*(3), 317–350.

Lemmon, M., & Zender, J. (2010). Debt Capacity and Tests of Capital Structure Theories. *Journal of Financial and Quantitative Analysis, 45*, 1161–1187.

Lindhe, T., Sodersten, J., & Oberg, A. (2004). Economic Effects of Taxing Different Organizational Forms under a Dual Income Tax. *International Tax and Public Finance*, 469–485.

Loughran, T., Ritter, J., & Rydquist, K. (1994). Initial Public Offerings: International Insights. *Pacific-Basin Finance Journal, 2*, 165–199.

Manyika, J. (August, 2011). *Google's CFO on Growth, Capital Structure, and Leadership*. McKinsey&Company, http://www.mckinsey.com/insights/corporate_finance/googles_cfo_on_growth_capital_structure_and_leadership.

Miglo, A. (2007). A Note on Corporate Taxation, Limited Liability and Asymmetric Information. *Journal of Economics (Springer), 92*(1), 11–19.

Miglo, A. (2011). Trade-Off, Pecking Order, Signaling, and Market Timing Models. In H. K. Baker,& G. S. Martin (Eds.), *Capital Structure and Corporate Financing Decisions: Theory, Evidence, and Practice* (pp. 171–191). Wiley and Sons.

Modigliani, F., & Miller, M. (1958). The Cost of Capital, Corporation Finance and the Theory of Investment. *American Economic Review, 48*(3), 261–297.

Pereira, T., & Sousa, M. (2017). Is There Still a Berlin Wall in the Post-Issue Operating Performance of European IPOs? *International Journal of Finance and Economics, 22*(2), 139–158.

Ritter, J. (2014). Initial Public Offerings: Updated Statistics. https://site.warrington.ufl.edu/ritter/files/2015/04/IPOs2013Underpricing.pdf

Schiantarelli, F., & Jaramillo, F. (2002). Access to Long Term Debt and Effects on Firms' Performance: Lessons from Ecuador No 3153, RES Working Papers from Inter-American Development Bank, Research Department.

Singh, P., & Kumar, B. (2008). Trade Off Theory or Pecking Order Theory: What Explains the Behavior of the Indian Firms? http://ssrn.com/abstract=1263226

Shyam-Sunder, L., & Myers, S. (1999). Testing Static Tradeoff against Pecking Order Models of Capital Structure. *Journal of Financial Economics, 51*(2), 219–244.

Wild, J., Shaw, K., & Chiappetta, B. (2014). *Fundamental Accounting Principles*. McGraw-Hill Education.

CHAPTER 2

Modigliani–Miller Proposition and Trade-off Theory

2.1 Three Ideas

This chapter considers the three basic ideas of capital structure. The capital structure irrelevance idea, the debt tax shield and the link between expected bankruptcy costs and optimal capital structure. All of these ideas attempt to provide an answer to the following question: can the firm increase its value by changing its capital structure? Each idea provides a different answer, which makes capital structure a complicated yet exciting topic at the same time.

The debt tax shield idea provides an interesting and powerful tool to businessmen around the world: by increasing the amount of debt, the firm creates a tax shield that can increase its value. Until recently it was not uncommon to think (especially in academic literature) that the debt tax shield, although theoretically important, does not seem to have any significant importance in capital structure decisions in practice. The situation is now changing. Faulkender and Smith (2016), for example, discuss tax strategies of international companies. It is mentioned that multinational groups are using significantly higher debt in high-tax jurisdictions,

Supplementary Information The online version contains supplementary material available at https://doi.org/10.1007/978-3-031-85459-0_2.

A. Miglo, *Capital Structure in the Modern World*,
https://doi.org/10.1007/978-3-031-85459-0_2

which is consistent with the tax shield idea, as we will see later in the chapter.[1]

The bankruptcy cost idea points out that increasing debt in a firm's capital structure increases its probability of bankruptcy. Since bankruptcy is a very costly process, the incentive to increase debt should depend on potential future bankruptcy costs. An interesting example represents the situation in the oil and drilling industry in the United States in 2014/2015. Oil prices fell quickly in the middle of 2014, weakening the futures of many companies in the industry. Gara (2015) described the situation in the industry and noticed that"...junk bond markets [were] decisively closed to the drilling industry and stock prices [were] trading at levels that [made] equity offerings extremely dilutive."[2] This is a classic example of indirect bankruptcy costs that, as we will see later, reduce the incentive for firms to issue debt. Even if a firm is not bankrupt, the market anticipates financial difficulties, which results in decreased credit conditions, reduced share price, loss of customers, etc.

Williams (1938) noticed that if a single individual or institutional investor owned all the bonds, stocks, and warrants issued by a corporation, it would not matter to this investor what the company's capitalization was. Modigliani and Miller (1958) further developed this idea, for which they won the 1985 Nobel Prize in economics, by proving the Modigliani–Miller (MM) theorem which states that when markets are perfect (no taxes and no bankruptcy costs among other things), the capital structure does not have any impact on the value of the firm. For example, a firm financed with 60% equity and 40% debt has the same value as a firm financed with 30% equity and 70% debt. The idea behind the MM theorem is that capital structure does not alter the total cash flows produced by a firm's assets (such as equipment, buildings, technology, patents, etc.) or their riskiness and that financial securities can only redistribute value and not create it.

[1] See also Loney (2015).

[2] Gara (November 25, 2015).

2.2 Modigliani–Miller Theorem

Assumptions underlying the MM (perfect market assumptions) analysis are as follows:

1. Perfect competition and minimal transaction costs
2. No asymmetric information among investors
3. No taxes
4. No bankruptcy costs
5. Contracts are easily enforced
6. No arbitrage opportunities.[3]

Proposition 2.1 ***(Modigliani–Miller Proposition)*** *Under the above assumptions, firms cannot increase their value by changing their capital structure. The value of the firm is independent of the debt ratio.*

Proof Suppose there are two identical firms with identical assets. The only difference between them is their capital structure. One firm is unlevered or completely equity financed (firm U) and the other one has a mix of debt and equity (firm L). Both firms produce the same earnings X. We will prove MM by contradiction assuming that the firms' values are different. Two cases will be analyzed: Case 1, where the value of the unlevered firm is greater than the value of the levered firm, and Case 2, where the value of the levered firm is greater than the value of the unlevered firm.

Case 1: The value of the unlevered firm is greater than the value of the levered firm. $V_u > V_L$. Figure 2.1 shows the balance sheets of firms U and L using notations introduced in Chapter 1. Consider an investor that holds a fraction α of firm U's shares. What is his optimal strategy? Should he keep the original fraction of shares or sell them and purchase a fraction of the shares of the levered firm?

Note that although X is risky (i.e., X is a random variable) debt is assumed to be risk-free and the risk-free interest rate equals r. In addition, the credit market is frictionless, by assumption, and investors and firms can borrow funds and invest them in bonds using the same interest rate. Later an extension with risky debt will be considered.

[3] An arbitrage opportunity is a situation where an investor is able to make a profit by simply selling and buying securities without incurring any additional investment cost.

Firm L

A	LC
V_L	Debt D
	Equity E_L

Firm U

A	LC		
V_U	Debt 0		
	Equity E_U	αE_U	Belongs to investor
		$(1-\alpha)E_U$	Belongs to other investors

Fig. 2.1 Balance sheets of firms U and L

Consider the following strategy for this investor: sell the shares for αE_U (note that since firm U does not have any debt, $E_U = V_U$), buy a fraction $\frac{\alpha V_U}{V_L}$ of company L's shares and buy a fraction $\frac{\alpha V_U}{V_L}$ of company L/s bonds. This strategy requires a net investment equal to $\alpha V_U - \frac{\alpha V_U}{V_L} E_L - \frac{\alpha V_U}{V_L} D$. Since $V_L = D + E_L$ the investment has zero cost. It also offers earnings from firm L/s shares and interest on firm L's bonds that equal in total $\frac{\alpha V_U}{V_L}(X - Dr) + \frac{\alpha V_U}{V_L} Dr = \frac{\alpha V_U}{V_L} X$. This is greater than αX (the investor's expected earnings in case of keeping firm U's shares) because by assumption $V_U > V_L$. Therefore, there is an arbitrage opportunity. Thus, the assumption that $V_U > V_L$ leads to a contradiction.

Case 2: The value of the levered firm is greater than the value of the unlevered firm. Let $V_U < V_L$. Consider an investor holding a fraction α of firm L's shares. This investor can either choose to keep the fraction of the levered firm's shares or sell them and buy the unlevered firm's shares.

Consider the following strategy: sell the shares for αV_L, borrow αD, buy a fraction $\alpha V_L / V_U$ of company U/s shares. This strategy requires a net investment equal to $\alpha(V_L - D) + \alpha D - \frac{\alpha V_L}{V_U} V_U = 0$. It also offers earnings equal to $\frac{\alpha V_L}{V_U} X - \alpha Dr = \alpha[X\frac{V_L}{V_U} - rD]$. This is greater than $\alpha[X - rD]$ (the investor's expected earnings in case of keeping firm L's shares) because by assumption $V_L > V_U$. Therefore, there is an arbitrage opportunity. Thus, the assumption that $V_L > V_U$ leads to a contradiction.

We have shown that any situation where $V_L \neq V_U$ leads to a contradiction. One can also show that if $V_L = V_U$ then any strategy with zero investment cost does not produce extra profit. Examples would be the two situations described above. In either case, if $V_L = V_U$, an investor using the strategies described above will not increase profits. The irrelevance of capital structure is the result of the investor's ability to undo any effects of the differences in the firms' capital structures when operating in a perfect financial market.

The following is a summary of the main ideas behind MM:

- If the shares of levered firms are priced too high, investors will borrow on their own and use the money to buy shares in unlevered firms. This is sometimes called homemade leverage.
- If the shares of unlevered firms are priced too high, investors will buy shares in levered firms and buy bonds.
- In order for capital structure to matter, there must be some market imperfections that create friction in the process of either selling or buying securities.

Example 2.1 Suppose two firms have the same assets that generate the same annual earnings and differ only in how they are financed: Firm U is unlevered ($V_u = \$220{,}000$). Firm L is levered; it has a long-term debt of \$80,000. Thus, the value of the equity is equal to: $E_L = V_L - D = V_L - \$80{,}000$. Next year, there are two possible economic scenarios: if growth is slow, the earnings will be \$4000; if the economy/growth is strong, then the earnings will be \$120,000. Interest rate is 10%. Suppose that $V_u > V_L = \$200{,}000$. Note that debt is not risk-free (the firm will not be able to repay the debtholders if growth is slow).

Consider two strategies of an investor holding 10% of firm U's shares. Strategy 1: To keep 10% of firm U/s shares. Strategy 2: Sell the shares for $0.1 * 220{,}000 = 22{,}000$, buy 11% of company L's shares (the value is $0.11 * 120{,}000 = 13{,}200$) and buy 11% of company L's bonds (the value is $0.11 * 80{,}000 = 8800$).

Table 2.1 Investments and earnings from strategies 1 and 2 in Example 2.1

	Strategy 1	*Strategy 2*
Investment	0	$22{,}000 - 13{,}200 - 8800 = 0$
Earnings if economy is weak	$400 = 0.1 * 4000$	$440 = 0.11 * 4000$
Earnings if economy is strong	$12{,}000 = 0.1 * 120{,}000$	$13{,}200 = 0.11 * (120{,}000 - 0.1 * 80{,}000) + 0.1 * 8800$

As shown in Table 2.1, earnings from strategy 1 include earnings from holding firm U's shares. Earnings from strategy 2 include earnings from holding firm L's shares and interest on firm L's bonds. One can see that strategy 2 provides higher earnings in each scenario and thus is definitely better than strategy 1.[4] When the economy is weak, there are no earnings from holding shares of firm U and interests on bonds are proportionally split between the debtholders. In conclusion, there is an arbitrage opportunity, which means that the described situation in not an equilibrium. Note that the arbitrage argument (and the MM proposition) still holds if debt is not risk-free, assuming no bankruptcy costs.

2.3 Bankruptcy Costs

A firm that is having financial difficulties and that cannot meet its debt obligations will usually organize a meeting (credit workout) with its creditors to renegotiate the debt conditions.[5] A credit workout is a contract between a firm and its creditors that describes the conditions that allow the firm to avoid bankruptcy that would imply a reorganization or liquidation of the firm's assets to pay off the debt. If no deal is reached, the firm may declare bankruptcy. Liquidation is the sale of a firm's assets. Reorganization is a restructuring of a firm's financial claims to keep it afloat; it involves keeping the firm as a going concern and compensating the creditors with new securities, including equity.

[4] More precisely we should say that strategy 2 dominates strategy 1 by first-order dominance (FOD). In Chapter 4 we discuss the concept of stochastic dominance in more details.

[5] http://www.investopedia.com/terms/w/workout-agreement.asp.

In the United States, corporations can file for either Chapter 7 bankruptcy, which leads to the liquidation of a firm's assets through a settlement of creditors' claims, or Chapter 11 bankruptcy, which allows the firm to restructure its debt and equity claims and continue to operate.[6] In the former case, the assets are distributed to the debtholders and any excess proceeds generated from the liquidation are distributed to the shareholders. In the latter case, the debtholder and equityholders receive new claims in exchange for their existing claims. Table 2.2 shows the largest bankruptcies in US History.

Restructurings are often successful. For example, Air Canada, an airline company, restructured its debt obligations in 2003 and reduced its debt from $12 billion to $5 billion, thus allowing the company to continue

Table 2.2 Largest bankruptcies in US history

Company	*Date*	*Value*	*Industry*	*Type of Bankruptcy*
Lehman Brothers Inc	2008	691,063,000,000	Investment Bank	Chapter 11
Washington Mutual	2008	327,913,000,000	Savings and Loans	Chapter 11
Worldcom, Inc	2002	103,914,000,000	Telecommunications	Chapter 11
General Motors	2009	82,290,000,000	Cars	Chapter 11
CIT Group	2009	71,000,000,000	Banking	Chapter 11
Enron Corp	2001	65,503,000,000	Energy, Gas	Chapter 11

Source of data "The 10 largest U.S. bankruptcies". *CNNMoney.com* (Cable News Network). 2009-06-01. p. General Motors
http://www.bankruptcydata.com/Research/Largest_Overall_All-Time.pdf. Retrieved 2016-01-22
"Washington Mutual, Inc. Files Chapter 11 *Case" (Press release). Washington Mutual, Inc. 2008-09-26*
http://www.businesswire.com/news/home/20080926005828/en. Retrieved 2016-01-22
"WorldCom to emerge from collapse." CNN. Monday April 14, 2003. http://edition.cnn.com/2003/BUSINESS/04/14/worldcom/. Retrieved 2016-01-22
Stoll, John D., and Neil King Jr. (July 10, 2009).GM Emerges From Bankruptcy. *The Wall Street Journal*. http://www.wsj.com/articles/SB124722154897622577. Retrieved 2016-01-22
de la Merced, Michael J. (November 1, 2009). "CIT Files for Bankruptcy". *New York Times*. http://dealbook.nytimes.com/2009/11/01/cit-to-file-for-bankruptcy-soon/. Retrieved 2016-01-22
Benston, George J. (November 6, 2003). "The Quality of Corporate Financial Statements and Their Auditors Before and After Enron". *Policy Analysis* (Washington D.C.: Cato Institute) (497): http://www.webcitation.org/5tZ00qIbE. Retrieved 2016-01-22

[6] US Securities and Exchange Commission, Investor publications. https://www.sec.gov/investor/pubs/bankrupt.htm.

operating.[7] This is not always the case: sometimes restructuring fails and the company is liquidated. Ideally, a firm should continue if it is worth more as a going concern than it would be in liquidation. However, a conflicts of interest between the lenders and the company may lead to a failure.

A company can be declared bankrupt by its owners (or directors) or it can be forced into bankruptcy via a court order petitioned by creditors. The assets of the firm are then sold by the company or by a trustee. The proceeds of the sale (excluding liquidator's fees) are distributed to the creditors. Creditors with the strongest claims are paid first and those with the weakest claims are paid last.

The order of payments in the case of bankruptcy is: secured creditors, unsecured senior debtholders, unsecured junior debtholders, preferred stockholders, and common stockholders.

There are two types of bankruptcy costs: direct and indirect. Direct bankruptcy costs are fees paid to the lawyers, liquidators, and other agents involved in the sale of the assets and the redistribution of the proceeds of the bankrupt firms. Indirect bankruptcy costs are costs incurred while the company is still in operation and stem from a general lack of stakeholder confidence in the firm.

Some examples of indirect costs include: a firm may lose orders for its products due to a possible inability to service them in the future, suppliers may demand cash or reduce the amount of credit offered to a firm, a firm may face high interest rates, or be unable to secure debt financing, a firm's managers may engage in actions that are harmful to their debtholders.

The famous Enron scandal led to the bankruptcy of the Enron Corporation, an American energy company based in Texas, at the end of 2001. It was also the main cause of Arthur Andersen's dissolution, which was one of the five largest audit firms in the world. Enron's complex financial strategies were not transparent enough to its shareholders and market analysts. In mid-July 2001, Enron's share price had decreased by more than 30% since the same quarter of 2000. While the company at that time was not bankrupt, the sharp decline in its stock price is an example of an indirect bankruptcy cost. On October 27 the company began buying back all of its commercial paper in an effort to calm investors. In addition, Enron financed the repurchase by depleting its lines of credit at

[7] McArthur and Jang (August 28, 2004).

several banks. The company's bonds were trading at levels slightly less, which made future sales problematic. The worsening credit line conditions, lower bond prices, and worsening commercial paper sales represent other examples of indirect bankruptcy costs.[8] Indirect Bankruptcy Costs are usually high for firms with large intangible assets and firms who sell products that require replacement parts and services.

Bhabra and Yao (2011) analyze the magnitude of indirect and total bankruptcy costs in different sectors and industries 3, 2, and 1 year prior to bankruptcy. Technology firms are an example of firms with large intangible assets and high indirect bankruptcy costs with total bankruptcy costs reaching more than 25% of the value of the assets one year before the bankruptcy. Bankruptcy costs are also quite large in the publishing industry.[9]

Intuitively, high bankruptcy costs should make borrowing more expensive and less attractive since the parties involved should anticipate these costs to arise at least with some probability implying a potential loss of revenue. Hence the value of levered firms (with risky debt and bankruptcy costs) should be lower than the value of unlevered firms. This means that in a market with only one imperfection, in the form of bankruptcy costs, the optimal capital structure is 100% equity. However, in practice, many firms use debt. One of the reasons for this is taxes. As we saw in Chapter 1: in contrast to dividends, interest paid on debt reduces the firm's taxable income.

2.4 Corporate Income Taxes and Capital Structure

Usually, interest on debt reduces a firm's earnings and its amount of corporate tax. There is a significant debate regarding the existence of corporate taxes in the economy. In general, there are two major arguments in favor of the tax. The first is a rent argument. The corporate tax can principally capture the rent earned by owners of fixed factors without distorting the investment decision. The second argument, the more popular one in corporate finance literature, is that the corporate tax is the price that corporations pay for limited liability of their shareholders.

[8] For more details about Enron's story see Palepu and Healy (2003).

[9] For more analysis of bankruptcy costs see, for example, Korteweg (2007).

This leads to what is called "double taxation" for corporations: the result of taxation at both the corporate and the household level. Meade (1978), for example, says that the legal construct of limited liability is a special benefit to incorporated firms and that it should be taxed. However, Musgrave and Musgrave (1980) argue: "the privilege of operation under limited liability is, of course, of tremendous value of corporations, but the institution of limited liability as such is practically costless to society and hence does not justify imposition of a benefit tax."[10]

Since interest paid on debt (unlike dividends) reduces taxable income, firms that use debt financing pay less taxes. This advantage is called the debt tax shield. Each \$1 of interest a firm pays, it saves \$$T$ dollars in taxes where T is the corporate tax rate. For example if $T = 35\%$, a firm will save 35 cents for each dollar of interest it pays, etc., note that the higher the tax, the higher the tax saving.

Corporate tax rates vary widely by country, leading some corporations to shield earnings within offshore subsidiaries or to redomicile within countries with lower tax rates. Corporate tax rates across the Organization for Economic Cooperation and Development are shown in Table 2.3. Rates within the OECD vary from a low of 8.5% in Switzerland to a high of 35% in the United States. The OECD average is 22%.[11]

2.5 Trade-off Theory

As mentioned before, in contrast to dividends, interest paid on debt reduces the firm's taxable income. Debt also increases the probability of bankruptcy. The trade-off theory suggests that capital structure reflects a trade-off between the tax benefits of debt and the expected costs of bankruptcy (Kraus & Litzenberger, 1973; Myers, 1989).[12] Under this theory, the firm's value equals the value of the unlevered firm (with the same assets) plus the benefits of the tax advantage of debt minus the

[10] More recent discussions about the link between limited liability and corporate taxation can be found for example in Miglo (2007).

[11] For more about corporate tax rates across different countries see, for example, Devereux et al. (2008).

[12] For a review see, for example, Frank and Goyal (2008), Miglo (2011) or Graham and Leary (2011). For early examples of related analysis see also Robichek and Myers (1966) and Scott (1976).

Table 2.3 Corporate tax rates in selected countries

Country	*2015 Corporate tax rate (%)*
Australia	30
Canada	15
France	34.43
Germany	15.83
Ireland	12.50
Israel	26.50
Italy	27.50
Korea	22
Mexico	30.00
Norway	27
Switzerland	8.50
United Kingdom	20
United States	35

Source of data OECD.Stat, http://stats.oecd.org//Index.aspx?QueryId=58204

expected bankruptcy costs.

$$V = V_U + TS(D, I, T) - BC(D, I, B)$$

Here V_U is the value of the unlevered firm (no debt), TS is the value of the firm's tax shield, which depends on the level of debt D, the firm's earnings I and the corporate tax rate T, and BC is the expected value of the bankruptcy costs, which depend on the level of debt, the firm's earnings and parameter B that reflects the magnitude of bankruptcy costs (B is low for example if the firm belongs to an industry with relatively low bankruptcy costs and vice versa). TS usually equals the amount of taxes saved from the fact that interests, in contrast to dividends, are tax-deductible. In a dynamic version of this model, TS would represent the present value of saved taxes over several periods of time. Usually it is assumed that

$$\frac{\partial TS(D, I, T)}{\partial D} \geq 0; \frac{\partial^2 TS(D, I, T)}{\partial D^2} \leq 0; \frac{\partial TS(D, I, T)}{\partial I} \geq 0; \frac{\partial^2 TS(D, I, T)}{\partial D \partial I} \geq 0 \quad (2.1)$$

$$\frac{\partial TS(D, I, T)}{\partial T} \geq 0; \frac{\partial^2 TS(D, I, T)}{\partial D \partial T} \geq 0; \frac{\partial BC(D, I, B)}{\partial D} \geq 0;$$

$$\frac{\partial BC(D, I, B)}{\partial B} \geq 0 \qquad (2.2)$$

$$\frac{\partial^2 BC(D, I, B)}{\partial D^2} \geq 0; \frac{\partial^2 BC(D, I, B)}{\partial D \partial B} \geq 0; \frac{\partial BC(D, I, B)}{\partial I} \leq 0;$$

$$\frac{\partial^2 BC(D, I, B)}{\partial D \partial I} \leq 0 \qquad (2.3)$$

Explanations regarding conditions (2.1)–(2.3) are usually the following. More debt means greater amounts of interest and larger taxable income reductions. This effect cannot last indefinitely, i.e., when taxable profit is approaching zero, a further increase in debt financing saves less taxes and in extreme cases, when there is no more taxable profit left, does not increase the tax shield. This explains condition (2.1). A greater corporate tax rate means larger tax savings from increased debt, which explains the first two conditions in (2.2). Higher debt increases the probability of bankruptcy. This explains the third condition in (2.2). The last condition in (2.2) comes from the definition of B. As debt increases, the probability of bankruptcy, as well as bankruptcy costs, especially indirect bankruptcy, have stronger effects since customers, banks, etc., tend to panic. The first two conditions in (2.3) have a similar spirit. An increase in the firm's income reduces the probability of bankruptcy. This explains the last two conditions in (2.3).[13]

Figure 2.2 shows marginal TS and BC. When D exceeds D' there is no benefit from increasing debt (profit is zero and further reductions do not make any contributions). The optimal level of debt D^* is achieved when the marginal benefit from a debt increase (marginal tax shield) equals the marginal cost of a debt increase (marginal expected bankruptcy costs).

Example 2.2 Consider a firm that generates a random cash flow R that is uniformly distributed between 0 and 100. The firm faces a constant tax rate of 0.3 on its corporate income. If the earnings are insufficient to cover the promised debt payment, D (for simplicity D represents interests only and the principal is equal to 0) there is a deadweight loss of $0.1 * D$ that is used up in the process. This loss can include direct bankruptcy

[13] See Van Binsbergen et al. (2010) about more details in constructing TS and BC using empirical data. In some of their graphs, there is a flat area for marginal benefit curve when the level of debt is very low and the tax rate is not affected by marginal debt changes. Qualitatively it does not affect our conclusions.

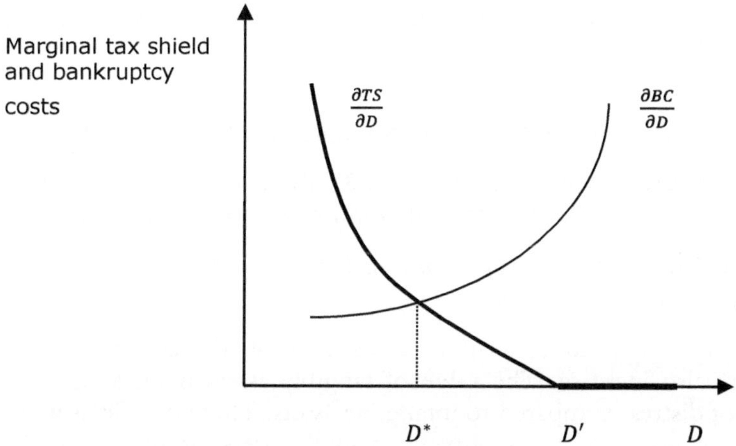

Fig. 2.2 Optimal level of debt under trade-off theory

costs such as fees paid to lawyers and indirect bankruptcy costs such as losses due to a general lack of confidence in the firm. If earnings are large enough ($R > D$), equityholders receive $(R - D) * (1 - 0.3)$. Otherwise, they receive nothing.

The value of unlevered firm can be found as follows: $V_U = 50 * (1 - 0.3) = 35$. Here $100/2 = 50$ are the average earnings of the firm and $50 * 0.7$ equals the expected net income.

$TS = 0.3 * \left(\frac{100-D}{100} * D + \frac{D}{100} * \frac{D}{2}\right)$. $\frac{100-D}{100}$ is the probability that $R > D$ and $\frac{D}{100}$ is the probability of default. If $R > D$, the debtholders receive D (tax savings equal $0.3 * D$) and they equal on average $\frac{D}{2}$, if the firm defaults.

$BC = \frac{D}{100} * \frac{D*0.1}{2}$. Here, $D/100$ is the probability of default. The bankruptcy costs equal, on average, $\frac{D*0.1}{2}$ if the firm defaults. The firm's value V equals

$$V = V_U + TS - BC$$
$$= 50 * 0.7 + 0.3 * \left(\frac{100 - D}{100} * D + \frac{D}{100} * \frac{D}{2}\right) - \frac{D}{100} * \frac{D * 0.1}{2}$$

The firm's choice of leverage is determined by maximizing V. The first-order condition with respect to D is $D = \frac{500*0.3}{2} = 75$.

2.6 Theory Predictions and Empirical Evidence

If B increases, then according to (2.3), the marginal cost of debt curve moves up in Fig. 2.3 and the equilibrium level of D is lowered.

Proposition 2.2 *Ceteris paribus, an increase in expected bankruptcy costs should result in lower debt.*

As the expected bankruptcy costs increase, the advantages of using equity also increase. The value of tangible assets is more stable in the case of distress compared to intangible assets. Therefore, firms with more tangible assets, such as airplane manufacturers or real estate companies, should have higher leverage compared to those that have more intangible assets, such as research firms or growth firms. Indirectly, this analysis implies that large conglomerates should have more debt than small entrepreneurial firms because they are more diversified and have a lower default risk.[14] Two remarks are noteworthy here. First, it has

Fig. 2.3 Optimal level of debt under trade-off theory when B increases

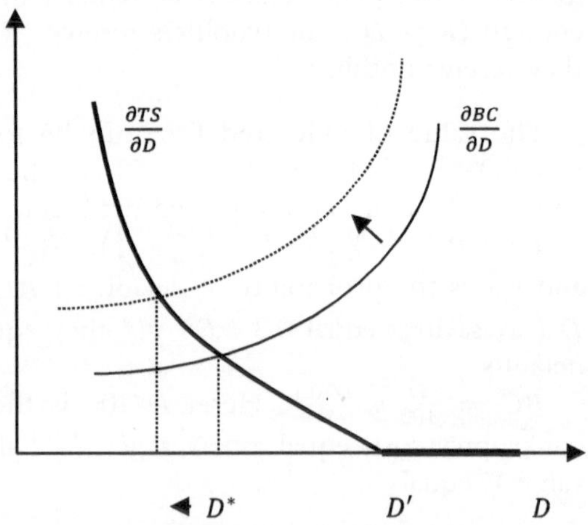

[14] For empirical support of these predictions see, for example, Frank and Goyal (2009).

been found in recent years that for small and start-up firms a positive relationship may exist between the amount of external debt (and consequently total debt) and growth opportunities (see, for example, Robb and Robinson (2012)). Secondly, Bulan and Sanyal (2009) investigate the impact of growth opportunities on the financing decisions of investor-owned electric utilities in the United States when the electricity sector was deregulated. They find that the relationship between leverage and growth opportunities may be positive or negative, depending on the nature of the growth opportunity.

When T increases in (2.2), the marginal benefit of debt curve moves up and debt should also increase because higher taxes lead to a greater tax advantage of using debt.

Proposition 2.3 *Firms with higher tax rates should have higher debt ratios compared to firms with lower tax rates.*

As mentioned in Miglo (2011), the empirical evidence regarding Proposition 2.3 is mixed. More recent literature (Philippon & Reshef, 2012, Strebulaev & Yang, 2013; Wright, 2004), and DeAngelo and Roll (2015)) began to closely analyze historical patterns in capital structure and whether or not they can be explained by traditional conclusions of trade-off theory, described above. For example, asset tangibility declined on average in the twentieth century but at the same time, the leverage ratio increased (Graham et al., 2015). Taxes increased sharply between the beginning of the twentieth century (starting from 15%) until 1950 when they reached 50% in the United States. The leverage increase during that period is consistent with the above predictions. In the 1980s, the corporate tax rate became around 35% but leverage continued to grow. More research is expected in this area.

As suggested in (2.3), if I increases, the marginal benefit curve moves up, the marginal cost curve moves down and D should increase.

Proposition 2.4 *More profitable firms should have more debt.*

Intuitively, the expected bankruptcy costs are lower and interest tax shields are more valuable for more profitable firms. Empirical studies, however, typically find a negative relationship between profitability and leverage (Fama & French, 2002; Frank & Goyal, 2009; Rajan & Zingales, 1995; Titman & Wessels, 1988). Danis et al. (2014) suggest that a positive correlation between debt and profitability may exist in times when firms are at or close to their optimal level of leverage.

Let's take a closer look at the last two conditions in (2.3). A firm's higher income definitely reduces the probability of bankruptcy, which supports these conditions. On the other hand, an increase in income may increase the value of potential losses for the firm in the case of bankruptcy. It is similar to: "If I'm poor I have nothing to lose and if I'm rich I have a lot to lose." This implies that the marginal cost curve can theoretically move in either direction depending on which effect is dominant (see Fig. 2.4).

If the marginal cost curve moves up and if this move is stronger than that of the marginal benefit curve, optimal debt may go down, which can explain the negative correlation between debt and profitability. In fact, Binsbergen et al. (2010) find that the marginal cost of debt is positively related to the firm's cash, which is consistent with the curve moving up in Fig. 2.4. Overall it seems like more research is required regarding the marginal cost of the debt curve.

The major challenge of classical trade-off theory remains empirical evidence about the negative correlation between debt and profitability because it does not directly follow the standard model. On the empirical side, papers addressing historical capital structure patterns over large periods of time with trade-off theory look interesting and promising.

Fig. 2.4 Optimal level of debt under trade-off theory when *I* increases

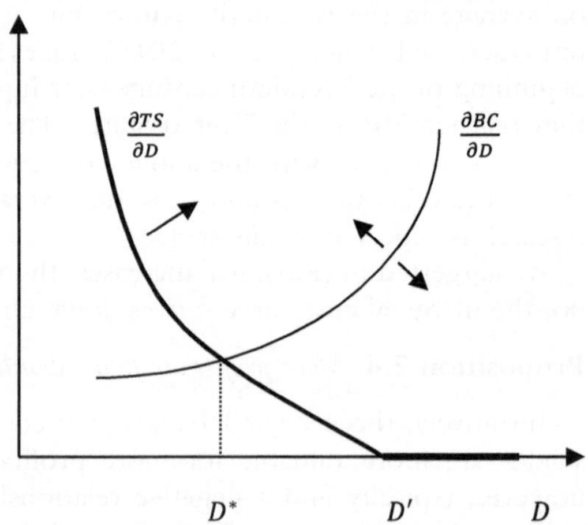

The basic trade-off theory model does not include retained earnings, transaction costs and costs of raising funds. These factors are usually important in what is called "dynamic trade-off theory". Hennessy and White (2005) analyze a model with equity flotation costs and show that a negative correlation between debt and profitability may be observed in some cases. Strebulaev (2007) analyzes a model where firms in distress have to sell their assets at a discount and therefore firms adjust their capital structure infrequently. The model's simulations can produce a negative correlation between debt and profitability. Hackbarth et al. (2006) and Bharma et al. (2010) present costly adjustment models that can account for the dynamic relation between leverage and macroeconomic characteristics. Danis et al. (2014) find that at times when firms are at or close to their optimal level of leverage, the cross-sectional correlation between profitability and leverage is positive. At other times, it is negative. Bolton et al. (2013) present a model of dynamic capital structure and liquidity choice where debt adjustments are costly. The authors focus on the debt servicing cost: debt payments drain the firm's valuable precautionary cash holdings and thus impose higher expected external financing costs on the firm. The model can replicate a negative correlation between debt and profitability.

In a review of empirical capital structure literature Graham and Leary (2011) suggested the following directions for improving trade-off theory results: fixing mismeasurement, for example calculations of marginal tax benefits and marginal bankruptcy costs should be significantly improved; new models are required in the area of partial adjustment toward optimal capital structure; dynamic trade-off theory models should still prove that they are indeed the primary drivers of capital structure changes; and the methods of value estimation for transactions related to capital structure changes should be more developed. To a large extent, these suggestions remain valuable. Note the following latest developments in the trade-off theory research. Izhakian et al. (2021) analyze the role of risk and ambiguity in the trade-off theory. The authors argue that risk and ambiguity may have different effects on the marginal benefits of tax and on the optimal level of debt. Hennessy and Chemla (2022) analyze difficulties in estimating the effect of changes in different parameters including tax rate on optimal levels of debt in existing literature taking into account differences in approaches from an econometrician and from a CFO point of view. Miglo (2024) analyzes the trade-off theory of capital structure with endogenous tax rates. In his model, the government first selects tax rates and then firms with investment projects select their capital structures driven by the trade-off between expected bankruptcy costs and the effective debt tax rate advantage. The model predicts, for example, that an equilibrium often emerges where the effective tax rate debt advantage equals 0. This is consistent with recent reduction in the corporate tax rate in the US and with low/zero effective rate of debt tax advantage mentioned in recent literature.[15] Abel (2018) develops a dynamic model of leverage with tax deductible interest and an endogenous cost of default. A firm borrowing constraint depends on lenders' disincentive to provide loans that would lead to immediate default. The author demonstrates that that there are cases when debt and profitability are negatively correlated. For an interesting analysis of firm adjustment towards the capital target that uses some ideas from traditional and dynamic trade-off theory see Chen and Frank (2022).

Questions and Exercises

1. M&M Proposition is the theory that the value of a firm is independent of its capital structure.
2. Indirect bankruptcy costs are very small for technology firms.
3. Tax shield decreases when the corporate tax rate increases.
4. In a world with bankruptcy cost and without taxes, the firm's value is maximized when the firm is financed by debt.
5. The proposition of Modigliani and Miller still holds if debt is risky but bankruptcy costs do not exist.
6. In a world with corporate taxes but without any other market imperfections firm should use debt as much as possible.
7. The static version of trade-off theory cannot explain the negative correlation between debt and profitability.
8. The trade-off theory predicts that the marginal tax benefit of debt should be equal to the marginal expected bankruptcy cost.
9. MM Proposition states that levered firms have greater value than unlevered firms.
10. Bankruptcy costs.

[15] More discussion will be provided in Chapter 14.

(a) Define direct bankruptcy costs and provide examples of direct bankruptcy costs.
(b) Define indirect bankruptcy costs and provides examples (at least 5) of indirect bankruptcy costs
(c) Provide examples of firms with high indirect bankruptcy costs? (Explanations required).

11. Trade-off theory.

(a) Describe the trade-off theory of capital structure (in words)
(b) According to this theory, which equation determines the firm's value?
(c) Describe empirical evidence that is consistent with the trade-off theory (provide at least 5 points). Explanations required.
(d) Describe empirical evidence that is not consistent with this theory (provide at least 4 points). Explanations required.

12. Suppose two firms have the same assets that generate the same earnings and differ only in how the assets are financed: Firm U is unlevered ($V_u = \$100{,}000$). Firm L is levered; it has a debt of \$40,000. Next year, there are two possible economic scenarios: if growth is slow, the earnings are \$4000; if the economy/growth is strong, then the earnings are \$150,000. Interest rate is 10%. Suppose that $V_u > V_L = \$80{,}000$.

    Suppose an investor X holds 10% of firm U shares. Explain why MM holds.
13. Consider a firm that generates a random cash flow R that is uniformly distributed between 0 and 1000. The firm faces a constant tax rate 0.2 on corporate income. If the earnings are insufficient to cover the promised debt payment, D (for simplicity D represents interests only and the principal is equal to 0) there is a deadweight loss of $0.2 * D$ that is used up in the process. Find optimal level of debt.

References

Abel, A. (2018). Optimal Debt and Profitability in the Trade-Off Theory. *The Journal of Finance, 73*, 95–143.

Bhabra, G., & Yao, Y. (2011). Is Bankruptcy Costly? Recent Evidence on the Magnitude and Determinants of Indirect Bankruptcy Costs. *Journal of Applied Finance & Banking, 1*(2), 39–68.

Bharma, H., Kuehn, L., & Strebulaev, I. (2010). The Aggregate Dynamics of Capital Structure and Macroeconomic Risk. *Review of Financial Studies, 23*(12), 4187–4241.

Bolton, P., Chen, H., & Wang, N. (2013). Market Timing, Investment, and Risk Management. *Journal of Financial Economics, 109*, 40–62.

Bulan, L., & Sanyal, P. (2009). Is There Room For Growth? Debt, Growth Opportunities and the Deregulation of U.S. Electric Utilities. http://ssrn.com/abstract=867004.

Chen, H., & Frank, M. (2022). Targets and the Trade-Off Theory of Capital Structure. https://ssrn.com/abstract=4031982

Danis, A., Rettl, D., & Whited, T. (2014). Refinancing, Profitability, and Capital Structure. *Journal of Financial Economics, 114*(3), 424–443.

DeAngelo, H., & Roll, R. (2015). How Stable Are Corporate Capital Structures? *Journal of Finance, 70*(1), 373–418.

Devereux, M., Lockwood, B., & Redoano, M. (2008). Do Countries Compete Over Corporate Tax Rates? *Journal of Public Economics, 92*(5–6), 1210–1235.

Fama, E., & French, K. (2002). Testing Trade-off and Pecking Order Predictions about Dividends and Debt. *Review of Financial Studies, 15*(1), 1–33.

Faulkender, M., & Smith, J. (2016). Taxes and Leverage at Multinational Corporations. *Journal of Financial Economics, 122*(1), 1–20.

Frank, M., & Goyal, V. (2009). Capital Structure Decisions: Which Factors Are Reliably Important? *Financial Management, 38*, 1–37.

Frank, M., & Goyal, V. (2008). Trade-off and Pecking Order Theories of Debt. In E. Eckbo (Ed.), *Handbook of Empirical Corporate Finance* (Vol. 2, pp. 135–202). Elsevier.

Gara, A. (2015, November 25). A Year After Oil's Black Friday, Consolidation in the Drilling Industry Nears. *Forbes/Investing*, http://www.forbes.com/sites/antoinegara/2015/11/25/a-year-after-oils-black-friday-consolidation-in-the-driling-industry-nears/

Graham, J., & Leary, M. (2011). A Review of Empirical Capital Structure Research and Directions for the Future. *Annual Review of Financial Economics, 3*, 309–345.

Graham, J., Leary, M., & Roberts, M. (2015). A Century of Capital Structure: The Leveraging of Corporate America. *Journal of Financial Economics, 118*, 658–683.

Hackbarth, D., Miao, J., & Morellec, E. (2006). Capital Structure, Credit Risk, and Macroeconomic Conditions. *Journal of Financial Economics, 82*, 519–550.

Healy, P., & Palepu, K. (2003). The Fall of Enron. *Journal of Economic Perspectives, 17*(2), 3–26.

Hennessy, C., & Chemla, G. (2022). Signaling, Instrumentation, and CFO Decision-Making. *Journal of Financial Economics, 144*(3), 849–863.

Hennessy, C., & White, T. (2005). Debt Dynamics. *Journal of Finance, 60*(3), 1129–1165.

Izhakian, Y., Yermack, D., & Zender, J. (2021). Ambiguity and the Tradeoff Theory of Capital Structure. *Management Science, 68*(6), 4090–4111.

Korteweg, A. (2007). *The Costs of Financial Distress Across Industries* (Working paper). http://ssrn.com/abstract=945425.

Kraus, A., & Litzenberger, R. (1973). A State-preference Model of Optimal Financial Leverage. *Journal of Finance, 28*(4), 911–922.

Loney, S. (2015). Corporate Leverage and Taxes around the World. All Graduate Plan B and other Reports. Paper 474. http://digitalcommons.usu.edu/gradreports/474.

McArthur, K., & Jang, B. (2004, August 28). How Air Canada got back on a new flight Path. *Globe and Mail*, http://www.theglobeandmail.com/report-on-business/how-air-canada-got-back-on-a-new-flightpath/article18272180/?page=all

Meade, J. (1978). The Structure and Reform of Direct Taxation, report of a committee chaired by Professor J. E. Meade. Allen and Unwin.

Miglo, A. (2007). Can Corporate Taxation be Explained by Limited Liability? *Journal of Current Issues in Finance, Business and Economics, 2*(4), 371–374.

Miglo, A. (2011). Trade-off, Pecking Order, Signaling and Market Timing Models. In H. K. Baker & G. S. Martin (Eds.), *Capital Structure and Corporate Financing Decisions: Theory, Evidence, and Practice* (pp. 171–190). Wiley.

Miglo, A. (2024). *Trade-Off Theory with Endogenous Taxes* (Working Paper), https://papers.ssrn.com/sol3/papers.cfm?abstract_id=4818421

Modigliani, F., & Miller, M. (1958). The Cost of Capital, Corporation Finance and the Theory of Investment. *American Economic Review, 48*(3), 261–297.

Musgrave, R., & Musgrave, P. (1980). *Public Finance in Theory and Practice.* McGraw-Tokyo.

Rajan, R., & Zingales, L. (1995). What Do We Know about Capital Structure: Some Evidence from International Data. *Journal of Finance, 50*(5), 1421–1460.

Myers, S. C. (1989). Still Searching for Optimal Capital Structure. In R. W. Kopke & E. S. Rosengren (Eds.), *Are the Distinctions Between Debt and Equity Disappearing*? Federal Reserve Bank of Boston.

Philippon, T., & A. Reshef. (2012). Wages and Human Capital in the U.S. Financial Industry: 1909–2006. *The Quarterly Journal of Economics*. First published online: October 9, 2012. https://doi.org/10.1093/qje/qjs030

Robb, A., & Robinson, D. (2012). The Capital Structure Decisions of New Firms. *The Review of Financial Studies, 1*(1), 1–27.

Robichek, A., & Myers, S. (1966). Problems in the Theory of Optimal Capital Structure. *The Journal Financial and Quantitative Analysis, 1*(2), 1–35.

Scott, J., Jr. (1976). A Theory of Optimal Capital Structure. *The Bell Journal of Economics, 7*(1), 33–54.

Strebulaev, I. (2007). Do Tests of Capital Structure Theory Mean What They Say? *Journal of Finance, 62*(4), 1747–1787.

Strebulaev, I., & Yang, B. (2013). The Mystery of Zero-Leverage Firms. *Journal of Financial Economics, 109*, 1–23.

Titman, S., & Wessels, R. (1988). The Determinants of Capital Structure Choice. *Journal of Finance, 43*(1), 1–21.

Van Binsbergen, J., Graham, J., & Yang, J. (2010). The Cost of Debt. *Journal of Finance, 65*, 2089–2136.

Williams, J. (1938). *The Theory of Investment Value*. Harvard University Press. 1997 reprint, Fraser Publishing.

Wright, S. (2004). Measures of Stock Market Value and Returns for the US Nonfinancial Corporate Sector, 1900–2002. *Review of Income and Wealth, 50*(4), 561–584.

CHAPTER 3

Asymmetric Information and Capital Structure

3.1 Finance and Asymmetric Information

It has been recognized for over 50 years, since at least Akerloff's (1970) publication about the used car market, that asymmetric information plays a role in the market. The resulting equilibrium, transactions, and prices depend on the degree of asymmetric information. Asymmetric information exists naturally since the seller of almost any item on the market has more information about the item than the buyer. The same is true in financial markets.

Unlike theorists, practitioners often wonder whether this is a theoretical problem that has already been solved on a big scale by existing laws of consumer protection, insider trading, etc., or a problem that is still relevant and will remain relevant in the future. Izabella Kaminska, in her article entitled "If you call it a blockchain, it's not an OTC story anymore," talks about the blockchain-enabled platform introduced by NASDAQ.[1] The platform facilitates the raising of equity by private companies. When discussing the ideas behind this innovation, the author

[1] Kaminska (October 30, 2015).

Supplementary Information The online version contains supplementary material available at https://doi.org/10.1007/978-3-031-85459-0_3.

A. Miglo, *Capital Structure in the Modern World*,
https://doi.org/10.1007/978-3-031-85459-0_3

mentioned the Stiglitz paradox. Stiglitz (along with Weiss, 1981) developed some research, in line with Akerloff's paper, with applications to credit markets with asymmetric information.[2] Applying this idea to the market for newly issued shares, under asymmetric information, the market may collapse because investors do not have enough information about the shares. Large companies who are traded publicly in large organized public markets spend a lot of money to inform the public about their companies: it is the way they raise public equity. This is something that is fairly expensive for small and private companies to do. NASDAQ's idea is to help these companies raise equity.

Another recent interesting topic is the IPO of the company called Block (formerly Square). Block, Inc. is an American technology company that deals with financial and merchant services including payment services. The company had an IPO in 2015 to finance its expanding operations. The IPO price was $9. By the end of the day, the share price was $13. The $9 price was below the last round of funding price so it was a loss value for the company. Evan Niu discussed the situation on Motley Fool.[3] As he argued, the situation was not unusual for IPO firms and by no means constitutes a sign of failure. As we will learn later in the chapter, this phenomenon is caused by asymmetric information between firms and investors and is called the "IPO underpricing" phenomenon.

3.2 Insiders and Outsiders

Information asymmetries are characterized by one person or organization having more information than another person or organization. Insiders may have private (exclusive) information about a firm that is unavailable to outsiders. In public corporations, insiders are typically managers; in closely held corporations, insiders are shareholders (initial shareholders) and often managers.

Insiders may not be able to fully disclose their information to the firm's claimholders. Grinblatt and Titman (2001) argue that among the reasons for this is that the information may be valuable to competitors; there is a risk of being sued by investors if they make forecasts that later turn out

[2] Akerloff and Stiglitz both won the Nobel Prize award for their contributions to asymmetric information research.

[3] Niu (November 21, 2015).

to be inaccurate[4]; and the managers may be reluctant to disclose "bad" information.

As a result, investors will try to incorporate indirect evidence in their valuation, which is done through the analysis of information-revealing actions (signals). These can include investment decisions, financing decisions, dividend decisions, etc. This chapter discusses some of the major ideas related to the problem of asymmetric information.

3.3 Pecking-Order Theory

Consider a firm that wants to raise money for a project. If it issues new equity for this project, it invites outsiders to share not only the new project but also all of its existing assets. Thus, outside investors will infer that existing assets are not very valuable. So, not knowing for sure what the firm is worth, outside investors will not be willing to pay much for this new equity. Therefore, if the firm is actually good, then its equity will have been underpriced. Because of that, a good firm should always rely on retained earnings to finance new projects. These ideas were put forth by Myers (1984) and Myers and Majluff (1984). In the next example, we will show how asymmetric information affects a firm's financing decisions.

Suppose a firm is raising funds for an investment project. The firm has internal funds i. The investment cost is $k, k \leq i$. The initial capital structure is 100% equity with n shares outstanding. The firms maximize the wealth of the existing shareholders (owners). To finance the project, the firm may use internal funds, issue debt or equity (Fig. 3.1).

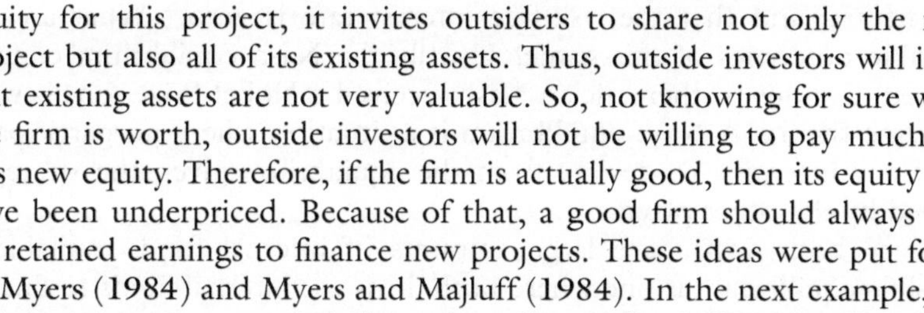

Fig. 3.1 Sequence of events

[4] See Stempel (December 18, 2013) for an example with Facebook's IPO.

To illustrate the idea we will assume that there are two types of firms on the market (both with equal probability) labeled with subscript 1 and 2. Owners learn the type (future expected earnings) of their firm in the beginning. The firm's type is not publicly observable. The public only knows that there are two firms on the market and one of them has potential earnings c_1 and the other c_2.

To solve this situation, game theory is typically used as the main tool. Players are: Firm 1, Firm 2 and the Investor. Firm 1 and 2 represent the existing shareholders of each firm's type. The Investor can provide financing or buy securities as long as the expected earnings cover the investment. It is usually justified by the assumption that the investor is risk-neutral and that the risk-free interest rate is zero.[5] What are the possible outcomes of this game? Usually the Nash equilibrium concept is used. Famous mathematician Nash received a Nobel Prize for his work in game theory. A Nash equilibrium is a situation where no participants have any incentive to deviate from the equilibrium given the strategies played by the other players.

Since both firms have large amounts of internal funds available, a possible equilibrium is one where both firms use internal funds to finance their projects. The payoff of the owners of firm t will be equal to $i + c_t - k, t = 1, 2$. The same holds for the situation where both firms use debt. Note that debt is risk-free in our model since firms have enough internal funds that can be used as an insurance fund to cover the initial investment. Now consider equity issues. Does the situation where both firms issue equity represent an equilibrium?

To answer this question, first consider a hypothetical situation where the Investor knows the firm's type (perfect information case) and Firm 1 issues equity. Since the Investor knows the firm's expected earnings, the Investor purchases Firm 1's shares at fair value. What fraction of the firm's shares will be sold? The Investor will receive $\alpha = \frac{k}{i+c_1}$. In this case, the Investor's expected earnings are: $\alpha = \frac{k}{i+c_1}(i + c_1) = k$. It equals the initial amount of investments. The initial owner's profit for Firm 1 is

$$(1 - \alpha)(i + c_1) = i + c_1 - k$$

[5] This assumption will be used in most models throughout the book unless specified otherwise.

It is the same profit that the owners of Firm 1 could get by using internal financing.

Now consider the case with imperfect information. What if the Investor believes that the firm is type 2 instead? Then the Investor will demand a fraction of equity equal to $\alpha = \frac{k}{i+c_2}$. The Firm 1 owner's payoff in this case is $(1-\alpha)(i+c_1) = (1-\frac{k}{i+c_2})(i+c_1)$.

As shown in Fig. 3.2 the payoff of the initial shareholders of Firm 1 depends on the expected earnings of Firm 2 and, respectively, the fraction of shares the Investor will ask for in exchange for their investment in the project. If $c_2 < c_1$, the Investor will perceive the firm to be of lower quality than it really is. The Investor will ask for a large fraction of shares and the payoff of the initial shareholders of Firm 1 will be lower than it would be in the case of perfect information (that could be achieved for example by using internal funds for financing the project).

Below we argue that a firm with higher expected earnings never issues equity in equilibrium. First consider a situation where firms use different strategies (separating equilibrium). Suppose that $c_2 > c_1$ and Firm 2 issues equity and Firm 1 uses internal funds or risk-free debt. Firm 1 owner's payoff equals $i + c_1 - k$. However, if Firm 1 decides to mimic Firm 2, its owners' payoff will increase as follows from Fig. 3.2. Therefore, this situation is not an equilibrium.

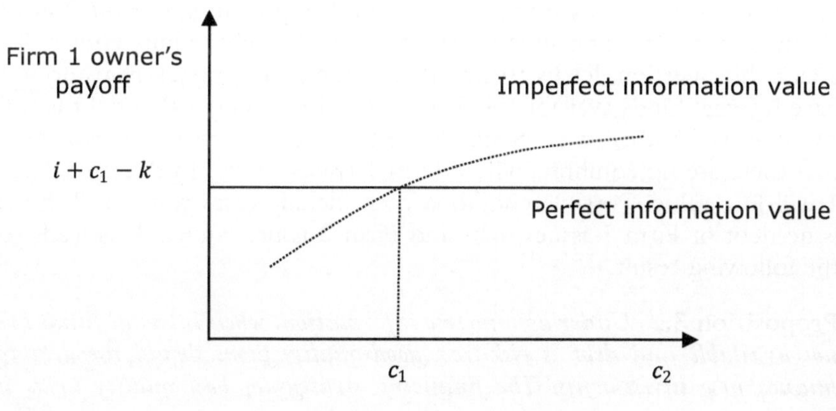

Fig. 3.2 The Firm 1 owner's payoff under imperfect information

Now consider a situation where both firms issue shares (also called pooling equilibrium since both firms use the same strategy) and suppose that $c_1 > c_2$. As was argued above, Firm 1 will issue equity only if the Investor is willing to buy shares for no more than $\alpha = \frac{k}{i+c_1}$ fraction of equity. In this case, however, the Investor loses money. The Investor will buy shares of Firm 1 with a probability 50% and make no losses in this case but with probability 50% the Investor will buy shares of Firm 2 and it will bring: $\frac{k}{i+c_1}(i + c_2)$, which is less than k because $c_2 < c_1$. Therefore, the situation where both firms issue equity is not an equilibrium.

So far, we have assumed that a firm can issue risk-free debt or equity with no cost. If we relax one of these assumptions, in order to avoid any loss of value, the higher quality firm needs to use internal funds. This leads to the following result.

Proposition 3.1 *Under asymmetric information, good-quality firms should first use internal funds to finance new investments because it is at least as good as external financing. If good-quality firms use internal financing, the financing strategy of bad quality firms is irrelevant.*

If good-quality firms use internal financing and if bad quality firms choose their financing randomly, then, on average, internal funds will be a dominant source of financing. On a large scale, this result appears to be true. If one considers the aggregate balance sheet of all-American corporations, one can see that internal funds represent about 60–70% of all investment financing sources. What about the debt/equity choice? To attack this question, let us assume that in the above model, firms do not have internal funds available or that $i = 0$. Also, suppose that debt is still risk-free, i.e. $k < c_2 < c_1$. Similarly, to the previous case, one can show that there are no equilibria where Firm 1 issues equity. In this case, Firm 1 will lose value. Possible equilibria then include cases when both firms issue debt or Firm 1 issues debt and Firm 2 issues equity. This leads to the following result.

Proposition 3.2 *Under asymmetric information, when internal funds are not available and debt is risk-free, good-quality firms should use debt to finance new investments. The financing strategy of bad quality firms is irrelevant.*

What if debt is not risk-free, which is usually the case in real life?! Assume for example that $c_2 < k < c_1$. In this case, Firm 1 cannot avoid losing value. Since debt is not risk-free and since the firm's type is private information, the Investor will charge a positive interest rate when providing debt financing. If the Investor provides a loan with zero interest rate assuming that it faces Firm 1 (which would be the case under perfect information), Firm 2 will mimic this strategy and ask for a loan with interest rate equal to zero and then the Investor will sustain a loss on average. So the only candidates left to be the equilibrium are cases when both firms issue debt or both firms issue equity. Some articles argue that equilibria with debt usually dominate ones with equity since value loss for a good-quality firm is typically smaller in the case of debt than in the case of equity. Intuitively, debt is a security that is less sensitive to value fluctuation (Nachman & Noe, 1994).

Propositions 3.1 and 3.2 lead to the so called pecking-order theory or POT (Myers, 1984; Myers & Majluff, 1984): under asymmetric information firms prefer to use internal funds, then debt, and equity is only a last resort.

Example 3.1 Consider a firm that has the opportunity to undertake an investment project. The project's cost is 70. The project will bring a revenue 90 and the firm will be liquidated. The risk-free interest rate is 0. The firm has issued 100 shares outstanding. The firm has 100 in cash when it makes the decision about the project. Since the firm has enough money to pay the cost of the new project, it can do so. It can also issue additional equity to finance the project.

If the firm decides to use internal funds, the shareholders' final profit will be $100 - 70 + 90 = 120$. . The shareholders will be interested in pursuing this strategy since their payoff is higher than in the case when the firm does not undertake the new project ($120 > 100$). In other words, the net present value of the new project is positive: $NPV = 120 - 100 = 20$.

Now consider the case when the firm issues equity. Outside investors know the amount of cash the firm has (100) and they also know the value of the earnings from the new project (90). When they buy equity and get a fraction α of the firm, their payoff is $\alpha 190$, which should be equal to 70 (investment cost), which implies: $\alpha = 70/190 = 7/19$. The initial shareholders' payoff is $(1 - \alpha)190 = 120$. Note that the initial shareholders' payoff is the same under any strategy (120). This is consistent with the spirit of the perfect market concept (capital structure irrelevance).

Now let us look at the asymmetric information case. Assume that earnings from the project can either be high (90) or low (30). Outside investors believe that its value will be 90 with a prior probability of 50%. Does a situation where both firms issue equity, or one firm issues equity and the other one uses internal cash for the project, represent an equilibrium?

If the shareholders use cash to finance the project, their final payoff for the high earnings firm is $100 - 70 + 90 = 120$ and for the low earnings firm is $100-70+30 = 60$. Now consider the case where the high-earnings firm issues equity and the low-earnings firm uses cash for the project. The fraction of equity sold to investors equals 7/19. The initial shareholders' payoff for the high-earnings firm is $(1-7/19)*(100+90) = 120$. However, it can not be an equilibrium. If the shareholders of the low earnings firm decide to issue equity as well (and "mimic" the high earnings firm), their payoff will be:$(1 - 7/19) * (100 + 30) = 82\frac{4}{19}$. This is definitely greater than what they can get by using cash for the project.

Now consider the case where both firms issue equity. Investors will rationally anticipate that they will invest in the high-earnings firm with only a 50% probability. So the minimum fraction of shares acceptable for outsiders is

$$\alpha = \frac{70}{100 + 0.5 * 30 + 0.5 * 90} = \frac{7}{16}$$

In reality, it should be even higher because there is no guarantee that the firm with a good project will also issue equity. Now consider the decision of the initial shareholders if they are informed that the value of the new project is 90. If they use internal funds their payoff is 120. If they issue equity their fraction of shares will be at most 9/16 and therefore their payoff will be $9/16 * (190)$, which is less than 120. Therefore, they will use internal funds and not issue equity.

In conclusion, high-quality firms will use internal funds and low quality firms will either issue equity or also use internal funds. Equity is dominated by internal funds: the basic idea of the pecking-order theory. Equity is considered "lemon" because it will only be issued by low-quality firms. The "lemon" problem was theorized by Akerloff, who was awarded the Nobel Prize in 2001 for his research (see, for example, Akerloff, 1970).

Consider the firm's stock price reaction to an equity issue announcement. As follows from the previous analysis, when Firm 2 issues equity the fraction of equity that belongs to new investors is $\frac{k}{i+c_2}$. Denote the number of newly issued shares byΔn. We have: $\frac{k}{i+c_2} = \frac{\Delta n}{n+\Delta n}$. This implies

$$\Delta n = \frac{kn}{i + c_2 - k} \tag{3.1}$$

We also have $p\Delta n = k$, where p is the price of newly issued shares. Along with (3.1) it implies:

$$p = \frac{i + c_2 - k}{n} \tag{3.2}$$

Proposition 3.3 *The market reaction on newly issued shares is negative.*

Indeed, initially, the market participants cannot distinguish between firms' types. They only know that firms have new projects and assets-in-place with value I. With regard to new projects the market believes that they will be high-earnings projects with probability 50% and low-earnings projects with probability 50%. So prior to the equity issue, the share price is

$$\frac{0.5 * (i + c_1 - k) + 0.5 * (i + c_2 - k)}{n} \tag{3.3}$$

However, after the issue is announced, the share price is given by (3.2) since only Firm 2 can issue shares in equilibrium. The price determined in (3.2) is smaller than in (3.3) because $c_2 < c_1$.

Proposition 3.4 *There is a negative correlation between debt and profitability.*

POT is usually considered to be a theory that can explain the, discussed in Chapter 2, famous negative correlation between debt and profitability that often fails the static trade-off theory. There are numerous interpretations of different predictions in POT and Trade-off theory, especially with regard to empirical strategies for testing these predictions. Frank and Goyal (2009) mentioned for example: "The theories are not developed in terms of standard accounting definitions. To test the theories, it is therefore necessary to make judgments about the connection between the observable data and theory. While many of these judgments seem uncontroversial, there is room for significant disagreement in some cases." The simple model presented in this section is not an exception. One can find very different interpretations of correlations between debt and profitability. One approach that is probably the most popular in literature is the following. Consider the link between the amount of assets-in-place (the variable i in our model; this can include cash and hence it is positively correlated with internal resources, retained earnings, and ultimately with the firm's profitability) and its link to the equilibrium capital structure choice. When $i > k$, the high-quality firm uses internal funds to finance the project (recall that the capital structure choice of the low-quality firm does not matter). When$i < k$, the high-quality firm will issue debt. So one should observe a negative correlation between the value of i and the amount of debt issued in this model, which proves Proposition 3.4.

Proposition 3.5 *A higher extent of asymmetric information reduces the incentive to issue equity.*

For example, if in the basic model $c_2 = c_1$, firms can issue equity without the risk of being misvalued, in this case, there is no negative reaction to equity issue announcement. However, when $c_2 \neq c_1$, Firm 1 will not issue equity in equilibrium.

As mentioned in Miglo (2011), the empirical evidence regarding firms following pecking order is mixed.[6] The negative reaction to equity issues, or in general to leverage reducing transactions, usually finds empirical support. The negative correlation between debt and profitability usually also finds empirical support as discussed in Chapter 2. The evidence regarding the link between the extent of asymmetric information and capital structure choice is mixed as well as some evidence exist that firms do not always follow the prescribed order of financing e.g., small firms (see e.g., Frank et al. (2020)). We will discuss possible reasons for that in Chapter 9 as well as consider some advanced developments of the effect of asymmetric information on capital structure in Chapters 7 and 11.

Among more recent articles note the following. De Jong et al. (2010) tests POT by separating the effects of financing surpluses, normal deficits, and large deficits. Using a panel of US firms over 1971–2005, it finds that POT works best for firms with surpluses and worst for firms with large financing deficits. These findings highlight a puzzle that small firms, although they have the highest potential for asymmetric information, do not behave according to POT. The authors argue that these results

[6] See, for example, Shyam-Sunder and Myers (1999), Frank and Goyal (2003) and Leary and Roberts (2010).

are consistent with the debt capacity in the pecking-order model. De Jong et al. (2011) tests the static trade-off theory prediction that a firm increases leverage until it reaches its target debt ratio, and the prediction of POT that debt is issued until the debt capacity is reached. It is found that POT is a better descriptor of firms' issue decisions than the static trade-off theory. Dong et al. (2012) study market timing and pecking order in a sample of debt and equity issues and share repurchases of Canadian firms from 1998 to 2007. They find that only when firms are not overvalued do they prefer debt to equity financing. Bhaduri (2015) tests POT for an emerging economy through a case study of the Indian Corporate sector that includes 556 manufacturing firms over the period 1997–2007. The study finds strong evidence in favour of the pecking-order hypothesis. Bhama et al. (2015) examine firms (of India and China) with normal as well as large deficits and surpluses. The study finds that Indian and Chinese firms frequently issue debt when they have normal deficits. The pecking-order results are less supportive for Indian firms with large deficits. Mogilevsky and Murgulov (2012) examine underpricing of private equity backed IPOs listed on a major US stock exchange between January 2000 and December 2009. The authors identify 265 private equity backed IPOs and compare these with concurrently listed venture capital (VC) backed and non-sponsored IPOs. The results indicate that, on average, private equity backed IPOs experience a significantly lower level of underpricing than venture capital backed and non-sponsored IPOs. Lemmon and Zender (2019) consider an asymmetric information model of capital structure with debt covenants that allow the lender to liquidate the firm in some cases. The liquidation is costly because of the lender's imperfect information about the firm. This creates a disincentive for the entrepreneur to issue debt as compared to the traditional pecking order.

Frank et al. (2020) argue that some evidence is consistent with pecking order e.g., that firms with moderate deficits favor debt issues and that firms with very high deficits often rely on equity while some evidence is not consistent with pecking order e.g., that many firms prefer equity over debt and that some firms with a surplus do issue equity. They suggest that a significant difference exists between capital structure policies of firms with surplus and firms with deficit and also between firms with different debt capacities and that more theory is required to explain these differences.

3.4 When Incumbent Shareholders are Risk-Averse

In traditional pecking-order models, like the one discussed in the previous section, good-quality firms are forced to use internal funds if available to avoid adverse selection problems and a loss in value. If internal funds are not available, these firms will issue debt. In the latter case, they are mimicked by low-quality firms. Therefore, in either case, good-quality firms cannot signal their quality by changing their capital structures. The following sections discuss models in which capital structure choice will indeed serve as a signal of a firm's quality (Leland & Pyle, 1977; Ross, 1977).

In Leland and Pyle (1977) the incumbent shareholders are risk-averse. It will be shown that if a firm's future is favorable, the shareholders may accept a bigger risk or a bigger fraction of ownership. This leads to a "risk-bearing" signaling idea.

Consider a firm owned by a risk-averse entrepreneur. The entrepreneur's expected utility is $Ew - 1/2\rho Varw$ where w is the entrepreneur's wealth.[7] The firm has assets-in-place that can bring a net return R_θ that is normally distributed with the mean θ and standard deviation σ. θ is the entrepreneur's private information and σ is the public information. The entrepreneur is considering selling shares on the market. Potential investors are risk-neutral. The risk-free interest rate is 0.

Perfect information

In this case, the entrepreneur definitely benefits from selling the firm to an investor. Since the investors are risk-neutral and the risk-free interest rate is 0, the price of the transaction (the entrepreneur's return) is: $P = \theta$. If the entrepreneur does not sell the firm, he will still have θ in expectation but it will involve some risk because the firm's return is stochastic. It is always better to sell the project because of risk aversion. The entrepreneur's wealth in this case is $w = \theta$ and the expected utility is θ.

The entrepreneur's wealth, if he sells α of the firm's equity, is $w = P + (1-\alpha)R_\theta$. Therefore $Ew = P + (1-\alpha)\theta$, $Varw = (1-\alpha)^2\sigma^2$.

[7] E and Var denote the expected value and variance respectively.

Also, since the information is perfect, the firm's price correctly reflects the firm's expected earnings: $P = \alpha\theta$.

Thus, the entrepreneur's expected utility is $\theta - 1/2\beta(1-\alpha)^2\sigma^2$. The optimum is attained when $\alpha = 1$.

Imperfect information (example)

Now consider the case when θ is the entrepreneur's private information (Fig. 3.3).

Example 3.2 To illustrate this idea, suppose there are two firms with the parameters of return described in Table 3.1:

As was argued above, if the information about the expected profits were public then Firm 1 would be sold for 100 and Firm 2 would be sold for 200. Suppose that the entrepreneurs sell their firms even if the information about expected returns is private. The price in this case will be 150. The investors will be ready to buy the firm for an average expected return. Consider the entrepreneurs' expected utilities. The entrepreneur of Firm 1 will obviously benefit from selling the firm for 150. His expected utility will be 150. If he keeps the firm, his expected utility is less than 100. What about the entrepreneur of Firm 2?

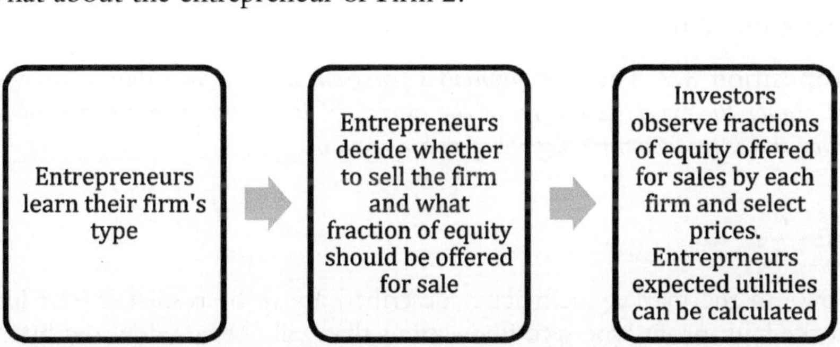

Fig. 3.3 The Sequence of Events Under Imperfect Information

Table 3.1 Expected profits and variances in Example 3.2

	Expected profit	*Variance*
Firm 1	100	100
Firm 2	200	100

If he does not sell the firm, his expected utility is $w_c = 200 - \frac{1}{2}\rho 100 = 200 - 50\rho$. If he sells, then it is 150. The entrepreneur is only interested in selling the firm if $\rho > 1$. Otherwise, he will keep his shares.

An implication of this result is that firms in industries with a high degree of asymmetric information (for example, research firms) are often characterized by entrepreneurs owning large fractions of equity.

Proposition 3.6 *The larger the extent of asymmetric information in the industry the greater the probability of quality firms losing money.*

Suppose there are two firms with expected profits θ_1 and θ_2, $\theta_2 > \theta_1$. The market only knows that $\theta = \theta_1$ with probability π_1 (Firm 1) and $\theta = \theta_2$ with probability π_2 (Firm 2). Similar to the argument in the above example, Firm 1 is always interested in selling the firm. Suppose, Firm 2 is also sold. Since the market cannot distinguish between the firms, it will pay the "average" price: $P = \theta_1\pi_1 + \theta_2\pi_2$.

The incentive to sell the firm depends on the following condition for the entrepreneur from Firm 2: $\theta_1\pi_1 + \theta_2\pi_2 \geq \theta_2 - \frac{1}{2}\rho\sigma^2$ that can be written as follows: $\pi_1(\theta_2 - \theta_1) \leq \frac{1}{2}\rho\sigma^2$. This condition is not necessarily satisfied. Firm 2 will not be sold if $\pi_1(\theta_2 - \theta_1) > \frac{1}{2}\rho\sigma^2$.

The larger the difference between the firms' expected profits the greater the probability of this condition being satisfied, this proves Proposition 3.6.

Proposition 3.7 The *entrepreneur's fraction of the firm's shares increases the higher the expected return of the assets, the lower the firm's risk and the lower the entrepreneur's degree of risk aversion.*

Signaling

How can the market inefficiency described above be resolved? The idea for the high-profit type is to find actions that will not be mimicked by the low-profit type. The market thus will be able to distinguish the types and pay a higher price for the shares of the high-profit type. Consider partial selling of the project. Denote the fraction of ownership retained by the entrepreneur with α. Suppose that Firm 1 sells the shares completely while Firm 2 sells only $(1-\alpha)$ of the shares. The payoff of the entrepreneur from Firm 1 is θ_1 while the wealth of the entrepreneur from Firm 2 is

$$(1 - \alpha)\theta_2 + \alpha R_{\theta_2} = \theta_2 - 1/2\rho\alpha^2\sigma^2 \quad (3.4)$$

If Firm 1 decides to mimic Firm 2, it will be able to sell the fraction $(1-\alpha)$ of Firm 1's shares for a higher price. However, the remaining shares will have to be held, which implies some risk-sharing with other shareholders. The separation condition (incentive for Firm 1 not to mimic Firm 2) is: $\theta_1 \geq (1-\alpha)\theta_2 + \alpha\theta_1 - 1/2\rho\alpha^2\sigma^2$. This condition can be written as

$$\frac{\alpha^2}{1-\alpha} \geq \frac{2(\theta_2 - \theta_1)}{\rho\sigma^2} \tag{3.5}$$

Note that according to (3.4) the payoff of the entrepreneur from Firm 2 is decreasing in α. Threfore, the optimal α for this entrepreneur would be minimal α which satisfies (3.5). It is given by

$$\frac{\alpha^2}{1-\alpha} = \frac{2(\theta_2 - \theta_1)}{\rho\sigma^2}$$

Since the left part of this equation increases with α, there is a positive correlation between θ_2 and α. Similarly, there is a negative correlation between α and the firm's risk (σ^2) and the entrepreneur's degree of risk aversion ρ. This proves Proposition 3.7.

Return to Example 3.2

Firm 1 sells all shares: $P_1 = 100$. Firm 2 sells partially. To find α, we need to solve the following equation: $\frac{\alpha^2}{1-\alpha} = \frac{2(200-100)}{\rho 100}$. Suppose that $\rho = 0.5$. The condition becomes: $\frac{\alpha^2}{1-\alpha} = 4$. Solving for α, given that $0 < \alpha < 1$, gives: $\alpha \geq\approx 0.75$. Therefore, the entrepreneur of Firm 2 should keep approximately 75% of the shares and sell 25%.

Since high-profit firms sell only partially, it can be interpreted as debt financing! Indeed suppose that instead of considering the sale of the entrepreneur's shares on the secondary market, the firm has a new investment project available and it needs to raise external funds to finance this project. Equity would be an optimal financing choice since it would provide the largest reduction of risk for the entrepreneur. In equilibrium, that would definitely be the choice for a low-quality firm. A high-quality firm will not be able to use equity financing exclusively since the share price will be below its true value and the value loss can outweigh the gains from the risk reduction. So a probable solution will be selling the shares partially and partially raising debt.

Leland and Pyle's (1977) idea that the entrepreneurs signal the qualities of their businesses by retaining larger fractions of equity is intuitively appealing. It has been used by banks and other financial institutions when screening entrepreneurs' demand for loans. Further the following evidence is consistent (directly or indirectly) with the spirit of this idea. For example, Conti et al. (2013) find that entrepreneur own investment has a positive impact on business angel investment. Further some examples of grants cited in Cumming and Hellmann (2013) require dual contribution (government and entrepreneur. The results of the analysis of initial public offerings (IPO) in Downes and Heinkel (1982) are also consistent with the entrepreneurial ownership retention idea.[8]

On the other hand, Ritter (1984) suggests that the evidence is ambiguous with respect to signaling idea (see also Krinsky and Rotenberg (2009) and Miglo (2022)). Further the main application of signaling theories for capital structure choice is that debt financing should serve as a positive signal for market participants. The empirical evidence regarding this prediction is mixed.[9] It is also not very well consistent with the negative correlation between debt and profitability.

The following papers are noteworthy. Grinblatt and Hwang (1989) extend Leland and Pyle idea to incorporate underpricing. Underpricing is a well-recognized phenomenon related to the issues of new shares including IPOs (see e.g., Ritter & Welsh, 2002). They develop a model with two signals that explains the underpricing of new issues. Garcia (2002) considers an optimal contracting problem between an informed risk-averse agent and a set of risk-averse principals. An informed entrepreneur approaches a group of outside investors to sell them an equity share in the firm motivated by risk-sharing gains. In contrast to the Leland and Pyle (1977) model, outside investors have bargaining power, and the investors and the entrepreneur also negotiate over a real investment decision in the firm. It is shown that the fraction of shares retained by the entrepreneur may not be increasing in the quality of private information. Varas (2014) analyzes a dynamic model involving Leland and Pyle's (1977) idea that an informed seller can use partial retention of an asset to signal quality. Retention is a credible signal only if the seller can

[8] See also Keloharju and Kulp (1996).

[9] See, among others, Eckbo (1986), Howton, Howton, and Perfect (1998), Antweiler and Frank (2006) and Miglo (2011).

commit not to trade again in the near future. The model considers trading dynamics if such a commitment is not possible. In equilibrium, the seller's holdings and the length of the trade delay are related and the expected delay between trades is a decreasing function of the fraction of the assets owned by the seller. The trading patterns are driven by the incentives to build a reputation of owning a high-quality asset.

3.5 Was Asymmetric Information Behind the 2007 Crisis?

Many economists consider the financial crisis of 2007–09, also known as the Global Financial Crisis to be the worst financial crisis since the Great Depression of the 1930s. It threatened the collapse of large financial institutions, prevented by government bailouts of banks, and stock markets dropped worldwide. The Dow Jones Industrial Average Index reached 14,093 in October 2007 and fell down to the level of the 1990s during the crisis: in March 2009 it was 6547. In many areas, the situation in housing markets involved foreclosures and unemployment. The crisis played a significant role in the failure of key businesses, leading to the 2008–2012 global recession and contributing to the European sovereign-debt crisis. The burst of the US housing bubble, which peaked in 2004, caused the values of securities tied to US real estate pricing to plummet, damaging financial institutions globally.

Many researchers agree that the main trigger of the financial crisis was the sharp increase in home ownership, easy access to loans for borrowers, and overvaluation of bundled subprime mortgages. The latter was mainly based on the theory that housing prices would continue to rise. An interesting question is whether it was a total (symmetric!) misunderstanding of real values in real estate markets or a case of asymmetric information when issuers or sellers of securities possess more (on average) information than the buyers of securities. If so, then it mirrors the materials discussed previously in this chapter. Or perhaps the market was not in equilibrium and investors were not rational?! Or did something else happen?

It is easy to assume that we indeed have a market with asymmetric information. In the primary market for mortgages, banks may not have a complete picture of the "quality" of their borrowers since the analysis of private borrowers is usually based on their credit history and does not take many other factors into consideration. In the secondary market, it is a pretty obvious assumption that financial institutions, including banks, have more information about the quality of mortgages in their portfolios than potential buyers. In the primary market, as in any other credit market with asymmetric information, interest rates should remain relatively high to limit the number of low-quality borrowers.[10] Any politically motivated downward pressure on interest rates or problems in the screening process will result in lower interest rates and a high number of low-quality borrowers. In the secondary market, when the extent of asymmetric information is significant enough, there is no equilibrium where good-quality items remain on the market (or good-quality shares as in the pecking-order model, or good-quality cars as in used car market of Akerloff). As the "lemon" model predicts, there are no deals for good-quality items (mortgages in this case) that are pushed off the market by bad quality items.

How should the market solve the problems of asymmetric information? First, any political pressure in markets with a high degree of asymmetric information can be very damaging and thus should be avoided. Secondly, as we know, in the market for used cars, sellers can purchase independent warrants or certificates that will describe the quality of their cars. Only good cars will be able to pass a test like this. In the market for new shares, there is a sophisticated due diligence process that involves professional underwriters, auditors, independent analysts, etc. Similar systems should probably exist in the market for mortgages and mortgage-backed securities.

Beltran and Thomas (2010) noted that a key feature of the 2007–2008 financial crisis was that for some classes of securities trade ceased. And where trade did occur, it appears that market prices were well below their intrinsic values. The authors argue that one explanation for this is that information is asymmetric, with the current holders having better information than potential buyers. They show how the resulting adverse selection problem can help explain why more complex securities trade at significant discounts to their intrinsic values. Kirabaeva (2011) argues that the complexity of structured financial products and the heterogeneity of the underlying asset pool gave their issuers an informational advantage in their evaluations.

[10] For more discussion, see next chapter.

Questions and Exercises

1. The pecking-order theory of capital structure suggests that firms should use internal funds under symmetric information between insiders and outsiders and they should issue equity when information is asymmetric.
2. Stock prices tend to decrease following the announcement of a new equity issue and tend to stay relatively stable following the announcement of a new debt issue.
3. The pecking-order theory of capital structure predicts negative correlation between debt and profitability.
4. The entrepreneur's fraction of firm's shares increases:

   a. the lower the expected return of the assets,
   b. the higher the expected return of the assets
   c. the higher the firm's risk
   d. the higher the entrepreneur's degree of risk aversion.

5. Consider a firm that has an opportunity to undertake an investment project. The project requires an investment $70 million. The project will bring $90 million and then the firm will be liquidated. The risk-free interest rate is 0. The firm has issued 12 million shares otstanding. The firm has assets-in-place which will bring $100 million. The firm needs to issue new equity to finance the new project.

   a. What would be the fraction of shares sold to new shareholders and the share price if the investors know the value of assets-in-place and that of new project?
   b. Should the firm undertake the project?
   c. Now let's look at the asymmetric information case. Assume that the initial assets can take two values, $40 million and $160 million. The true value of this is unknown in the beginning but is soon known by the entrepreneur (insider). Outside investors have a prior probability of 50% that the value equals $160 million. Analyze the situation where both types of firm issue equity and invest.
   d. Now analyze the situation where only one type of firms issues equity and invests.

e. Describe the share price dynamics. Find the share price (1) before the information about the project is known to the public; (2) at the moment when the market knows about the project but the firms have not issued equity yet; (3) at the moment when firms issue equity.
f. Which two phenomena are illustrated here?

6. Consider a firm owned by a risk-averse entrepreneur. The entrepreneur's expected utility is $Ew - 1/2\rho Varw$ where w is the entrepreneur's wealth. The firm has assets-in-place that can bring a net return R_θ, that is normally distributed with the mean θ and standard deviation σ. θ is the entrepreneur's private information and σ is the public information. Potential investors are risk-neutral. The risk-free interest rate is 0. There are two types of firms (the fraction of each type is 50%): one with $\theta = 20$ (Firm 1) and the other with $\theta = 100$ (Firm 2). $\sigma^2 = 50$ and it is publicly observable information.

a. Assume that θ is common knowledge. Which strategy is the best for the entrepreneur in this case? Explain.
b. What is the entrepreneur's utility? Calculate separately for each type.
c. Now suppose that the firm's type is the entrepreneur's private information. Suppose that the entrepreneurs of both types sell shares in total. Find the condition for this equilibrium to exist.
d. Provide an intuitive explanation for this condition.
e. Suppose $\rho = 1$. Describe possible equilibrium.

References

Akerlof, G. (1970). The Market for "Lemons": Quality Uncertainty and the Market Mechanism. *The Quarterly Journal of Economics, 84*(3), 488–500.

Antweiler, W., & Frank, M. (2006). *Do U.S. Stock Markets Typically Overreact to Corporate News Stories?* (Working Paper). University of British Columbia and University of Minnesota.

Beltran, D., & Thomas, C. (2010). Could Asymmetric Information Alone Have Caused the Collapse of Private-Label Securitization? Board of Governors of the Federal Reserve System International Finance Discussion Papers N. 1010.

Bhaduri, S. (2015). Why Do Firms Issue Equity? Some Evidence from an Emerging Economy, India. *Journal of Emerging Market Finance, 14*(1), 59–85.

Bhama, V., Jain, P., & Yadav, S. (2015). Does Firms' Pecking Order Vary during Large Deficits and Surpluses? An Empirical Study on Emerging Economies. *Procedia Economics and Finance, 30*, 155–163.

Conti, A., Thursby, M., & Rothaermel, F. (2013). Show Me the Right Stuff: Signals for High Tech Startups. *Journal of Economics & Management Strategy, 22*(2), 341–364.

Cumming, S., & Hellmann, T.: Non-Dilutive Funding Opportunities for Entrepreneurs in British Columbia, Canada. Project Report. Sauder School of Business.

De Jong, A., Verbeek, M., & Verwijmeren, P. (2011). Firms' Debt–Equity Decisions when the Static Tradeoff Theory and the Pecking Order Theory Disagree. *Journal of Banking and Finance, 35*(5), 1303–1314.

De Jong, A., Verbeek, M., & Verwijmeren, P. (2010). The Impact of Financing Surpluses and Large Financing Deficits on Tests of the Pecking Order Theory. *Financial Management, 39*(2), 733–756.

Dong, M., Loncarski, I., ter Horst, J., & Veld, C. (2012). What Drives Security Issuance Decisions: Market Timing, Pecking Order, or Both? *Financial Management, 41*(3), 637–663.

Downes, D., & Heinkel, R. (1982). Signaling and the Valuation of Unseasoned New Issues. *Journal of Finance, 37*(1), 1–10.

Eckbo, B. E. (1986). Valuation Effects of Corporate Debt Offerings. *Journal of Financial Economics, 15*(1), 119–151.

Frank, M., & Goyal, V. (2003). Testing the Pecking Order Theory of Capital Structure. *Journal of Financial Economics, 67*(2), 217–248.

Frank, M., & Goyal, V. (2009). Capital Structure Decisions: Which Factors Are Reliably Important? *Financial Management 38*, 1–37.

Frank, M., Goyal, V., & Shen, T. (2020). The Pecking Order Theory of Capital Structure. In *Oxford Research Encyclopedia of Economics and Finance.*

Garcia, D. (2002). Retained Equity, Investment Decisions and Private Information, Tuck School of Business Working Paper No. 01-05. http://ssrn.com/abstract=289801

Grinblatt, M., & Hwang, C.-Y. (1989). Signalling and the Pricing of New Issues. *Journal of Finance, 44*, 393–420.

Grinblatt, M., & Titman, S. (2001). *Financial Markets and Corporate Strategy* (2nd Edition). McGraw-Hill/Irwin.

Howton, S. D., Howton, S. W., & Perfect, S. (1998). The Market Reaction to Straight Debt Issues: The Effects of Free Cash Flow. *Journal of Financial Research, 21*(2), 219–228.

Kaminska, I. (2015, October 30). If You Call It a Blockchain, It's Not an OTC Story Anymore. *FT Alphaville.* http://ftalphaville.ft.com/2015/10/30/2143421/if-you-call-it-a-blockchain-its-not-an-otc-story-anymore/.

Keloharju, M., & Kulp, K. (1996). Market-to-Book Ratios, Equity Retention, and Management Ownership in Finnish Initial Public Offerings. *Journal of Banking and Finance, 20*(9), 1583–1599.

Kirabaeva, K. (2011). Adverse Selection and Financial Crises. *Bank of Canada Review, 2010–2011*(Winter), 11–19.

Krinsky, I., & Rotenberg, W. (2009, April 6). *Signalling and the Valuation of Unseasoned New Issues Revisited*. Published online by Cambridge University Press.

Leary, M. T., & Roberts, M. (2010). The Pecking Order, Debt Capacity, and Information Asymmetry. *Journal of Financial Economics, 95*(3), 332–355.

Leland, H. E., & Pyle, D. (1977). Information Asymmetries, Financial Structure, and Financial Intermediation. *Journal of Finance, 32*(2), 371–378.

Lemmon, M., & Zender, J. (2019). Asymmetric Information, Debt Capacity, and Capital Structure. *Journal of Financial and Quantitative Analysis, 54*, 31–59.

Miglo, A. (2011). Trade-off, Pecking Order, Signaling and Market Timing Models. In H. K. Baker & G. S. Martin (Eds.), *Capital Structure and Corporate Financing Decisions: Theory, Evidence, and Practice* (pp. 171–190). Wiley.

Miglo, A. (2022). Theories of Financing for Entrepreneurial Firms: A Review. *International Review of Entrepreneurship, 20*(2), 301–330.

Mogilevsky, V., & Murgulov, Z. (2012). Underpricing of Private Equity Backed, Venture Capital Backed and Non-Sponsored IPOs. *Investment Management and Financial Innovations, 9*(3), 47–59.

Myers, S. C. (1984). The Capital Structure Puzzle. *Journal of Finance, 39*, 575–592.

Myers, S. C., & Majluf, N. (1984). Corporate Financing and Investment Decisions When Firms Have Information That Investors Do Not Have. *Journal of Financial Economics, 13*(2), 187–221.

Nachman, D., & Noe, T. (1994). Optimal Design of Securities under Asymmetric Information. *Review of Financial Studies, 7*(1), 1–44.

Niu, E. (2015, November 21). Did Square Underprice Its IPO? *The Motley Fool*, http://www.fool.com/investing/general/2015/11/21/did-square-underprice-its-ipo.aspx.

Ritter, J. R. (1984). Signaling and the Valuation of Unseasoned New Issues: A Comment. *The Journal of Finance, 39*(4), 1231–1237.

Ritter, J. R., & Welch, I. (2002). A Review of IPO Activity, Pricing, and Allocations. *The Journal of Finance, 57*(4), 1795–1828.

Ross, S. A. (1977). The Determination of Financial Structure: The Incentive Signaling Approach. *Bell Journal of Economics, 8*(1), 23–40.

Shyam-Sunders, L., & Myers, S. (1999). Testing Static Tradeoff against Pecking Order Models of Capital Structure. *Journal of Financial Economics, 51*(2), 219–244.

Stempel, J. (2013, December 18). Facebook, Zuckerberg, Banks must Face IPO Lawsuit: Judge. *Reuters*, http://www.reuters.com/article/us-facebook-ipo-lawsuit-idUSBRE9BH0VD20131218

Stiglitz, J., & Weiss, A. (1981). Credit Rationing in Markets with Imperfect Information. *The American Economic Review, 71*(3), 393–410.

Varas, F. (2014). *Trading Dynamics of Financial Assets Under Asymmetric Information* (Working Paper). Duke University. Fuqua School of Business.

CHAPTER 4

Credit Rationing and Asset Substitution

4.1 Shareholders versus Creditors: Capital Structure Battle

Agency problems exist between shareholders and managers. In this relationship, shareholders are the principal and they do not have direct control over the managers' actions (agent). This chapter analyzes shareholders–creditors agency problems where creditors (principal) cannot control the actions of the shareholders (firm's owners) responsible for major decisions.

Recall that in a perfect market the firm undertakes projects with positive NPVs. Also, in a perfect market, contracts are easily enforceable and shareholders' decisions are easily contractible. So creditors and shareholders will write a contract according to which the creditors will get their investments back and shareholders will choose projects with positive NPVs or, when projects are mutually exclusive, the shareholders will choose the project with maximal NPV. Both shareholders and creditors have the same goal: to maximize the value of their investment. This goal is achieved when firms use the policy described above. But this mutual

Supplementary Information The online version contains supplementary material available at https://doi.org/10.1007/978-3-031-85459-0_4.

A. Miglo, *Capital Structure in the Modern World*,
https://doi.org/10.1007/978-3-031-85459-0_4

goal is the cause of their conflicting interests when markets are imperfect. Throughout this chapter, and the next chapter, we will discuss the reasons why creditors and shareholders often support different corporate decisions in order to maximize the values of their claims. Two kinds of distortions may arise from agency problems between creditors and shareholders. This chapter considers the shareholders' tendency to invest in very risky projects, possibly even in projects with negative NPVs. The next chapter will look at situations when the shareholders–creditors conflict leads to underinvestment in positive NPV projects.

Potential conflicts between creditors and shareholders explain many interesting phenomena in financial markets. One of them is called "credit rationing." Josef Stiglitz and Andrew Weiss described it in their 1981 article (Stiglitz was awarded the Nobel Prize in 2001 for his contribution to imperfect market theories). Credit rationing is a situation where financial institutions, such as banks, refuse to increase interest rates clearing the demand for loans, even when the demand is coming from firms with profitable projects. This is an unusual situation for market economies because, traditionally, prices (interest rates in a market for loans) were supposed to be flexible enough to equalize demand and supply. In November 2015, Ruth Simon published an article in the *Wall Street Journal* entitled "Big Banks Cut Back on Loans to Small Business." The article argues that the biggest banks in the United States are making far fewer loans to small businesses than they did a decade ago thus ceding market share to alternative lenders that charge significantly higher rates. Together, 10 of the largest banks issuing small loans to businesses lent $44.7 billion in 2014, down 38% from a peak of $72.5 billion in 2006, according to an analysis of the banks' federal regulatory filings. The largest banks "have essentially abandoned the small business market," said Dr. Cole, DePaul University finance professor. Some entrepreneurs had to borrow online where interest rates are as high as 80%.[1] This chapter will provide some insight into these phenomena.

[1] Simon (November 26, 2015).

4.2 Asset Substitution and Risk-Shifting

Usually, a creditor's claim is maximized when the probability of the claim being honored is maximized. In most cases this means creditors prefer lower risk. However, shareholders of high-leveraged firms may gain when business risk increases, especially the shareholders of firms with low equity value. If the project fails, the shareholders will not be worse off. But if the project succeeds, there will be more than enough earnings to pay off the debt, and the surplus will go to the shareholders.

Investments are usually risky but sometimes conflicts of interests lead shareholders to invest in overly risky projects. Investors demand high returns in good times to offset the chance of low returns in bad times. The degree of risk is different from investment to investment and corporations have an almost unlimited choice with regard to how much risk they want to take on. Asset substitution arises when a firm takes on an investment that transfers wealth from creditors to shareholders. This is done for the most part by taking on a risky investment. Due to limited liability, shareholders are able to avoid most of the consequences of a bad investment and reap much more reward when an investment works out compared to the creditors. This incentivizes the shareholders to take on more risk. Creditors are never paid more than the principal plus interest, so when a risky investment pays off, they are unable to receive any excess profit. When the same investment fails and the firm is forced into bankruptcy, creditors have no insurance against being paid less than their principal plus interest. As a result, creditors desire investments with low risk.

Therefore, when a firm takes on a risky project, it can create wealth for the shareholders and take away wealth from the creditors. The effects of asset substitution and risk shifting were first introduced by Jensen and Meckling (1976). It is considered to be one of the most important concepts in corporate finance. Many authors consider some leveraged-buyouts in the 1980s to be examples of risk-shifting, including the case of RJR Nabisco, which was one of the largest buyouts in history. When the firm entered financial distress in the late 1980s, the share price went down and the firm's managers undertook a risky investment in the form of a leveraged buyout. It made many of the existing debtholders furious. The result was quite surprising for many analysts. Nabisco's share price went up and its bond's price went down: reflecting the negative impact of the risky investment on the creditors' value.[2]

There are quite a few ways to measure risk. The main theoretical way to measure risk is with the mean-preserving spread criterion (MPS) or increasing risk dominance (IR).[3] If one stochastic variable dominates another by the MPS or IR criterion, then it is considered less risky.

To illustrate the idea of asset substitution, consider a company that is deciding between two projects. A project j brings cash flow R_j, $j = 1{,}2$. The company has debt with a face value D. R_1 is distributed according to the distribution function F and density function f and R_2 is distributed according to the distribution function G and density function g.

The timing of events in this situation (and most other situation considered in this chapter and Chapter 5) is shown in Fig. 4.1. The key aspect of this model is that creditors do not have direct control over the shareholders' actions. Even if the firm gets financing from creditors, it is up to the shareholders to make the final decisions. In contrast to the models with asymmetric information from Chapter 3, This chapter and Chapter 5 analyze models with moral hazard.

The shareholders' payoff is 0 when $R < D$ and it is $R - D$ otherwise. Then the difference between the shareholders' expected payoffs from undertaking projects 1 and 2 are

$$\Delta_T = \int_D^{\overline{R}} (R - D) f(R) dR - \int_D^{\overline{R}} (R - D) g(R) dR$$

Fig. 4.1 The sequence of events

[2] See Warga and Welch (1993) about wealth shifting during 1980s buyouts. Also see http://www.investopedia.com/articles/stocks/09/corporate-kleptocracy-rjr-nabisco.asp.

[3] See Appendix for more information about stochastic dominance, mean-preserving spread condition etc.

$$= \int_D^{\overline{R}} (R - D)(f(R) - g(R))dR$$

Let $v = R - D$ and $du = (f(R) - g(R))dR$. Then

$$\Delta_T = (R - D)(F(R) - G(R))|_D^{\overline{R}} - \int_D^{\overline{R}} (F(R) - G(R))dR$$

$$= \int_D^{\overline{R}} (G(R) - F(R))dR \tag{4.1}$$

If $F(R)$ dominates $G(R)$ by FOD then $G(R) \geq F(R)$ for any R. This leads to the following proposition.

Proposition 4.1 *If Project 1's cash flow distribution first-order dominates that from Project 2, the shareholders will choose Project 1 regardless of its level of debt.*

Now suppose that $F(R)$ dominates $G(R)$ by increasing the risk criterion (IR). We can rewrite (4.1) as $\int_0^{\overline{R}} (G(R) - F(R))dR - \int_0^D (G(R) - F(R))dR$.

From the definition of IR it follows that the first term equals 0 and the second term is non-negative implying $\Delta_T \leq 0$. It means that in most cases the shareholders will choose project 2, which has greater risk. In some cases they will be indifferent between the two projects. Galai and Masulis (1976) and Green (1984) were one of the first to analyze a leveraged firm's investment choice when dealing with two projects with equal expected earnings one of which has lower variance or dominates the other by the MPS condition.

Since in many cases Δ_T is strictly negative, the above conclusions may hold even if the expected cash flow from project 2 is lower than that from project 1.

Proposition 4.2 *If Project 1 dominates Project 2 by the mean-preserving spread condition, the Project 2 is at least as good as Project 1 for the shareholders.*

Example 4.1 The following example will illustrate the shareholders' incentive to undertake projects with low or even negative NPVs. Consider a company that is deciding between two one-year projects, A and B. Both projects have the same investment cost, \$70,000, but are expected to generate different earnings. The amount of earnings depends on the state of nature. There are two states of nature: good (g) and bad (b), with equal probability. For simplicity, assume that there are no bankruptcy costs. Also assume that a banker exists that is ready to finance the firm's investment by providing a $70,000 one-year loan with 5% interest so the company has a debt due in one year with a face value of $73,500.

The payoffs from the projects and their expected earnings are indicated in Table 4.1. Clearly, project B has higher expected earnings and a higher NPV because both projects have the same investment cost. Furthermore, the NPV of project A is negative regardless of the interest rates because the expected earnings are smaller than the investment cost. Nevertheless, the project that is undertaken by the firm is the one that will yield the greatest payoff to the shareholders (see Table 4.2).

Therefore, project A will be chosen even though project B has a higher NPV. The reason is that project A has more risk. Its cash flow is either too high or too low. It is the "too high" situation that made this project attractive to shareholders. The projects are such that given the firm's debt, both projects bring nothing to shareholders in bad times while in good times project A is definitely better.

Note that if project A brings $25,000 in state b, Project B dominates Project A by the MPS condition: the projects' expected earnings are equal but Project A has a higher risk. The shareholders will choose Project A, which illustrates Proposition 4.2. Alternatively, suppose that in the initial

Table 4.1 Projects and earnings in Example 4.1

	b (Pr = 0.5)	*g (Pr = 0.5)*	*Expected earnings*
Project A	$5000	$125,000	$65,000 = 1/2*5000 + 1/2*125,000
Project B	$65,000	$85,000	$75,000 = 1/2*65,000 + 1/2*85,000

Table 4.2 Shareholders' payoff in Example 4.1

	b (Pr = 0.5)	*g (Pr = 0.5)*	*Expected payoff to the shareholders*
Project A	$0	$51,500 = 125,000–73,500	$36,750
Project B	$0	$11,500 = 85,000–73,500	$5750

situation, Project B brings \$125,000 in state g. One can check that in this case Project B dominates project A by FOD. One can also check that in this case, the shareholders would choose Project B, which illustrates Proposition 4.1.

Finally, note that if one investment dominates another investment by the second-order dominance criterion, no conclusions regarding the shareholders' incentive for asset substitution can be reached without further analysis (see e.g., Su & Zhang, 2017). The reason for this is that $G(R)$ can be larger than $F(R)$ for some values of R and vice versa for other values of R and therefore the sign of the expression in (4.1) depends on each individual case.

Debt Level and Assets Substitution

What are the implications of the asset substitution effect on capital structure? An interesting question, for example, is how the shareholders' incentive to choose riskier projects depends on the level of the firm's debt? As was noted above, if one project dominates another by FOD, asset substitution will never take place. In the case of MPS, the firm will always substitute assets. What about other cases? To analyze this question, let us note that common sense in finance suggests that riskier projects should have a higher probability of bankruptcy compared to safer projects. In other words, $G(D) > F(D)$. Let us now return to (4.1). We have $\frac{\partial \Delta_T}{\partial D} = G(D) - F(D) > 0$ suggesting that the likelihood of asset substitution increases when debt increases.[4] This leads to the following proposition.

Proposition 4.3

As long as the probability of bankruptcy with a riskier project exceeds that with a safer project, a higher level of debt increases the likelihood of asset substitution.

This result implies that by changing the level of debt firms can control the incentive for an asset substitution problem. So one would expect that firms with a greater potential to have an asset substitution problem should have smaller debt.

[4] See Gavish and Kalay (1983) and Green and Talmor (1986) for further analysis of this topic.

Table 4.3 Projects and earnings in Example 4.2

	b (*Pr* = 1 − *p*)	*g* (*Pr* = *p*)	*Expected earnings*
Project A	X_1	X_2	$pX_2 + (1 - p)X_1$
Project B	Y_1	Y_2	$pY_2 + (1 - p)Y_1$

Example 4.2 There are two states of nature: g with probability p and b with probability $1 - p$. Consider a firm with two investment projects available with earnings shown in the table along with their expected earnings (Table 4.3).

Projects are mutually exclusive. We make the following assumptions: (1)$Y_2 > X_2 > X_1 > Y_1$; (2) $X_2 + (1 - p)X_1 > pY_2 + (1 - p)Y_1$ (the interpretation of these assumptions is that project A has a higher NPV and Project B is riskier); and (3) The company has issued debt with a face value D.

If $D < Y_1$, the shareholders will select Project A. Their payoff in this case is $pX_2 + (1 - p) X_1 - D$ which is greater than Project B's: $pY_2 + (1 - p) Y_1 - D$.

Consider D such that $X_1 > D > Y_1$. The shareholder's payoff if A is chosen is $pX_2 + (1 - p)X_1 - D$ and if B it is $p(Y_2 - D)$. The latter can be written as: $pY_2 + (1 - p)Y_1 - D + (1 - p)D - (1 - p)Y_1$. This is greater than $pX_2 + (1 - p) X_1 - D$ because $D > Y_1$. We can then conclude that project B will be chosen. The conclusion is the same for the case when $X_2 > D > X_1$. The shareholder's payoff if A is chosen is $p(X_2 - D)$ and if B it is $p(Y_2 - D)$. Project B will be chosen since $Y_2 > X_2$. This illustrates Proposition 4.3. Note that the case $D > X_2$ does not make too much sense since Project A can not be considered a safer project because the probability of bankruptcy with Project A is 100%.

In conclusion, we find that when the debt level is low and there is no incentive for asset substitution. When the debt level increases, then it changes. Anticipating an asset substitution problem, the creditors will charge a higher than normal interest rate. This leads to a loss for the shareholders (agency cost of debt).

Table 4.4 New and existing projects' earnings

	b (*Pr* = *0.5*)	*g* (*Pr* = *0.5*)
Firm	\$20 mln	\$100 mln
Project 1	\$0 mln	\$18 mln

Debt Seniority and Overinvestment

A special case of the risk shifting problem is overinvestment. In the example below, a firm has debt with a face value of 50 and has assets-in-place that will generate 20 in the bad state and 100 in the good state. The firm is able to take on a project in the first period that costs 10 and will generate the payoffs according to the table below. As one can see the project has a negative NPV: $0.5 * 0 + 0.5 * 18 - 10 = -1$. Let us consider now that the shareholders will be willing to undertake the project. Assume that to finance the new project, the firm can only offer a senior debt with a face value of 10 (Table 4.4).

If the firm does not undertake the new project, the shareholders' payoff will be $0.5 * (100 - 50) + 0.5 * 0 = 25$. If the firm undertakes the project then it will be: $0.5 * 58 + 0.5 * 0 = 29$ (note that 58 represents the shareholders' earnings in the good state: $100 + 18 - 10 - 50$). Hence, the shareholders will choose to undertake the project even though it has a negative NPV. Note that everybody is happy in this scenario except the initial debtholders. Without the project, their expected payoff is $0.5 * 50 + 0.5 * 20 = 35$. With the project it is: $0.5 * 50 + 0.5 * 10 = 30$.

In conclusion, the shareholders' decision will dilute the initial (junior) creditors' claims. They will only receive 10 in the bad state when they could potentially have received 20.

We have seen in this section that the asset substitution or risk shifting problem can potentially damage a firm's investment decisions and reduce its value. It can be caused by either investing in projects that have too much risk or investing above the optimal level (the overinvestment problem). How can this situation be prevented? In general, how can the firm mitigate the negative effect of the asset substitution problem on its value? First, we need to understand that the problem arises not because the shareholders are "bad" people by definition and they do not care about creditors money. The shareholders undertake actions from a rational decision-maker point of view, i.e., actions that maximize the value of their claims. A distortion here comes from the fact that markets are imperfect, there is a moral hazard problem between different economic agents and it is virtually impossible to write comprehensive contracts that will describe all possible circumstances.

The asset substitution theory explains the usage of some financing strategies. All strategies listed below help prevent asset substitution problems. These strategies are: using debt with financing covenants, using debt with dividend covenants, asset covenants or binding covenants, using loans with protective loan covenants, using bank debt and using convertible debt or warrants (for more analysis of this issue see Green (1984)).

The idea of convertible debt is that if shareholders undertake a strategy that can potentially shift value from creditors to shareholders, the creditors can threaten to convert bonds into shares. Bank debt is usually accompanied by better monitoring from the lender, therefore, the shareholders ability to undertake value diminishing projects decreases. Some corporations have limited the asset substitution problem by issuing warrants and options. In some cases, firms split off the safe part of the business. In a recent paper, Batten et al. (2021) study financing strategies of multinational corporations and argue that first they use a larger variety of debt securities than domestic firms that increase their risk including the extent of agency problems and asset substitution problems and secondly the usage of convertible securities helps to mitigate these problems.

Protective loan covenants are restrictions placed on the firm by the debtholders and can include: prohibition of new debt financing, the maintenance of certain financial ratios, etc. Sometimes covenants restrict firms from selling their assets, undertaking new businesses and taking new loans. Firms that violate these covenants are in technical default and debtholders are allowed to intervene in the company's business. Loan covenants make debts safer, and therefore increase their values. This undermines the whole idea of asset substitution consisting of value shifting from equityholders to debtholders.

There is evidence that risk-shifting incentives of insolvent banks can significantly deplete assets. For example, Barrow and Horvitz (1993) studied insolvent savings and loans operated by the, now defunct, Federal Savings and Loan Insurance Corporation from 1985 to 1988. The firms that operated under government conservatorship adopted much less risky strategies and on average depleted the deposit insurance fund less than insolvent savings and loans that were allowed to continue operating under their existing management.

During the recent financial crisis, many companies and banks were saved via bailouts by the government. The United States executed two stimulus packages, totaling nearly $1 trillion during 2008 and 2009.[5] Wilson and Wu (2010) studied bank incentives for risk shifting. If a bank is facing insolvency, it will be tempted to reject good loans and accept bad loans so as to shift risk onto its creditors. If bailing out banks deemed "too big to fail" involves buying assets at above fair market values, then these banks are encouraged ex ante to purchase bad assets. The authors argue that buying up common (preferred) stock is always the most (least) efficient type of capital infusion.

Note that empirical evidence about asset substitution is ambiguous. For example, Graham and Harvey (2001) found that the majority of finance executives do not think that asset substitution is a very important factor in capital structure decisions.

Some attempts have been made to incorporate asset substitution into capital structure analysis along with other factors. For example, Ikeda (2005) demonstrates that equityholders' risk-shifting incentives are not necessarily monotonically increasing in leverage in a stochastic interest rates environment. Equityholders will substitute less risky negative net present value projects for riskier positive net present value projects if the correlation coefficient between the firm value and interest rate is sufficiently negative. Tsuji (2009) analyses the joint effect of the bankruptcy cost of debt and agency cost of debt including asset substitution. The results are consistent with the capital structure behaviour of Japanese firms.

4.3 Credit Rationing

Two famous economists Stiglitz and Weiss published a paper together in 1981 on credit rationing (which is closely related to asset substitution), which was part of Stiglitz's Nobel Prize package in 2001! Their idea was that banks ration credit rather than increase borrowing rates.

In contrast to a classical upward-slopping supply curve, the loans supply curve may not necessarily be like that. At some point, a further increase in the interest rate may cause biased investment decisions

[5] "BBC – Stimulus Package 2009". BBC News. February 14, 2009. http://news.bbc.co.uk/2/hi/business/7889897.stm. Retrieved January 22, 2016.

by borrowers, which can result in a loss for the financial institution. Figure 4.2 illustrates this point.

Banks will not increase the interest rate above r^* and as a result some firms will not get loans. The following example demonstrates this idea.

Assume that a firm can choose between two projects, A and B, both costing 50. The firm seeks debt to finance the project. There are two states of nature (bad, good) with equal probability. The risk-free rate is 0. What is the link between the interest rate and the choice of project?

The earnings in the two states are as follows (Table 4.5):

Considering a debt with face value 50, the shareholders' payoffs are as follows. If A: $0.5 * 40 + 0.5 * 40 = 40$. If B: $0.5 * (125 - 50) + 0.5 * 0 = 37.5$. Therefore, project A will be chosen. The creditors will be interested

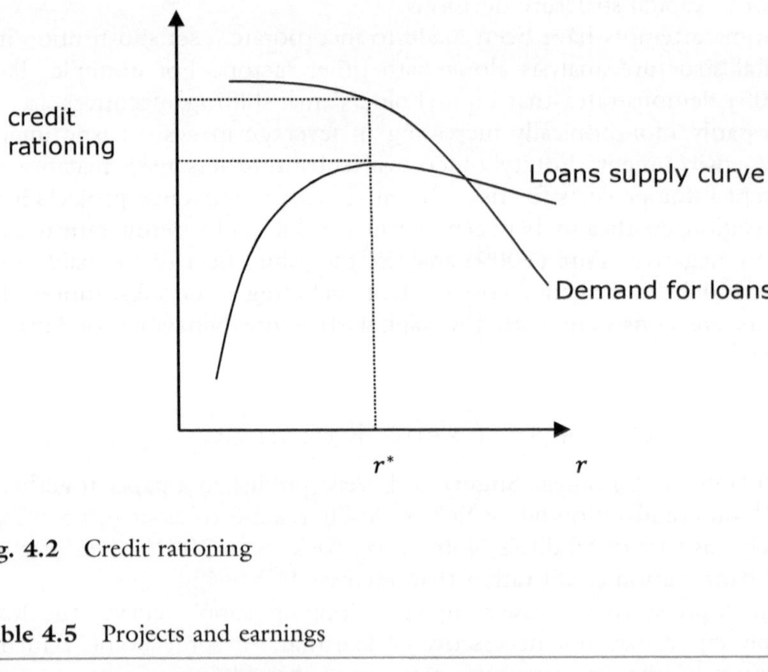

Fig. 4.2 Credit rationing

Table 4.5 Projects and earnings

	b (Pr = 0.50)	*g (Pr = 0.50)*	*Expected earnings*
Project A	90	90	90
Project B	0	125	62.5

in providing the firm with the needed funds because debt is essentially risk-free when the firm takes project A.

Now suppose that the risk-free interest rate is 50%. In order to be able to raise debt, the firm needs to convince potential creditors that they can earn at least 50% (on average). Otherwise the creditors would prefer to invest in risk-free government bonds. If the debt face value is 75 (the debt face value plus 50% interests), the shareholders' expected payoffs will be as follows. If A: $0.5 * 15 + 0.5 * 15 = 15$. If B: $0.5 * 0 + 0.5 * 50 = 25$. Therefore, project B will be chosen. In this case, the creditors' expected payoff is $0.5 * 75 + 0.5 * 0 = 37.5$, which is less than the cost of the investment. As a result, they will not be willing to lend the money. In fact, the maximal possible face value of debt is 125 (otherwise the shareholders do not receive any profit). Therefore the maximal expected payoff to the creditors is $0.5 * 125 = 62.5 < 75$. So there is no equilibrium where creditors can count on earning at least a minimal expected rate of return.

We have seen some positive NPV projects that were very attractive from the creditors' point of view but that were not undertaken in favor of riskier projects. Creditors could charge higher interest rates on their debt. This leads to a vicious cycle where creditors keep charging higher interest rates and firms keep taking on riskier projects. Instead, some creditors will refuse to lend to firms when interest rates are too high, regardless of the interest payments the firm agrees to make. This phenomenon is called credit rationing (it can also exist because of asymmetric information).[6]

When interest rates are below their equilibrium level, there is an excessive demand for credit. Banks, however, will not necessarily increase the interest rate in order to equalize demand and supply. Perhaps this explains why bankers are often described as "very conservative people." Perhaps this also explains why the volume of credit seems to be much less than necessary in developing countries where demand for credit is very high but the average quality of borrowers is low. It can also explain why more loans are collateralized when treasury rates rise (banks expect a decrease in the quality of borrowers). The model of credit rationing was also used

[6] For a review see e.g., Miglo (2022). Bester (1985) argues that collateral by high-quality borrowers can be used as a screening device by banks. Some recent papers aanalyze credit rationning under both asymmetric inormation and agency problems and argue that adverse selection is less important (Arnold & Riley, 2009; Coco, 1997; Su & Zhang, 2017).

by Kaufman (1996) to explain aspects of Argentina's economic crisis of 1995–96.[7]

Among recent research note Eckbo et al. (2022) that argues that the non-interest terms (e.g., up-front fees) in bank loans can be used to mitigate the credit rationing problem and Jin and Zhang (2019) that analyzes links between credit rationing and firm size when different bank screening methods are used. As mentioned in Miglo (2022) it seems that most researchers agree on the importance of credit rationing in general (especially regarding small firms financing[8]), while two issues seem to be most debatable. One is a discussion about whether moral hazard or asymmetric information is the most important driver of credit rationing (see e.g., Arnold & Riley, 2009; Banerjee & Duflo, 2014; Berger & Udell, 1992; Su & Zhang, 2017). The other one is the connection between interest rate and collateral (e.g. Berger & Udell, 1992; Godlewski & Weill, 2011; John et al., 2003; Niinimäki, 2018). Most studies find a negative relationship between interest rates and collateral consistent with Bester (1985) but some papers argue that collateral may lead to borrowers' complacency and other negative effects.

Acharya and Viswanathan (2011) build a model of the financial sector to explain why an adverse asset shock can lead to a sharp decrease in the level of cash. Financial firms raise short-term debt in order to finance asset purchases. When market conditions worsen, debt provides an incentive for asset substitution, which can lead to credit rationing by banks. Firms then may sell assets to better-capitalized firms in order to reduce leverage. Short-term debt is relatively cheap to issue in good times. As a result many firms with high leverage and low capital can be created in the financial industry. The following illustrates this point.

We will continue with Example 4.2. This time suppose that each project has its own probability of success denoted p_A and p_B and also $X_1 = Y_1 = 0$. We consider a firm that initially invested in Project A. The cash flow from projects will be realized in Date 2. The sequence of events is presented below (Fig. 4.3).

Also assume that initially the firm has some debt outstanding. On Date 1, the firm has to rollover existing debt because liquidating projects on Date 1 is not profitable. Also, on Date 1 the firm can switch to Project B.

[7] See Hashi and Toçi (2010) for credit rationing analysis in south-European countries.

[8] More discussion is provided in Chapter 9.

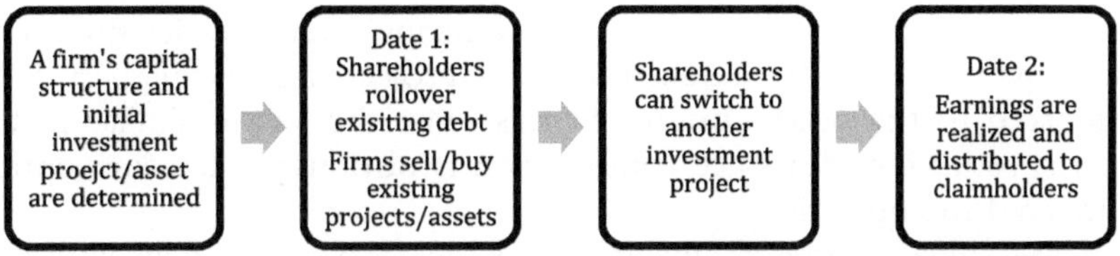

Fig. 4.3 Sequence of events

Banks have no control over the project choice. As was mentioned in the previous subsection, the project choice depends on the level of debt after Date 1. The critical level of debt is determined by the following equation: $p_A(X_2 - D) = p_B(Y_2 - D)$. Let $D^* = \frac{p_A X_2 - p_B Y_2}{p_A - p_B}$. A firm with a level of debt below this will not shift to a riskier project and vice versa. What is then the critical level of debt in Date 1 that can be rolled over. The bank will have to provide financing D to cover the firm's period 1 debt but the expected payoff in Date 2 is Dp_A (assuming that the firm does not change projects). So the critical level of the date 1 debt is $D^* p_A$.

As was mentioned above, the inability to rollover debt on Date 1 is damaging to the firm. Assume that the firm can partially sell its assets/projects on Date 1. Suppose that the asset price is p. If the firm can sell the project for a price higher than a certain level p, it would be able to rollover the debt. Suppose the firm sells a fraction x of the project. Then the firm's debt capacity is $xp + (1 - x)D^* p_A$. And it should be equal to the initial debt: $xp + (1 - x)D^* p_A = D$. It follows that the fraction of the project that should be sold is: $x = \frac{D - D^* p_A}{p - D^* p_A}$. This fraction decreases with the price of asset p, and increases with the initial level of debt D. The latter result leads to the point that although the probability of a financial crisis is lower in good times, its severity in terms of potential asset sale and evaporation of market liquidity can be greater. This is because in good times the ability to accumulate debt is high.

4.4 Other Related Ideas

Since the shareholders get nothing in case a leveraged company is liquidated and the firm's assets' value is smaller than the value of the debt, the shareholders may have an incentive to continue the firm's operations in hopes of miracle luck or recovery. Even the slightest probability of success can make not liquidating the company a rational decision. This can happen even if the liquidation, as a project, has the highest NPV compared to the other options. In this sense the idea is similar to the asset substitution idea since continuation is obviously the riskier option compared to liquidation.[9]

The following example illustrates this idea. A firm has debt with face value $D = 110{,}000$. The firm has two options. One is to liquidate the company for a value $L = 100{,}000$. The firm can also continue business in the next period and receive $R = 150{,}000$ in the good state of the economy or 0 in the bad state with a probability of 0.5. What will the shareholders do?

Liquidation has a higher value for debtholders. If the firm liquidates, it will receive 100,000; however, if it choose to continue, the expected value of the debt will be $0.5 * 110 + 0.5 * 0 = 55{,}000$, which is much less than 100,000. If there is a liquidation in the first period, shareholders receive nothing since the liquidation value is less than the debt value; however, if they continue, the expected payoff for the shareholders will be $0.5*(150 - 110)+0.5*0 = 20$. Therefore, the shareholders will choose to continue even though it is detrimental to the senior debtholders.

Real-life examples of this problem include a prolonged liquidation of Eastern Airlines during the recession of 1989.[10] A more recent example is the case of Cyprus bank FBME, where the shareholders were seemingly resisting the bank's liquidation.[11] In fact, Bernie Madof's Ponzi scheme can also be seen as a variation of the situation described above. The company was never voluntarily liquidated but instead continued to support its risky investments without actually informing investors about the real destinations of their investments. Some other examples can be found in the recent credit crisis in 2008. Not many companies wanted to end their operations and liquidate. For example, General Motors (just like many other car producers, banks and financial companies) had a continuation strategy and it was looking for a sponsor to get through the recession. Finally it received some support from the government.

[9] See, for example, Titman (1984).

[10] Grinblatt and Titman (2001). Also see "*Eastern Airlines*". *US Centennial of Flight Commission*.

http://www.centennialofflight.net/essay/Commercial_Aviation/EasternAirlines/Tran13.htm. Retrieved 22 January 2016.

[11] http://in-cyprus.com/hope-for-fbme-deposits/.

Although the idea of liquidation resistance is appealing theoretically, it seems that after the series of large-scale corporate scandals related to the misuse of corporate funds and miscommunication of information to investors, corporate managers of companies in financial distress are not just trying to "fool" investors by investing in riskier and riskier projects but are trying to deal with debt renegotiations and debt restructuring, which we consider in the next chapter.

Brander and Lewis (1986) show that issuing risky debt induces firms to be more aggressive in the product market. This effect of risky debt can be considered a special form of the asset substitution effect. Brander and Lewis consider the traditional Cournot model. The firms choose simultaneously their respective output levels and, given these quantities, the price of the good is determined in the product market according to the demand curve. Quantities in the Cournot model are strategic substitutes: when firm 1 becomes more aggressive, firm 2 becomes softer, and vice versa. It is beneficial for each firm to commit itself to an aggressive behavior in the product market by adopting a strategy that will shift its reaction curve outward (i.e., commit the firm to produce a larger quantity for each quantity produced by the rival). Increasing output in equilibrium also increases the variance of the firm's profit. Since the marginal benefit increases in a good state, the shareholders gain significantly in good states. On the other hand, marginal losses are highest in bad states. It is similar to the asset substitution effect where what matters most for the shareholders are the gains in good states.

Brander and Lewis' (1986) follow-up paper included bankruptcy costs and produced similar results. Subsequent theoretical and empirical literature produced mixed results regarding connections between debt level and a firm's production strategy. Maksimovic (1988) argued that the firms become more aggressive while Chevalier and Scharfstein (1996) argued that they become less aggressive. Povel and Raith (2004) analyze the interaction of financing and output market decisions in a duopoly in which one firm is financially constrained. Unlike most previous work, debt is derived as an optimal contract. Compared with a situation in which both firms are unconstrained, the constrained firm produces less while its unconstrained rival produces more. Empirical literature finds that industrial concentration is an important variable in the interaction between the financial market and the product market (see, for example, Kovenock and Philips (1997)). It also finds that the close rivals can increase their market share while the leveraged firms lose out both in terms of investments and market shares (see, for example, Opler & Titman, 1994). Chowdhury (2006) argues that the relation between debt and firm competitive behavior is not monotonic.

Questions and Exercises

1. There are two projects available to a firm, F and S. The cost is the same for each project: $B = 50$. Project F will generate cash flows of 60 in both the bad and good state, and project S will generate 20 and 90 in the bad and good states, respecticely.

   a. What is the NPV of each project?
   b. Suppose the firm can raise the 50 by issuing a bond with a face value of 50. Which project would the shareholders prefer and what are the payoffs to the creditors?
   c. Now suppose the debt face value is $80 million, which project will the company select?

2. Consider a corporation that has two projects available. Project 1 generates 10 with probability 1. Project 2 yields a random return: 15 in a good state of economy (with probability 1/2) and 3 otherwise. The projects are mutually exclusive. To finance one of the projects, the firm issues debt (denote its face value by D). The lenders are not able to control the project's choice by shareholders. Assume that the shareholders are risk-neutral.

   a. Which project will be chosen?
   b. Explain your answer in (a) intuitively.
   c. Which phenomenon is illustrated in this example?
   d. Comment on some of your answers by (a) using your knowledge of stochastic dominance and the link between stochastic dominance and the phenomenon illustrated in this exercise.
   e. Suppose that the investment cost is 6 for each project. Lenders are risk-neutral. Find D.
   f. What is the shareholders' expected payoff?
   g. Continue to assume that the investment cost is 6 and financing was provided by creditors and that a project was chosen by the shareholders. Suppose that after all these decisions have been made but before cash flow from the project is realized, a firm gets an unpredictable opportunity to make an additional investment. The cost of this investment is 2 and the return is 3 in the

good state and 0 otherwise. Explain the problem that may arise if debt raised for financing the first project was junior.

3. A corporation has two projects available. The projects are mutually exclusive. Each project costs B. If Project 1 is undertaken, the cash flow is K if the project is unsuccessful and it is R_1 otherwise, $R_1 > B > K$. The probability of success is p_1. If project 2 is undertaken, the cash flow is K if the project is unsuccessful and it is R_2 otherwise, $R_2 > B$. The probability of success is p_2. Everybody is risk-neutral and the risk-free interest rate is f. Finance is provided by a standard debt contract. There exists perfect competition among lenders and they have a competitive payoff in equilibrium. The firm acts in the shareholders' interests.

   a. Suppose the debt face value is D. Write the condition that determines whether project 1 or project 2 will be chosen.
   b. Further, use $K = 100$, $B = 200$, $R_1 = 260$, $p_1 = 80\%$, $R_2 = 300$, $p_2 = 20\%$. What is the NPV of each project?
   c. Write the condition that determines whether project 1 or project 2 will be chosen.
   d. Find D as a function of f if the lenders know that project 1 will be chosen.
   e. Find D as a function of f if the lenders know that project 2 will be chosen.
   f. Now suppose that the lenders can't control the choice of the project by the shareholders. Find the maximum value of f when the firm will make an investment.
   g. Which phenomenon is illustrated here?

4. The following is not one of the ways a firm can mitigate an asset substitution problem.

   a. Protective loan covenants
   b. Better monitoring
   c. Convertible debt
   d. Callable bonds.

5. Asset substitution

   a. Describe (in words) the asset substitution problem
   b. Which facts or empirical data can illustrate this problem?

c. Suppose the firm has two mutually exclusive projects available. The probability of success is p in both of them. The first project generates F_2 in the case of success and F_1 otherwise. $F_1 < F_2$; the second one generates cash flow S_2 in the case of success and S_1 otherwise, $S_1 < S_2 < F_2$. Also, $pF_2 + (1-p)F_1 = pS_2 + (1-p)S_1$. Projects have the same investment cost. Prior to making the decision as to which project to undertake, the firm borrowed funds sufficient for financing one project. The face value of the debt is D. Assume risk neutrality and that the firm acts in the interests of its existing shareholders. Which project will be chosen if:
   c1) D is very small? (For simplicity, suppose that $D = 0$)
   c2) $\max\{F_2, S_2\} > D > \max\{F_1, S_1\}$?
d. Now assume that F_2 decreases by a marginally small amount ε. It means the first project produces F_{2new} in the good state: $F_{2new} = F_2 - \varepsilon > S_2$. Which project will be chosen if:
   d1) $D = 0$? Comment.
   d2) $\max\{F_{2new}, S_2\} > D > \max\{F_1, S_1\}$? Comment.
e. Consider a more general setup. Suppose the first project generates cash flow R_1, where R_1 is distributed according to the distribution function $F(R_1)$; the second project generates cash flow R_2, where R_2 is distributed according to the distribution function $G(R_2)$. The firm has debt equal to $D > 0$. Describe (in words) the asset substitution problem when:
   e1) $F(R_1)$ first order dominates $G(R_2)$;
   e2) $F(R_1)$ dominates $G(R_2)$ by MPS;
   e3) $F(R_1)$ dominates $G(R_2)$ by second-order stochastic dominance
f. How can a firm prevent an asset substitution problem?

6. Consider two projects which cost 90 each but have different probabilites of success and different cash flows. Projects' cash flows and the probabilites aof success are shown in the table below. Which project will the firm choose? (assume risk-neutrality)

   a. Which project has higher NPV?
   b. Which project will be chosen if the risk-free interest rate is 0?
   c. Analyze the situation if the risk-free interest rate is 30%.

	Cash Flow		
	Failure	*Success*	*Pr(success)*
Project A	80	130	0.8
Project B	0	140	0.2

7. Assume that there is a firm and that it will go bankrupt if it has insufficient cash flows to meet its debt obligation or it is unable to borrow a sufficient amount to meet its debt obligations. The firm has a senior debt of 1150 and a coupon payment worth 150 due immediately. The firm can either choose to liquidate for a value of 1100 or continue operating by borrowing an additional 150 to repay the senior debt to the bank and promise him 250 next year and have a cash flow of either 1500 or 500 with equal probability. Assume that all investors are risk-neutral and the risk-free interest rate is 10%. Which option will the firm choose?
8. Consider a firm with two potential projects: F and S. The cost is the same for each project: $B = 20$. There are two states of nature b = bad and g = good and the discount rate is 0.

	b (Pr = 0.5)	*g (Pr = 0.5)*	*Expected cash flow*
Project F	60	60	60
Project S	20	90	55

   A bank considers a potential loan to the firm. What is the link between the interest rate and the project choice? What is optimal loan policy for the bank?
9. Assume that a firm can choose between two projects, A and B, both costing 40. The firm seeks debt to finance the project. There are two states of nature (bad, good) with equal probability. The risk-free rate is 0.

   The earnings in the two states are as follows:

	b (P = 0.50)	*g (P = 0.5)*	*Expected earnings*
Project A	80	80	80
Project B	0	110	55

a. What project has higher NPV?
b. What project will be chosen if the debt face value is 40?
c. Now suppose that the risk-free interest rate is 50%. Describe the scenario if the lenders offer a loan with 50% interest rate.
d. Is there any equilibrium in this case?

10. Explain the idea in Acharya and Viswanathan (2011).

Appendix 1. Stochastic Dominance

Stochastic Variable

A stochastic (random, probabilistic) variable X is characterized by a cumulative distribution function (*c.d.f.*) $F(x)$ such that $F(x) = Pr(X < x)$.

A discrete variable can take values $x_1, x_2, \ldots\ldots x_n$ with probabilities $p_1, p_2, \ldots\ldots p_n$, respectively. For a discrete variable, we have

$$F(x) = \sum_{x_i \le x} p(x_i)$$

A continuous variable has a density function $f(x)$. For a continuous variable,

$$F(x) = \int_{-\infty}^{x} f(z)dz$$

where f is the density function. The expected value of X is determined as follows:

$$EX = \int_{-\infty}^{\infty} xf(x)dx$$

First-order Stochastic Dominance

Consider the stochastic variable X with distribution function $F(x)$ and Y with $G(y)$ (Fig. 4.4). X dominates Y in the first-order sense if

$$F(z) \leq G(z), \forall z$$

The possible payoffs (z) are along the x-axis and the values of the cumulative distribution functions are on the y-axis. The dotted line (G) lies above F. Hence, X first-order dominates Y.

Example 4.3 Example with discrete variables. Consider the following projects X and Y, which are subject to the following profit scenarios with the given probabilities. How would one find which project dominates the other by first-order dominance? (Table 4.6).

To compare X and Y, we build the following table (Table 4.7):

The probabilities for each value of z are taken from the previous table; $F(z)$ is the cumulative probability (or cumulative distribution function) for X; $G(z)$ is CDF for Y, and Δ is the difference between F and G. If Δ is non-positive (non-negative), then X dominates $Y(Y$ dominates $X)$ by FOD.[12]

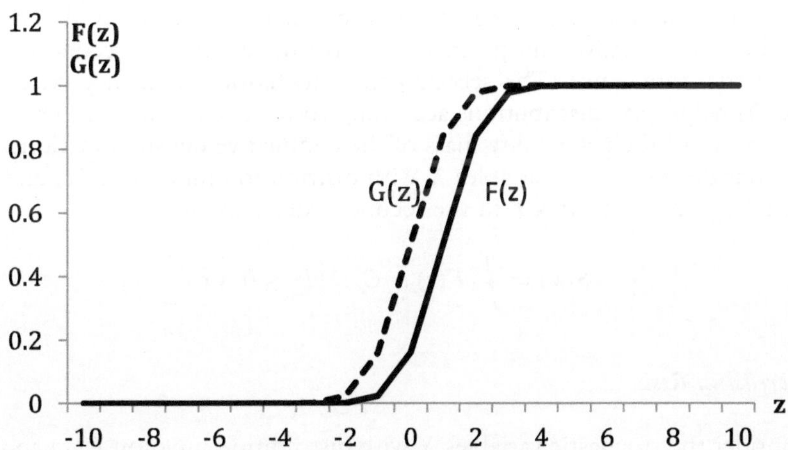

Fig. 4.4 First-order stochastic dominance (FOD)

[12] This method works if one keeps the same lag for values of z in the table.

Table 4.6 Projects and profits in Example 4.3

	Probability of outcomes		
	Low profit = 1	*Average Profit = 2*	*High Profit = 3*
X	0	0.1	0.9
Y	0.9	0.1	0

Table 4.7 Stochastic dominance analysis in Example 4.3

z	*Prob. X*	*Prob. Y*	*F(z)*	*G(z)*	*Δ*
1	0	0.9	0	0.9	−0.9
2	0.1	0.1	0.1	1	−0.9
3	0.9	0	1	1	0

Second-Order Dominance

We saw that FOD is a very strong criterion. All investors immediately chose options that dominated others by FOD. Unfortunately, not all cases involve FOD between available alternatives. In order to solve the problem where the differences between the two cumulative probability functions can be both negative and positive, we have to rely on the second-order stochastic dominance. The second-order stochastic dominance criterion (SOD) helps rank distributions according to relative riskiness in terms of the spread of the probability mass of the cumulative density functions.

Consider stochastic variables X with distribution function $F(x)$ and X with $G(y)$. X dominates Y in the second-order sense if

$$S(x) = \int [F(z) - G(z)]dz \leq 0, \forall x$$

Increasing Risk

Consider the stochastic variables X with distribution function $F(x)$ and Y with $G(y)$, $X < b$, $Y < b$. X dominates Y in the increasing risk sense (IR) if

$$S(x) = \int [F(z) - G(z)]dz \le 0, \forall_x$$

$$S(b) = 0$$

It can be shown mathematically that IR is similar to SOD graphically. However, under IR two lotteries have the same expected outcome.

Example 4.4 Example with discrete variables. Consider the following projects X and Y, which are subject to the following outcomes with the given probabilities (Table 4.8).

To compare X and Y, we build the following table (Table 4.9):

Here, $\sum F(z)$ and $\sum G(z)$ are sums of the numbers in columns $F(z)$ and $G(z)$ and $\Delta = \sum F(z) - \sum G(z)$. If Δ is non-positive (non-negative), then X dominates $Y(Y$ dominates $X)$ by SOD.

If Δ is non-positive (non-negative) and $\Delta(z_{max}) = 0$, then X dominates $Y(Y$ dominates $X)$ by IR (note that it also dominates by SOD).

Finally note the following rules regarding the different types of stochastic dominance: FOD implies SOD (compare definitions of SOD

Table 4.8 Projects, outcomes and probabilities in Example 4.4

Probabilities of outcomes				
Outcomes	*1*	*2*	*3*	*4*
X	0	0.3	0.7	0
Y	0.1	0.2	0.6	0.1

Table 4.9 Stochastic dominance analysis in Example 4.4

z	*Prob.X*	*Prob.Y*	$F(z)$	$G(z)$	$\sum F(z)$	$\sum G(z)$	Δ
1	0	0.1	0	0.1	0	0.1	–0.1
2	0.3	0.2	0.3	0.3	0.3	0.4	–0.1
3	0.7	0.6	1	0.9	1.3	1.3	0
4	0	0.1	1	1	2.3	2.3	0

and FOD); SOD does not imply FOD; IR implies SOD (check comments in Example 6); SOD does not imply IR.

For more analysis of stochastic dominance approach see Abhyankar et al. (2006) and Levi (1992).

References

Abhyankar, A., Ho, K., & Zhao, H. (2006). Value versus Growth: Stochastic Dominance Criteria. Cass Business School Research Paper. http://ssrn.com/abstract=793204.

Acharya, V., & Viswanathan, S. (2011). Leverage, Moral Hazard and Liquidity. *Journal of Finance, 66*, 99–138.

Arnold, L., & Riley, J. (2009). On the Possibility of Credit Rationing in the Stiglitz Weiss Model. *American Economics Review, 99*, 2012–2021.

Banerjee, A., & Duflo, E. (2014). Do Firms Want to Borrow More? Testing Credit Constraints Using a Directed Lending Program. *Review of Economic Studies, 81*(2), 572–607.

Barrow, J., & Horvitz, P. (1993). Response of Distressed Firms to Incentives: Thrift Institution Performance Under the FSLIC Management Consignment Program. *Financial Management, 22*(3), 176–184.

Batten, J., Khaw, K.L.-H., & Young, M. (2021). Convertible debt and asset substitution of multinational corporations. *Journal of Corporate Finance, 67*, 101843.

Berger, A., & Udell, G. (1992). Some Evidence on the Empirical Significance of Credit Rationing. *Journal of Political Economy, 100*, 1047–1077.

Bester, H. (1985). Screening vs. Rationing in Credit Markets with Imperfect Information. *American Economic Review, 75*, 850–855.

Brander, J., & Lewis, T. (1986). Oligopoly and Fianncial Structure: The Limited Liability Effect. *American Economic Review, 76*(5), 956–970.

Chevalier, J., & Scharstein, D. (1996). Capital Market Imperfections and Counter Cyclical Markups: Theory and Evidence. *American Economic Review, 86*, 703–725.

Chowdhury, J. (2006). *Limited Liability Effect with Endogenous Debt and Investments* (Working Paper). http://ssrn.com/abstract=901080

Coco, G. (1997). Credit rationing and the welfare gain from usury laws. Discussion Paper in Economics - University of Exeter, 15/97.

Eckbo, B. E., Su, X., & Thorburn, K. (2022). Penalty-Free Prepayments, Credit Rationing, and the Use of Upfront Fees in Bank Loans, https://ecgi.global/sites/default/files/working_papers/documents/eckbosuthorburnfinal_1.pdf

Galai, D., & Masulis, R. (1976). The Option Pricing Model and the Risk Factor of Stock. *Journal of Financial Economics, 3*, 53–81.

Gavish, B., & Kalay, A. (1983). On the Asset Substitution Problem. *Journal of Financial and Quantitative Analysis, 18*, 21–30.

Godlewski, C. J., & Weill, L. (2011). Does Collateral Help Mitigate Adverse Selection? A Cross-Country Analysis. *Journal of Financial Services Research, 40*(1–2), 49–78.

Graham, J., & Harvey, C. (2001). The Theory and Practice of Corporate Finance: Evidence from the Field. *Journal of Financial Economics, 60*(2–3), 187–243.

Green, R. (1984). Investment Incentives, Debt, and Warrants. *Journal of Financial Economics, 13*(1), 115–136.

Green, R., & Talmor, E. (1986). Asset Substitution and the Agency Costs of Debt Financing. *Journal of Banking and Finance, 10*(3), 391–399.

Grinblatt, M., & Titman, S. (2001). *Financial Markets & Corporate Strategy* (2nd Edition). McGraw-Hill/Irwin.

Hashi, I., & Toçi, Z. (2010). Financing Constraints, Credit Rationing and Financing Obstacles: Evidence From Firm-Level Data In South-Eastern Europe. *Economic and Business Review, 12*(1), 29–60.

Ikeda, M. (2005). *Risk Shifting Incentive of the Firm when its Value is Correlated with Interest Rates* (Waseda University Working Paper).

Jensen, M., & Meckling, W. (1976). Theory of the Firm: Managerial Behavior, Agency Costs and Ownership Structure. *Journal of Financial Economics, 3*, 305–360.

Jin, Y., & Zhang, S. (2019). Credit Rationing in Small and Micro Enterprises: A Theoretical Analysis. *Sustainability, 11*, 1330.

John, K., Lynch, A., & Puri, M. (2003). Credit Ratings, Collateral, and Loan Characteristics: Implications for Yield. *The Journal of Business, 76*(3), 371–410.

Kaufman, M. (1996). *An Incursion into the Confidence Crisis-Credit Rationing-Real Activity Channel: Evidence from the Argentine 'Tequila' Crisis* (Working Paper Central Bank of Argentina).

Kovenock, D., & Phillips, G. (1997). Capital Structure and Product Market Behavior: An Examination of Plant Exit and Investment Decisions. *Review of Financial Studies, 10*, 767–803.

Levi, H. (1992). Stochastic Dominance and Expected Utility: Survey and Analysis. *Management Science, 38*(4), 555–593.

Maksimovic, V. (1988). Capital Structure in Repeated Oligopolies. *Rand Journal of Economics, 19*, 389–407.

Miglo, A. (2022). Theories of Financing for Entrepreneurial Firms: A Review. *International Review of Entrepreneurship, 20*(2), 301–330.

Niinimäki, J.-P. (2018). Collateral in Credit Rationing in Markets with Asymmetric Information. *The Quarterly Review of Economics and Finance, 68*, 97–102.

Opler, T., & Titman, S. (1994). Financial Distress and Corporate Performance. *Journal of Finance, 49*, 1015–1040.
Povel, P., & Raith, M. (2004). Financial Constraints and product Market Competition: Ex-ante vs Ex post Incentives. *International Journal of Industrial Organization, 22*, 917–49.
Simon, R. (2015, November 26). Big Banks Cut Back on Loans to Small Business. *Wall Street Journal.* http://www.wsj.com/articles/big-banks-cut-back-on-small-business-1448586637.
Stiglitz, J., & Weiss, A. (1981). Credit Rationing in Markets with Imperfect Information. *The American Economic Review, 71*(3), 393–410.
Su, X., & Li, Z. (2017). A Re-Examination of Credit Rationing in the Stiglitz and Weiss Model. *Journal of Money, Credit and Banking, 49*(5), 1059–1072.
Titman, S. (1984). The Effect of Capital Structure on a Firm's Liquidation Decision. *Journal of Financial Economics, 13*(1), 137–151.
Tsuji, Y. (2009). Measuring the Agency Costs of Debt: A Simplified Approach. http://ssrn.com/abstract=997222
Warga, A., & Welch, I. (1993). Bondholders Losses in Leveraged Buyouts. *Review of Financial Studies, 6*(4), 959–982.
Wilson, L., & Wu, Y. (2010). Common (Stock) Sense about Risk-Shifting and Bank Bailouts. *Financial Markets and Portfolio Management, 24*(1), 3–29.

CHAPTER 5

Debt Overhang

5.1 Debt Overhang

The asset substitution problem occurs when firms invest in projects with negative NPVs, while the debt overhang problem occurs when firms do not invest in projects with positive NPVs. Equityholders may underinvest: pass up profitable investments because the firm's existing debt captures most of the project's benefits (Myers, 1977).

This can happen in different ways. Shareholders may decide to distribute large dividends instead of investing in profitable projects. Or they can decide to transfer assets away from companies with large amounts of debt to other companies. The latter is often accompanied by legal battles between shareholders and creditors who claim that the shareholders artificially reduce the values of their claims.

Famous Caesars Entertainment Corp. was struggling to deal with its high level of debt after it was purchased in a $30.7 billion leveraged buyout put together by Apollo Global Management LLC and TPG Capital at the peak of the last takeover boom in 2008. It created a debt overhang, or distressed debt problem, as described by Sridhar Natarajan

Supplementary Information The online version contains supplementary material available at https://doi.org/10.1007/978-3-031-85459-0_5.

A. Miglo, *Capital Structure in the Modern World*,
https://doi.org/10.1007/978-3-031-85459-0_5

and Christopher Palmeri in the article from April 2014 entitled: "Caesars Uses $100 Million Lure for Asset Shift: Distressed Debt."[1]

Caesars offered $100 million to negotiate with lenders to finance a plan that would transfer the most valuable casino assets to a unit called Caesars Growth Partners. Caesars had $1.18 billion worth of term loans due in March 2021. Some debtholders were very unhappy with this transaction; they argued that the shift of assets would exert pressure on the existing lenders, enabling Caesars' management to carry out a favorable restructuring of its high-cost bonds.

Debt overhang may also be a result of large investments (including the repurchasing of a firm's own shares) in the recent past and together with large amounts of debt it may lead to a loss of financial flexibility. As reported by Amey Stone in 2015, too many acquisitions and share repurchases caused Standard & Poor's Ratings Services to downgrade the debt of famous cereal producer Kellogg.[2] Its investment grade rating dropped to triple-B from triple-B-plus. Some examples of Kellogg's investments prior to that included paying $450 million to buy a 50% stake in Multipro, a sales and distribution company in Nigeria and Ghana, and buying Mass Food Group, Egypt's leading cereal company.

To better understand the debt overhang phenomenon, let's consider a firm with an investment opportunity available. The firm has some debt outstanding. The timing of events is as follows (Fig. 5.1).

Proposition 5.1 *In some cases, a firm with debt may pass up positive NPV investments.*

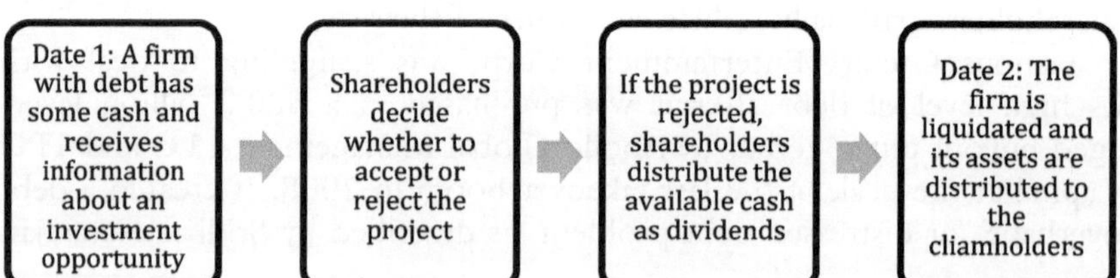

Fig. 5.1 Sequence of events

[1] Natarajan and Palmeri (April 2, 2014).

[2] Stone (November 5, 2015).

To prove this proposition, simply consider the following example. Consider a firm with $5000 debt due at Date 2. The firm's available cash at Date 1 is $3000. The firm has the opportunity to undertake a project costing $3000 that will generate a cash flow of $4000 at Date 2. Will the firm undertake this positive NPV project or distribute $3000 as dividends at Date 1?

If the firm distributes dividends at Date 1, shareholders receive $3000. If the firm undertakes the new project, shareholders get zero at dates 1 and 2. So the project will not be undertaken.

Debt overhang arises when shareholders refuse to invest in positive NPV projects because the existing debt captures most of the project's benefits. Recall that the NPV of a project is sometimes different for shareholders and creditors. Since the board of directors usually acts in the interest of the shareholders, a firm will choose projects with the highest earnings for shareholders. The problem is that projects with positive NPVs (for the firm as a whole) sometimes have low payoffs to the shareholders and junior creditors. By its very nature debt has priority over equity in cases when earnings are not sufficient to satisfy every claimholder and senior debt has priority over junior debt. In the real world, debt typically has covenants preventing issues of new debt of the same or higher seniority as the existing debt. Although one would think that the existing creditors would be willing to renegotiate these terms, since the investment makes everyone better off, it does not usually happen.

Financially distressed firms represent a good practical implication of the debt overhang problem. It is very difficult for firms to obtain new funds when they are in financial distress and the existing debtholders have a high risk of losing their money. These firms have to cut capital expenditures and R&D. It has been found that firms that are financially constrained may have a harder time responding to competition because firms with higher leverage cannot respond to competitors' price changes.[3] This is because any price decrease is in fact an investment because the firm loses funds in the short term. Evidence of this can be found in studies in the supermarket industry and the trucking industry.

[3] Opler and Titman (1994).

5.2 How Does the Type and the Level of Debt Affect the Underinvestment Problem

In this section, we demonstrate how the level of debt influences the underinvestment problem. Suppose a firm owns the following project (project-in-place). At $t = 1$, cash flow from the project may be equal to $R > 0$ with probability p_1 or 0 otherwise. At $t = 0$, the firm is given the opportunity to make an investment B that increases the probability of p_1 to p_2. This investment has a positive NPV, i.e., $(p_2 - p_1)R - B > 0$. The firm has issued senior debt with total amount D. The timing of events is presented in Fig. 5.2.

Proposition 5.2 *Higher debt increases the likelihood of debt overhang.*

The following illustrates the proof of Proposition 5.2. Without the new project the shareholders' expected profit is $p_1(R - D)$. If the firm invests in the new project, the shareholders' expected profit will be: $p_2(R - D) - B$. This is equal to the firm's expected cash flow (the new probability of success multiplied by the net income, i.e., earnings reduced by the amount of payment to the senior debtholders) minus the payment to the outside investors, which will be either junior debt or equity. In any case, the expected payment to investors should be equal to the cost of the investment. Comparing the shareholders' payoff without the investment and with the investment we find that the firm will invest if $(p_2 - p_1)(R - D) - B > 0$. Since $p_2 > p_1$, the left side of the above inequality is negatively correlated with D. If D increases, the likelihood of debt overhang increases. This is because the presence of existing risky claims reduces the incentives for existing shareholders to invest in that project since it increases the value of the existing debt and not the value of the shares, which is the essence of the debt overhang problem.

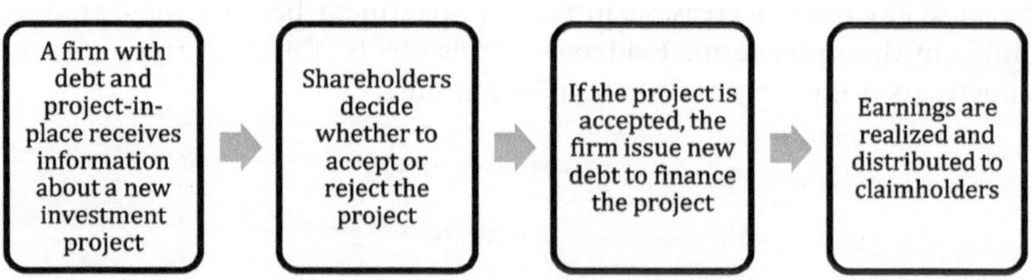

Fig. 5.2 Sequence of events

Example 5.1 A firm has a project-in-place that can generate earnings $R = 10,000$ with probability $p_1 = 0.5$. There is a new project available. The cost of the project is $B = 1000$. If the investment is undertaken, the probability increases by 0.2. Will the new project be undertaken if the firm's debt equals D?

First, note that the NPV of this project is positive for the firm. The firm's expected earnings increase by $10,000 * 0.2 = 2000$ which is greater than the 1000 investment cost. So the NPV of the project for the firm equals $10,000 * 0.2—1,000 = 1000$.

The answer to the question in Example 5.1 depends on the value of D. Consider two different debt levels: $D = 3000$ and $D = 6000$. Proposition 5.2 predicts that the project will not be undertaken if $(p_2 - p_1)(R - D) - B < 0$. Or $0.2 * D > 1000$. And this is the case when $D = 6000$.

Without the new project, the shareholders' earnings are: $(10,000 - D) * 0.5$. If $D = 3000$, the shareholdrs' expected earnings are $(10,000 - 3000) * 0.5 = 3500$. If the firm undertakes the new project the shareholders' expected payoff will be $(10,000 - 3000) * 0.7 - 1000 = 3900 > 3500$ so the project will be undertaken.

Consider $D = 6000$.Without the new project the shareholdrs' expected earnings are $(10,000 - 6000) * 0.5 = 2000$. If the firm undertakes the new project the shareholders' expected payoff will be $(10,000 - 6000) * 0.7 - 1000 = 1800 < 2000$ so the project will not be undertaken.

Let us now analyze whether the debt overhang problem depends on the type of the existing debt. Consider a firm with an amount D of debt (senior) due at date 1. The firm's cash flows at date 1 are stochastic and depend on the state of nature. In the good state they will be R_2; in the bad state they will be R_1,$R_2 > D > R_1$; the probability of the good state is p. The firm has an opportunity to undertake a project costing B that will generate cash flows of X in both states. $X > B$ and $D > R_1 + X$. This means that the new project has a positive NPV but earnings in the bad state are not sufficient to cover the existing debt. Will the firm undertake this positive NPV project?

Proposition 5.3 *In some cases a senior debt will lead to debt overhang but junior debt will not.*

Without the new project, the shareholders' expected payoff is: $p(R_2 - D)$. Now consider the new investment opportunity. The cost is

1500 and cash flow is 2000 in each state. Suppose the project is financed with debt (junior since the initial debt is senior). Will the firm undertake the project?

Let F be the face value of the new debt. Since the initial debt is senior and $D > R_1 + X$, the new (junior) debtholders receive nothing in the bad state. Hence, the expected payoff to new debtholders equals pF, which implies $F = B/p$. The shareholders' payoff is $p(R_2 + X - D - B/p)$. If $X < B/p$, the shareholders' payoff with the new project is less than without the new project. Thus, the project will not be undertaken.

Now suppose the initial debt is junior and the firm can issue senior debt to finance the new project. The face value of the new senior debt is B (since the total earnings are greater than B in both states). So the shareholders' expected payoff, if the new project is undertaken, is: $p(R_2 + X - D - B)$. This is greater than the shareholders' payoff without the new project because $X > B$. So the new project will be undertaken.

5.3 Debt Overhang Implications and Prevention

Renegotiating with Existing Creditors

We have seen that a firm's shareholders are unwilling to finance positive NPV projects with funds (in the form of junior debt) provided by outside creditors. The same conclusion holds if the firm issues new equity to outside investors or when the firm uses internal financing. But what about other kinds of financing? The firm can, for example, ask existing (incumbent) creditors for additional financing.

Proposition 5.4 *In some cases a debt overhang problem can be solved* via *renegotiation with existing creditors.*

Let us return to the set-up of Proposition 5.3. Suppose the incumbent debtholders agree to finance the new project with a new (junior) debt with a face value (including principal and interests) $B + i$, $B + i < X$. Recall that without the new project, the shareholders' expected payoff is: $p(R_2 - D)$. Now suppose the shareholders accept financing from incumbent creditors. The cost is B and cash flow is X in each state. The shareholders' payoffs with the new project will be $p(R_2 + X - D - i - B)$. This is greater than $p(R_2 - D)$ because $X > B + i$. Hence the shareholders will be interested in having a deal with incumbent creditors. Now consider the incentive of creditors. Without the new project their expected payoff is $pD + (1 - p)R_1$. With the project it is: $p(D + B + i) + (1 - p)(R_1 + B + i) - B = pD + (1 - p)R_1 + i$. So the deal is beneficial for both shareholders and creditors.

The example below illustrates Propositions 5.3 and 5.4.

Example 5.2 Consider a firm with a 5000 debt (senior) due at date 1. The firm's cash flows in the good state will be 8000; in the bad state they will be 3000; each state has an equal probability. The firm has the opportunity to undertake a project costing 1500 that will generate cash flows of 2000 in both states.

Without the new project, the shareholders' expected payoff is: $0.5 * (8000 - 5000) + 0.5 * 0 = 1500$. Now consider the new project. Let F be the face value of the new debt. The expected payoff to the new debtholders equals $0.5 * F = 1500$, which implies $F = 3000$. The shareholders' payoff is $0.5 * (10000 - 5000 - 3000) = 1000$. This is less than the shareholders' payoff without the new project. Thus, the project will not be undertaken.

Now suppose the initial debt is junior and the firm can issue senior debt to finance the new project. The face value of the new senior debt is 1500 (since the total earnings are at least 2000 in both states). So the shareholders' expected payoff, if the new project is undertaken, is: $0.5 * (10000 - 5000 - 1500) = 1750$. This is greater than 1500. So the new project will be undertaken. This illustrates Proposition 5.3.

Now suppose the initial debt is senior but the incumbent debtholders agree to finance the new project with a new (junior) debt with a face value (including principal and interests) of 1500. Recall that without the new project, the shareholders' expected payoff is: $0.5 * (8000 - 5000) + 1.2 * 0 = 1500$. Now suppose the shareholders accept financing from the incumbent creditors. The cost is 1500 and cash flow is 2000 in each state. The shareholders' payoffs with the new project will be $0.5 * (10,000 - 5000 - 1500) = 1750$. This is greater than 1500 and hence the shareholders will be interested in making a deal with incumbent creditors. Now consider the incentive for the creditors. Without the new project, their expected payoff is $0.5 * 5000 + 0.5 * 3000 = 4000$. With the project it is: $0.5 * (5000 + 1500) + 0.5 * 5000 - 1500 = 4250$. So the deal is beneficial for both the shareholders and the creditors.

Similarly, lenders can commit to additional financing when the first loan is granted. This can also help resolve debt overhang problems.

Costly Renegotiation

Why can't the firm always avoid costs of financial distress by renegotiating with creditors? The firm could negotiate with creditors to write down a new debt, postpone interest, or ease covenants in exchange for additional interest or some equity in the company. However, these negotiations are costly and sometimes not feasible.[4] The reasons for this are that creditors are often dispersed, making it hard for all of them to negotiate, and that they face conflicts of interest among themselves. One other problem that occurs is that creditors have doubts that their funds will be used for a "good" project.

To illustrate this, let us again consider Example 5.2. The shareholders can rationally realize that the new project is valuable to incumbent creditors; they can calculate that the creditors will accept the deal even if the face value of the new debt is below 1500, for example, 1250. The creditors' expected payoff is 4125, in this case, which is still higher than 4000 in the case without the new project. However, if the number of initial debtholders is large, then the free-rider problem can appear: it is in the interest of the initial debtholders to put up the money collectively, but it is not in the interest of any one of them to do it alone because the new debt has a negative NPV (face value of debt is below the cost of investment). So the shareholders may find it hard to convince the creditors to invest in the new project.

Pawlina (2010) shows that shareholders' option to renegotiate debt in a period of financial distress exacerbates the underinvestment problem at the time of the firm's expansion. This result is a consequence of a higher wealth transfer from shareholders to creditors occurring upon investment in the presence of the option to renegotiate. This additional underinvestment is eliminated when bargaining power belongs to creditors.

Favara et al. (2015) focus on connections between bankruptcy laws and debt renegotiation frictions. They develop a model that includes firms' choices of investments, asset sales, and risk-taking. It is shown that bankruptcy laws favoring debt renegotiation reduce underinvestment, limit asset sales, and decrease incentives for risk-taking when firms are

[4] See, for example, Gertner and Scharfstein (1991).

near insolvency. The model is tested on a panel of 19,466 firms across 41 countries with different bankruptcy codes and finds and a good amount of support.

Other Implications of the Debt Overhang Problem

A special case of the debt overhang problem arises when firms are inefficiently biased toward short-term earnings for shareholders instead of investing in more profitable long-term projects. This may take place when a firm has long-term risky debt and investing in a long-term project would create value for long-term creditors and not for shareholders. An example of this phenomenon is an inefficient dividend policy. The shareholders may choose to distribute large dividends and pass up this positive NPV project if future earnings from the project will be mostly used to pay back existing (long-term) debt. Similarly, the shareholders may prefer to invest in a less profitable shorter term project rather than invest in a more profitable long-term project if the firm has issued long-term debt and investing in long-term projects is more beneficial to creditors.

Opler and Titman (1994) suggest that highly levered firms lose market share to their less levered rivals during industry downturns for several reasons. Distressed firms that face underinvestment problems (debt overhang) are forced to sell off assets and reduce their selling efforts. Low-levered firms, assumed to have deep pockets, can engage in predatory practices especially in a highly competitive environment designed to financially exhaust highly levered rivals and drive them out of the market. A highly levered firm might be vulnerable to predation from low-levered competitors because low-levered competitors can purposefully reduce their prices and keep this strategy for a long time to drive the highly levered firm out of business.

A way to prevent inefficient dividend policy is to have dividend covenants, which are restrictions that do not allow dividends to be paid until the claim is paid to debtholders. Other ways to prevent a debt overhang problem in general include using bank and privately placed debt, and using project financing and the debtor-in-possession rule in US Chapter 11 Bankruptcy Code. We will discuss it in detail in Chapter 9. Firms can also use short-term debt to mitigate debt overhang.

Rajan (1992) argues that while informed banks make flexible financial decisions that prevent a firm's projects from going away, the cost of this credit is that banks have bargaining power over the firm's profits once projects have begun (hold-up problem). Vilanova (2004) argues that a bank with a senior claim at the onset of financial distress benefits from having strong bargaining power in subsequent debt restructurings and can exploit this enhanced power to hold up other claimants (the firm and junior lenders). It allows the senior bank with an initial impaired claim to rule out the repayment risk. The concentration of liquidation rights in the hands of the bank also leads to more favorable debt restructurings for low-quality borrowers. On the contrary, the ex post strong bargaining power of a senior bank might lower its incentives to monitor at the early stages of financial distress.

Some papers analyze links between the structure of firm debt and debt overhang problem. For example, Gertner and Scharfstein (1991) show that, conditional on ex post financial distress, making a fixed promised debt payment due earlier (i.e., shorter term) raises the market value of the debt and thus the firm's market leverage, leading to more debt overhang ex post. Diamond and He (2015) show that reducing maturity may increase or decrease overhang. With an immediate investment, shorter term debt typically imposes a lower overhang. Future overhang is more volatile for shorter term debt. Gan et al. (2022) combine debt overhang problem and the trade-off theory elements and argue that a mix of market debt and bank debt can accelerate investments and reduce the debt overhang problem.

Another line of research analyzes the impact of macroeconomic conditions on the debt overhang problem. Chen et al. (2017) analyze connections between macroeconomic risks and agency problems of financing including debt overhang. The distortions caused by agency problems during bad times affect investors more than in booms and the extent of debt overhang problem depends positively on the riskiness of debt that rises in bad times. Demirgüç-Kunt et al. (2023) find that shareholders of highly leveraged firms benefit less compared to bondholders from quantitative easing[5] by monetary authorities during COVID-19 crisis and argue that it suggests an additional cost of debt consistent with debt overhang. Firms more heavily impacted by the crisis gain less from same actions,

[5] Quantitative easing is a policy consisting of increasing the amount of money in the economy (e.g., when the government buys back its previously issued bonds) that usually increases the overall amount of firms' investments in the economy.

which is also consistent with debt overhang. Blickle and Santos (2020) argue that debt overhang during the COVID recession could lead to an up to 10 percent decrease in growth for firms in most affected industries.

5.4 Flexibility Theory of Capital Structure

Firms in the development stage need financial flexibility. There is a lot of uncertainty because they consider a lot of investment projects, including their financing strategies, which requires a lot of flexibility. Having too much debt in the capital structure will not help here (similar to a debt overhang problem). In addition, firms in the development stage have little favorable track record (i.e., credit ratings) of borrowing (Diamond, 1991) and are most likely to be turned down for credit when they need it the most. Hence firms in the development stage that have little financial flexibility will abstain from issuing risky debt and will instead issue equity. Firms in the maturity stage begin generating positive earnings and have more financial flexibility than developing firms. Accordingly, these firms rely more on debt financing to fund their investments as they face less financing constraints as they expect to repay their debt with their growing future earnings.

Flexibility theory finds a lot of support in empirical studies (Byoun, 2008), in managers' surveys (Graham & Harvey, 2001) and interviews as well. In addition to Google CFO interview example from Chapter 1 note a more recent with the CFP of famous Swedish manufacturing concern ABB Timo Ihamuotila who mentioned that after a significant reduction debt/equity ratio after conducting several significant steps in capital structure policy the firm now enjoys a much better level of flexibility.[6] This theory helps explain why small and risky firms issue equity and why these firms do not follow the pecking-order theory. Gamba and Triantis (2008) develop a theoretical model that analyzes optimal capital structure policy for a firm that values flexibility in the presence of personal taxes and transaction costs. The importance of financial flexibility, as compared to major theories of capital structure, remains an open question. More work that compares flexibility theory with other theories is expected. It was also noted that many young firms especially venture firms do not

[6] Dittli (01.04.2021).

issue common equity but rather convertible preferred equity which resembles debt more than equity. DeAngelo et al. (2011) argue that empirical evidence shows that leverage-related cost includes the opportunity cost of firm future problems with new borrowings. This cost implies that target capital structures are more conservative as compared to ones prescribed by traditional trade-off theory and hence are consistent with flexibility idea of capital structure.

In recent years, zero-debt policy research has been an increasingly growing area of interest (see also, Strebulaev & Yang, 2013; Dang, 2013; Bessler et al., 2013, Sundaresan et al., 2015; Byoun & Xu, 2013). Strebulaev et al. (2013) call it the "zero-leverage puzzle". The standard trade-o§ theory of capital structure does not explain situations when debt is totally absent because optimal debt is the trade-off between tax advantage of debt and bankruptcy cost so a zero-debt would only be possible if tax rate is zero which is not considered in traditional trade-off theory.[7] Pecking-order theory suggests that debt should be used if internal funds are not sufficient. Firms usually do not have sufficient funds to cover all their investment needs and further zero-debt policy is used not only by financially constrained firms (see, for example, Leary & Roberts, 2005). Miglo (2020) presents a model based on flexibility idea of capital structure that is consistent with zero-debt puzzle.[8]

Life cycle theory of capital structure argues that besides financial flexibility there are other factors that can explain financing patterns of firms in different stages of their developments (Damodaran, 2003). Start-up firms do not have much profit, so the tax advantage of debt is not as important to them as it is for a mature firm. Start-up firms do not require incentives for managers since there is no large separation between ownership and management like in the case of big public corporations. This leads to the idea that mature firms value debt more than start-up firms. To what extent does the life cycle theory represent a separate theory of capital structure rather than a combination of arguments from other theories remains an open question. More discussions about life cycle theory will be provided in Chapter 9.

[7] Miglo (2024) discusses trade-off theory with endogenous taxes and argues that the case with factually zero-taxes can arise (we provide more discussion in Chapter 14).

[8] For zero-debt puzzle related alternative models see also Morellec et al. (2012) and Lotfaliei (2018). We provide more discussion in Chapter 8.

Sundaresan et al. (2015) consider a life cycle model of a firm that includes tax benefit of debt, bankruptcy costs, and debt overhang problem and argue that the firm consistently chooses conservative leverage in order to mitigate the debt-overhang effect. They also suggest that debt seniority and debt priority structures have different debt-overhang implications.

5.5 Debt Overhang in Financial Institutions

Since the financial crisis of 2007–2009, regulators have been pushing for an increase in capital requirements for banks, so that a greater share of their investments is funded by equity (Basel Committee on Banking Supervision, 2009). The advantage of more equity funding is that it can reduce agency costs of debt, which is especially important for banks who have large amounts of debt on their balance sheets. Bankers however often resist changes related to capital increase. Admati et al. (2012) discuss these issues and explain why banks may not be interested in reducing leverage with more equity. The following example demonstrates one of the ideas. It closely follows the examples from this chapter but this time corporate taxes are considered so the shareholders may lose some corporate tax benefit as a result of leverage reduction. Consider a firm with a 5000 debt due at date 1. The firm's earnings at date 1 are stochastic and depend on the state of nature. In the good state they will be 8000; in the bad state they will be 0; both states have an equal probability. The corporate tax rate is 30%. The firm has an opportunity to issue new shares in order to repurchase the existing debt. As usual, assume that investors are risk-neutral and the risk-free interest rate is 0.

Debtholders will sell their debt for 2500. To see this, note that in the current situation debtholders will receive: $0.5 * 5000 + 0.5 * 0 = 2500$. Will shareholders repurchase the debt? Currently, the shareholders' expected payoff (given that corporate tax is 30%) is: $0.5 * (8000 - 5000) * (1 - 0.3) + 0.5 * 0 = 1050$. The new shareholders will be able to pay \$2500 for newly issued shares if they get 25/28 of the firm's equity. To see this note that the firm's net income after the debt repurchase in the bad state will still be 0 and that in the good state it will be $8000 * 0.7 = 5600$. Since this occurs with a 50% probability, new shareholders will need 5000 in that state. So their fraction should be equal to 5000/5600. The initial shareholders' fraction of equity is then 3/28 and their expected payoff is $3/28 * 5600 = 600$, which is less than 1050. Note that if the government provides a subsidy in the case of bankruptcy, a share repurchase will further reduce the shareholders' expected benefit.

Black and Scholes (1973) mentioned that previously issued debt by a firm creates a financial option i.e., the shareholders earnings in the future depend on whether the firm assets are greater or less than the firm debt; respectively the present values of equity and debt can be viewed as the prices of options and further than any changes in capital structure are affected by previously issued debt. Admati et al. (2018) further developed this point by introducing the debt ratchet effect term that means that the firm capital structure is affected by the history of its capital structure changes. They further argue that in the absence of prior commitments or regulations, shareholder-creditor conflicts may induce shareholders to resist debt reductions. In a dynamic context, since leverage becomes effectively irreversible, firms may limit leverage initially but then ratchet it up in response to shocks. The authors study shareholders' preferences of different ways to adjust leverage. A benchmark result gives conditions for shareholder indifference, but generally, shareholders have clear rankings of the alternatives. For example, shareholders often prefer reducing leverage by selling assets even at distressed prices. Further they discuss the applications of their analysis to banking and the role of capital regulation. For example, minimum capital requirements for banks can be interpreted as a counterforce to the leverage ratchet effect mandating that the leverage reductions should be done via new equity issues and not via costly fire sales.

Wilson (2012) shows that when a bank is subsidized ("too big to fail") by regulators, it may be tempted to buy risky assets. The paper analyzes bank bailouts involving the purchases of toxic assets, preferred stock, and common stock when the government wants to encourage efficient lending. It finds that preferred stock recapitalizations are the least efficient method of correcting debt overhang problems from both an ex post and ex ante perspective. In contrast, efficient lending and voluntary participation can be best achieved without the subsidy by purchasing either toxic assets or common stock. Nevertheless, troubled banks must be subsidized if they are to voluntarily participate in any recapitalization.

Questions and Exercises

1. A firm has assets-in-place that can generate earnings $R = 100{,}000$ with probability $p_1 = 0.4$. There is a new project available. The cost of the project is $B = 30{,}000$. If the investment is undertaken, the probability increases by 0.4. Initially, the firm has debt (senior) with face value $D = 20{,}000$. Everybody is risk-neutral in this economy. The risk-free interest rate is zero.

   (a) Find the NPV of new project
   (b) Will the new project be undertaken?
   (c) Now suppose that 60,000. Same question.
   (d) What phenomena are illustrated in this example?

2. Consider a firm with a 6000 debt (senior) due at date 1. The firm's cash flows in the good state will be 10,000; in the bad state they will be 4000; each state has an equal probability. The firm has an opportunity to undertake a project costing 2000 that will generate cash flows of 3000 in both states. The investors are risk-neutral and the risk-free interest rate is 0.

   (a) Find the new project NPV?
   (b) Will the firm undertake new investment?
   (c) Now suppose the initial debt is junior. The same question.
   (d) Now suppose the initial debt is senior but the incumbent debtholders agree to finance the new project with a new (junior) debt. The same question.
   (e) Find the minimal acceptable face value of new debt for creditors. Find the maximal acceptable face value of debt for shareholders.
   (f) What can prevent this situation happening?

3. Consider a firm with a 10,000 debt due at date 1. The firm's earnings at date 1 depend on the state of nature. In the good state they will be 18,000; in the bad state they will be 0; both states have an equal probability. The corporate tax rate is 40%. The firm has an opportunity to issue new shares in order to repurchase the existing debt. As usual, assume that investors are risk-neutral and the risk-free interest rate is 0. Are shareholders interested in repurchasing the firm's debt by selling equity?
4. *Debt overhang*

(a) Briefly describe (in words) a debt overhang problem.
(b) Provide examples of debt overhang problem.
(c) In general, how can a firm prevent a debt overhang problem?
(d) If a firm that faces a debt overhang problem increases its investments, who does usually benefit most from it: shareholders or bondholders?
(e) Discuss the empirical evidence related to debt overhang during COVID-19 crisis.

5. Since a firm usually faces a lot of uncertainty especially if it deals with a lot of (potential) investment projects, it needs a lot of flexibility. Firms that need flexibility would usually issue debt rather than equity.
6. Zero-debt puzzle refers to situations when the pecking order is reversed.

References

Admati, A., DeMarzo, P., Hellwig, M., & Pfleiderer, P. (2012). *Debt Overhang and Capital Regulation, Rock Center for Corporate Governance at Stanford University* (Working Paper No. 114). MPI Collective Goods Preprint, No. 2012/5. Available at SSRN. http://ssrn.com/abstract=2031204

Admati, A., DeMarzo, P., Hellwig, M., & Pfleiderer, P. (2018). The Leverage Ratchet Effect. *Journal of Finance, 73*(1), 145–198.

Basel Committee on Banking Supervision. (2009). *Enhancements to the Basel II Framework*. Bank for International Settlements.

Bessler, W., Drobetz, W., Haller, R., & Meier, I. (2013). The International Zero-leverage Phenomenon. *Journal of Corporate Finance, 23*, 196–221.

Black, F., & Scholes, M. S. (1973). The Pricing of Options and Corporate Liabilities. *Journal of Political Economy, 81*, 637–654.

Blickle, K., & Santos, J. (2020). The Costs of Corporate Debt Overhang Following the COVID-19 Outbreak, Liberty Street Economics 20201201, Federal Reserve Bank of New York.

Byoun, S. (2008). *Financial Flexibility and Capital Structure Decision* (working paper). Available at SSRN. http://ssrn.com/abstract=1108850

Byoun, S., & Xu, Z. (2013). Why Do Some Firms Go Debt-Free? *Asia-Pacific Journal of Financial Studies, 41*, 1–38.

Chen, H., & Manso, G. (2017). Macroeconomic Risk and Debt Overhang. *Review of Corporate Finance Studies, 6*(1), 1–38.

Dang, V. (2013). An Empirical Analysis of Zero-leverage Firms: New Evidence from the UK. *International Review of Financial Analysis, 30*, 189–202.

DeAngelo, H., DeAngelo, L., & Whited, T. M. (2011). Capital Structure Dynamics and Transitory Debt. *Journal of Financial Economics, 99*, 235–61.

Demirgüç-Kunt, A., Horváth, B., & Huizinga, H. (2023). Corporate QE in Europe During the COVID-19 Crisis and Debt Overhang. *Journal of International Money and Finance, 135*, 102855.

Dittli, M. (2021, Apr 1). ABB: «We Have Billions of Financial Capacity if Needed» The Market, https://themarket.ch/interview/abb-we-have-billions-of-financial-capacity-if-needed-ld.3943

Damodaran, A. (2003). *Corporate Finance: Theory and Practice*. Wiley Series in Finance.

Diamond, D. (1991). Monitoring and Reputation: The Choice Between Bank Loans and Directly Placed Debt. *Journal of Political Economy, 99*(2), 689–721.

Diamond, D., & He, Z. (2015). *A Theory of Debt Maturity: The Long and Short of Debt Overhang* (Working Paper Chicago Booth).

Favara, G., & Imbs, J. (2015). Credit Supply and the Price of Housing. *American Economic Review, 105*(3), 958–992.

Gamba, A., & Triantis, A. (2008). The Value of Financial Flexibility. *Journal of Finance, 63*(5), 2263–2296.

Gan, L., Xin, X., & Zhang, H. (2022). Debt Structure and Debt Overhang. *Journal of Corporate Finance, 74*, 102200.

Gertner, R., & Scharfstein, D. (1991). A Theory of Workouts and the Effects of Reorganization Law. *The Journal of Finance, 46*(4), 1189–1222.

Graham, J., & Harvey, C. (2001). The Theory and Practice of Corporate Finance: Evidence from the Field. *Journal of Financial Economics, 60*(2–3), 187–243.

Leary, M., & Roberts, M. (2005). Do Firms Rebalance Their Capital Structures? *Journal of Finance, 60*, 2575–2619.

Lotfaliei, B. (2018). Zero Leverage and the Value in Waiting to Issue Debt. *Journal of Banking and Finance, 97*, 335–49.

Miglo, A. (2020). Zero-Debt Policy Under Asymmetric Information, Flexibility and Free Cash Flow Considerations. *Journal of Risk and Financial Management, 13*(12), 296.

Miglo, A. (2024). *Trade-Off Theory with Endogenous Taxes* (Working Paper). https://papers.ssrn.com/sol3/papers.cfm?abstract_id=4818421

Morellec, E., Nikolov, B., & Schürhoff, N. (2012). Corporate Governance and Capital Structure Dynamics. *The Journal of Finance, 67*(3), 803–848.

Myers, S. (1977). Determinants of Corporate Borrowing. *Journal of Financial Economics, 5*, 147–175.

Natarajan, S., & Palmeri, C. (2014, April 2), Caesars Uses $100 Million Lure for Asset Shift: Distressed Debt. BloombergBusiness. http://www.bloomberg.com/news/articles/2014-04-02/caesars-uses-100-million-lure-for-asset-shift-distressed-debt

Opler, T., & Titman, S. (1994). Financial Distress and Corporate Performance. *Journal of Finance, 49*(3), 1015–1040.

Pawlina, G. (2010). Underinvestment, Capital Structure and Strategic Debt Restructuring. *Journal of Corporate Finance, 16*(5), 679–702.

Rajan, R. (1992). Insiders and Outsiders: The Choice between Informed and Arm's-Length Debt. *Journal of Finance, 47*(4), 1367–1400.

Stone, A. (2015, November 5). Kellogg Downgraded Due to Too Much Debt. *Barron's*. http://blogs.barrons.com/incomeinvesting/2015/11/05/kellogg-downgraded-due-to-too-much-debt/

Strebulaev, I., & Yang, B. (2013). The Mystery of Zero-Leverage Firms. *Journal of Financial Economics, 109*, 1–23.

Sundaresan, S., Wang, N., & Yang, J. (2015). Dynamic Investment, Capital Structure, and Debt Overhang. *Review of Corporate Finance Studies, 4*, 1–42.

Vilanova, L. (2004). Bank Seniority and Corporate Debt Restructuring. (EFA 2004 Maastricht Meetings Paper No. 2880). Available at SSRN. http://ssrn.com/abstract=554602

Wilson, L. (2012). Debt Overhang and Bank Bailouts International. *Journal of Monetary Economics and Finance, 5*(4), 393-414.

CHAPTER 6

Capital Structure, Behavioral Finance, and Incomplete Contracts

6.1 Capital Structure and Managerial Optimism and Overconfidence

The capital structure ideas discussed in previous chapters can be divided in two large groups: one related to what we call "the perfect market concept" (e.g., Modigliani–Miller ideas discussed in Chapter 1 and 2) and one related to traditional imperfect market ideas (asymmetric information, agency problems, bankruptcy costs, and taxes). As we have learned, the second group helps to explain a lot of different puzzles about capital structure. Yet, most theories in traditional imperfect market framework have their limitations. For example, the traditional pecking-order theory (Chapter 3) cannot explain why good-quality firms often issue equity: this is considered an empirical puzzle. The signaling theory of capital structure predicts that good firms issue debt as a signal of quality, which contradicts the well documented negative correlation between debt and profitability. In the last 20–30 years a couple of approaches have made significant contributions to the area of capital structure: the behavioral finance approach where (as opposed to the traditional imperfect

Supplementary Information The online version contains supplementary material available at https://doi.org/10.1007/978-3-031-85459-0_6.

A. Miglo, *Capital Structure in the Modern World*,
https://doi.org/10.1007/978-3-031-85459-0_6

approach) it is often assumed that the decisions-makers are not always totally rational and the incomplete contract approach where it is often assumed that contracts are not always enforced without cost. This section analyzes the role of behavioral finance in explaining the major empirical puzzles of capital structure mentioned above as well as some others. One of the most popular approaches is based on managerial overconfidence. By their nature, firm managers are often energetic and optimistic people. However, this often leads to overconfidence (Hackbarth, 2008; Malmendier et al., 2011). The following illustrates some basic ideas about how overconfidence can affect firm capital structure decisions.

Consider a firm that has an investment project with a positive net present value.[1] The project costs B. The probability of project success is p. In the case of success the project generates earnings X and in the case of project failure earnings equal 0. Average earnings generated by the project equal $M = pX > B$. The firm belongs to an entrepreneur who owns 100% of the firm's equity. The entrepreneur can undertake the project by issuing debt or equity. Everybody is risk-neutral and the risk-free interest rate is normalized to zero. The investors provide funds as long as the expected earnings cover their cost and the entrepreneur maximizes his expected profit. In addition, the entrepreneur is biased and this bias is two-dimensional: with regard to the average return from the project and with regard to the project risk (probability of success).[2] More specifically, the entrepreneur thinks that the average earnings from the project are $M + \varepsilon$, where ε measures the degree of the entrepreneur's bias. $\varepsilon > 0$ means that the entrepreneur is overconfident with regard to project earnings, $\varepsilon < 0$ means that the entrepreneur is pessimistic and $\varepsilon = 0$ means that the entrepreneur is unbiased (rational). In addition the entrepreneur thinks that the probability of project success equals $p+\gamma$. Respectively, the entrepreneur expects that in the case of success the project generates $\frac{M+\varepsilon}{p+\gamma}$ while objectively this value equals M/p (Fig. 6.1). The sequence of events is as follows:

We start by considering the case with rational entrepreneurs ($\varepsilon = \gamma = 0$) and symmetric information, i.e., all parties share the same information and all variables are public knowledge. If debt is selected (we will denote

[1] Based on Miglo (2024).

[2] For a literature review regarding risk and overconfidence see, for example, Bilgehan (2014). See also Reyes, Miranda and Vera-Martínez (2019).

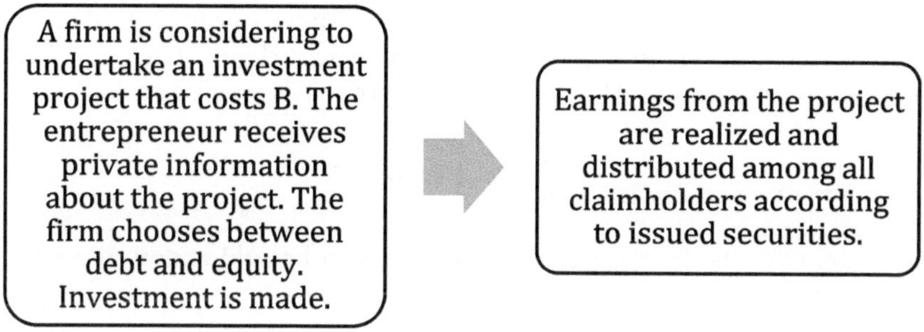

Fig. 6.1 Sequence of events

this decision/strategy by d for shortness), the entrepreneur's expected profit equals

$$p(X - F) = p\left(\frac{M}{p} - F\right)$$

where F is the face value of debt. The entrepreneur's expected profit from the project equals the difference between earnings from the project and face value of the debt multiplied by the probability of project success. If equity is selected (this strategy is denoted by e), the entrepreneur's profit is

$$(1 - \alpha)M \tag{6.1}$$

where α is the fraction of equity sold to new shareholders.

Lemma 6.1 Under symmetric information and rational entrepreneurs, the firm is indifferent between debt and equity.

Proof For strategy d, the face value of debt is determined by the following condition:

$$X \geq F$$

$$B = Fp$$

The first condition means that the face value of debt should not be greater than the amount of earnings the firm earns if the project succeeds and the second condition means that the expected earnings that the bank is going to receive covers their investment/loan. They can hold simultaneously because $M > B$. The entrepreneur's profit equals

$$p\left(\frac{M}{p} - F\right) = M - B \tag{6.2}$$

For strategy e, the fraction of shares that has to be sold is determined by the following condition:

$$\alpha M = B \tag{6.3}$$

Substituting α from (6.3) into (6.1) leads to the following:

$$\left(1 - \left(\frac{B}{M}\right)\right)M = M - B \tag{6.4}$$

Equations (6.2) and (6.4) are equal. This result is not surprising. It is consistent with the spirit of classical literature on firm financial decision-making in a perfect market (Modigliani & Miller, 1958) as discussed in Chapter 2.

Biased Entrepreneurs

Now suppose that entrepreneurs are biased. First consider the case $\gamma = 0$. The entrepreneur thinks that the average project's earnings are $M + \varepsilon$.

Proposition 6.1. *1) If* $\varepsilon > 0$, *the entrepreneur prefers d; 2) if* $\varepsilon < 0$, *the entrepreneur prefers e.*

Proof If d is selected, then, objectively, the entrepreneur's profit equals $p\left(\frac{M}{p} - F\right)$. The entrepreneur, however, thinks that it is.

$$p\left(\frac{(M + \varepsilon)}{p} - F\right) \tag{6.5}$$

From the lenders' point of view, the expected payoff should cover the amount of investment/loan: $B = pF$. Substituting F into (6.5) implies that the entrepreneur's expected profit (from his point of view)[3] equals

$$p\left(\frac{(M+\varepsilon)}{p} - F\right) = p\left(\frac{(M+\varepsilon)}{p} - B/p\right) = M + \varepsilon - B \tag{6.6}$$

If e is selected, the entrepreneur's expected earnings equal $(1-\alpha)(M+\varepsilon)$. From the investors' point of view, the expected payoff should cover the amount of investment: $B = \alpha M$, which implies that $\alpha = B/M$. So the entrepreneur's profit equals

$$\left(1 - \left(\frac{B}{M}\right)\right)(M+\varepsilon) \tag{6.7}$$

The difference between (6.7) and (6.6) equals $B\varepsilon/M$. If $\varepsilon > 0$, it is positive and vice versa.

Proposition 6.1 is generally consistent with Fairchild (2005) and Malmendier et al. (2011) where an overconfident manager prefers d (our case $\varepsilon > 0$). Now consider the case $\varepsilon = 0$. The entrepreneur thinks that the probability of project's success equals $p + \gamma$.

Proposition 6.2 *1) If $\gamma > 0$, the entrepreneur prefers e; 2) if $\gamma < 0$, the entrepreneur prefers d.*

Proof If d is selected, then, objectively, the entrepreneur's profit equals $p\left(\frac{M}{p} - F\right)$. The entrepreneur, however, thinks that it is $(p+\gamma)\left(\frac{M+\varepsilon}{p+\gamma} - F\right)$. Again, from the lenders' point of view, the expected payoff should cover the amount of investment/loan: $B = Fp$. Hence, the entrepreneur's expected profit equals

$$(p+\gamma)\left(\frac{M}{p+\gamma} - \frac{B}{p}\right) = M - (B(p+\gamma)/p) \tag{6.8}$$

If e is selected, the entrepreneur's expected earnings equal $(1-\alpha)M$. From the investors' point of view, the expected payoff should cover the

[3] Further if we use the term "entrepreneur's expected profit" it will be assumed that it is expected profit from his point of view (that can be different from the objective value of expected profit). We will omit this clarification for brevity unless further comments are required.

amount of investment: $\alpha M = B$, which implies that $\alpha = B/M$. The entrepreneur's profit equals

$$EW = \left(1 - \left(\frac{B}{M}\right)\right)M = M - B \tag{6.9}$$

The difference between (6.9) and (6.8) equals $B\gamma/p$. If $\gamma > 0$ then it is positive and vice versa.

Finally, consider the case with $\varepsilon > 0$ and $\gamma > 0$.

Proposition 6.3 *1) If $\varepsilon/M > \gamma/p$, the entrepreneur prefers d; 2) if $\frac{\varepsilon}{M} < \gamma/p$, the entrepreneur prefers e.*

Proof If d is selected, then, objectively, the entrepreneur's profit equals $p\left(\frac{M}{p} - F\right)$, where as previously $F = B/p$. The entrepreneur, however, thinks that it is $(p + \gamma)\left(\frac{M+\varepsilon}{p+\gamma} - F\right)$ or

$$(p + \gamma)\left(\frac{M + \varepsilon}{p + \gamma} - \frac{B}{p}\right) = M + \varepsilon - (B(p + \gamma)/p) \tag{6.10}$$

If e is selected, the entrepreneur's expected earnings equal $(1 - \alpha)(M + \varepsilon)$, where $\alpha = B/M$. Hence, the entrepreneur's expected profit equals

$$\left(1 - \left(\frac{B}{M}\right)\right)(M + \varepsilon) = M - B - \frac{B\varepsilon}{M} \tag{6.11}$$

The difference between (6.11) and (6.10) equals B $B(\frac{\varepsilon}{M} - \frac{\gamma}{p})$. If $\varepsilon/M > \gamma/p$, it is positive and the entrepreneur prefers d and vice versa.

The Model Implications

First consider the case $\gamma = 0$. It means that entrepreneurial bias is not related to risk estimation but only to overestimating the average expected earnings from the project. In this case Proposition 6.1 predicts that an overconfident manager prefers debt which is in general consistent with the spirit of e.g., Heaton (2002) and some empirical evidence e.g., Malmendier et al. (2011). The case $\varepsilon = 0$ means that entrepreneurial bias is only related to project risk estimation but not to the average expected earnings from the project. Since γ is related to the probability of project success the case where managers underestimate the risk of their projects is $\gamma \geq 0$ (i.e., they overestimate the probability of success and underestimate the probability of project failure). This case also generates interesting predictions compared to existing theories. This is consistent with the spirit of results in Bukalska (2019) and Vivian and Xu (2018) where more overconfidence leads to more equity if overconfidence is related to risk assessment.

Miglo (2024) combines behavioral finance and asymmetric information and suggests that there are cases when equilibrium exists where a separating equilibrium may exist where high-quality issues equity and low-quality issues debt that may be consistent with such phenomena as reverse pecking order (i.e., when firms prefer equity to debt under asymmetric information) and negative correlation between debt and profitability discussed previously in this part of the book. Ji and Miglo (2019) provide an analysis of the case with $\varepsilon = 0$ for high-quality type and find empirical support.

The assumption about managerial overconfidence used in this section is consistent with findings and ideas of literature that managerial behavior Barros and Silveria (2008), Griffin and Tversky (1992), March and Shapira (1987) and Larwood and Whittaker (1977). As we have seen overconfidence usually leads managers to believe that the equity of their firms is undervalued leading them to prefer internal funds followed by (which is also undervalued in their opinion but to a lesser degree than equity) which is in general consistent with traditional POT. However, Hackbarth (2008) argues that in a more complete modeling, firms may prefer equity which is consistent with the spirit of some results presented in this chapter.

Fairchild (2005) examines the combined effects of managerial overconfidence (overconfidence in their model is interpreted as a bias estimation of a firm's investment project success probability), asymmetric information and the moral hazard problem on the manager's choice of financing (debt or equity). It is shown that the effect of overconfidence on managerial moral hazard is ambiguous. It has a positive effect by inducing higher managerial effort. However, it may lead to excessive use of debt and higher expected bankruptcy costs. For more information about managerial biases and their impact on different financing decisions including capital structure see for example, Baker and Wurgler (2012), Fairchild (2010) and Shefrin (2001).

6.2 Other Types of Behavioral Biases and Capital Structure

The Irrational Investor Approach. In the previous section, managers were assumed to be biased. An alternative approach is to assume that investors are biased. The theoretical modeling of the approach of the rational manager adapting to the irrationality of financial markets (also known as the irrational investor approach or market timing theory) is essentially derived from the work of Stein (1996), but also has its roots in the work of Blanchard et al. (1993), De Long et al. (1989), Fischer and Merton (1984), Morck et al. (1990). It was then taken over by Baker et al. (2002) and dynamic considerations were added to it by Bolton et al. (2013). Why is it important for firms' capital structure policies?!

First, investors are supposed to influence the prices of securities. Secondly, managers are supposed to be smart enough to be able to see/ estimate the differences between actual market prices of securities and their fundamental values (or prices in the case of fully rational investors) (Baker et al., 2002). There are 3 possible aspects of manager policy that can affect firm capital structure. First, managers maximize firm long-term value; second, they take advantage of short term mispricing to transfer wealth to existing shareholders; and third, they maximize short-term value (maximize current share price relative to value).

Second, the overvaluation of equities by an irrational market is an important reason for the issuance of shares. Companies would be tempted to issue shares when their values are excessively high. Doing so benefits current shareholders at the expense of new shareholders. Similarly, the timing of repurchasing the company's own shares is often done when stocks are undervalued. In this context, Stein (1996) was among the first to provide a useful framework for reflecting on this idea and showed that when the stock price of a company is too high, the rational manager should issue more shares to take advantage of investors' bias. In their study of the implications of investor irrationality on the managers' choice of capital structure, Baker and Wurgler (2002) assume capital structure is largely the cumulative result of past attempts to adapt to equity market valuations (market timing). Graham and Harvey (2001) found that 2/ 3 of CFOs believe that mispricing is important in the decision to issue new stock. The market is sluggish in rationally incorporating information in managers' market timing motivation for external financing. The slow assimilation of information can be because of investors' information processing biases. Lowry et al. (2017) finds that mispricing/overvaluation of shares is the second most important reason for issuing shares.[4]

Empirical evidence related to the securities' returns following external financing have some behavioral explanations. For example, low long-terms returns (3 years) following equity offerings, debt offerings, and bank borrowings are consistent with securities mispricing (overvaluation) when they are issued. The same implies to high returns following share repurchases. Managers seem to time external financing transactions to exploit mispricing. Further market's immediate reaction to the financing decisions is incomplete (underreaction to public announcements of voluntary decisions). The market gradually reacts over the following one-to-three years which is inconsistent with market efficiency and consistent with some of the information-processing biases.

In Chapter 2 we mentioned a recent paper by Izhakian et al. (2021) that analyzes the role of risk and ambiguity in the trade-off theory. The ambiguity is a situation where economic agents are facing an uncertain outcome but in contrast to a more traditional risky situation (where risk-aversion plays a crucial role) under ambiguity they do not know the probability distribution. The authors argue that risk and ambiguity (using both investors and managers' bias in their model) may have a different effect on marginal benefits of tax and on the optimal level of debt. They argue that greater ambiguity—the uncertainty over the probabilities associated with the outcomes—leads firms to increase leverage. It to some extent contrasts the intuition of the traditional risky outcome situation prediction (e.g., in the trade-off theory) that ceteris paribus greater risk usually leads to lower leverage.

Capital Structure and Corporate/National Culture

Kreps (1990) argues that corporate culture is the result of transaction/communication costs inside the firm. Hermalin (2001) argues that corporate culture is an important determinant of corporate governance and corporate finance. One prediction of this theory is that capital structure policy of a firm with a parent company can be explained by the

[4] More discussion about the connections between the market timing idea and capital structure is provided in the next chapter.

capital structure policy of the parent company because they usually have similar corporate cultures. This prediction finds some support in Cronqvist et al. (2009). Another prediction of this theory is that corporate culture can be more important for the capital structure policy in large and mature firms. Lemmon et al. (2008) argue that a major determinant of capital structure is debt policy and more specifically debt structure prior to the IPO. Firms with low leverage prior to their IPOs tend to have low leverage subsequently and vice versa. Bruer et al. (2015) analyze the relationship between the corporate debt choice (either bank or bond financing) and cultural value types—in particular Autonomy (countries that value freedom, creativity, broadmindedness, and curiosity) and Embeddedness (countries that value respect for tradition, social order, national security, reciprocation of favors, self-discipline, wisdom, moderation, honoring of parents and elders, preserving public image, obedience, devotion, forgiveness, and cleanliness). Referring to the importance of specific human capital investments and individuals' future orientations, the authors show that firms in Autonomy cultures tend to prefer bank finance, whereas firms in Embeddedness cultures show a preference for financing by issuing bonds. Empirical evidence from 71 countries confirms the results. Griffin and Li (2009) investigate the role of the managers' countries of origin in leverage decisions using data on foreign joint ventures in China. It was found that national culture has significant explanatory power in the financial leverage decisions of foreign joint ventures in China. Country-level variation is evident in capital structure and appears to work through choices of firm characteristics, industry affiliation, ownership structure, and region of investment. Cao and Mauer (2010) investigate the effect of corporate culture on capital structure policy. They find that cultural changes brought by new CEOs have significant impacts on the continuation of firms' existing debt policies. Firms with a recent CEO replacement tend to switch their debt policy. Firms that never change their debt policy over their history have significantly fewer CEO turnovers than firms with policy changes, which is consistent with the idea that new CEOs induce capital structure changes. Hilgen (2014) examines the impact of cultural clusters on the capital structure decisions made by European retailers. The paper finds a significant difference between the mean capital structures of the different cultural clusters. Overall links between capital structure and corporate/national culture look like promising research areas.

6.3 Financing Strategy and Incomplete Contracts

This section considers the role of incomplete contracts in explaining some capital structure phenomena. Under standard moral hazard problems considered for example in Chapters 4 and 5, the parties cannot write a contract that will describe some of the decision-maker's actions. The incomplete contracts approach takes this one step further: the parties cannot write a contract that will describe some of the decision-maker's actions nor can they write contracts (financial contracts) that will be contingent on a firm's profit. The firm's profit is observable but not verifiable! So in many situations, the only contracts that can be written are property rights allocation or unconditional payments. This leads to the so called "property rights approach" (Grossman & Hart, 1986; Hart, 1995; Hart & Moore, 1990). The following model provides an illustration of these ideas.

An entrepreneur E and an investor I can produce a good. E has an idea but does not have funds to finance the production of the good (the required amount is B). I has resources but lacks ideas (or does not want to exploit his own ideas). The value of the good $v(i_1, i_2)$ depends on the level of investment provided by each party (i_1 provided by E and i_2 provided by I).[5] We assume $v(i_1, i_2) = pi_1 + (1 - p)i_2$. p reflects the productivity/efficiency of each party i.e. if $p > 1/2$ then E can contribute potentially more and vice versa. The cost of investment is $c(i_k) = i_k^2, k \in \{1,2\}$. The amount of investments made by each party is non-verifiable. Hence, the parties cannot write a complete contract specifying the levels of effort because it cannot be enforced.

The interaction between the parties is as follows. It involves 3 stages that will be called initial contracting, investment, and production (see Fig. 6.2). The two parties meet at the beginning of stage 1 and bargain about the financing contract. If the decision is not reached, the utility of both parties is zero. Otherwise, I provides financing B and the parties sign a contract. This contract is denoted by a pair (σ; P). σ = E means that E owns the firm, σ = I means that I owns the firm, σ = J means joint property. P is the promised payment from the firm's owner to another party,

[5] The entrepreneur's investment is time, skills development etc. The investor's investment may include the firm monitoring and performance analysis. Also the production process can be multi-stage which may require additional investments in later stages. For simplicity we do not focus on these details.

$P \geq 0$. If $\sigma = J$, $P = 0$. The financial interpretation of these contracts is as follows. $\sigma = E$ implies debt financing. Since I is not participating in the ownership of the firm the only way to make him interested is to promise some future payment. $\sigma = I$ means that the firm will be sold to I. If $P \neq 0$ in this case it means that the firm will have debt owed to E. $\sigma = J$ means equity financing since I will become a co-owner of the firm. In stage 2, the parties choose i_1 and i_2. In the beginning of stage 3, the parties observe i_1 and i_2 and the potential value of the good $v(i_1, i_2)$, which can be created if they agree. The parties meet again to discuss profit distribution. Writing complete contracts (i.e. enforced with no cost) is possible now. If an agreement is reached, the parties write a contract which determines their payoffs w_1 and w_2. If the agreement fails at the beginning of stage 3, the parties do not cooperate. If the parties disagree then the payment P should be made. If earnings are not sufficient the firm belongs to the investor/creditor. In the case of joint ownership if the ownership fraction of E is x and respectively that of the investor is $1-x$ then earnings should be split at the same proportions. Firm earnings if the parties do not cooperate depend on who owns the firm. The firm revenue is pi_1 if E owns and $(1-p)i_2$ if I owns.[6] It means that if E owns the firm, he will be able to produce and sell the good for the value pi_1 which is in general less than the value when (the parties cooperate in the production stage $(v(i_1, i_2))$).

Initially, if the parties are able to write a contract (enforceable with no cost) which specifies the levels of effort i_1 and i_2 (complete contracts scenario), then the first-best effort levels will be achieved. The ex ante efficient effort level maximizes the total expected surplus. If we denote the efficient effort levels by i_1^* and i_2^* then $(i_1^*, i_2^*) = argmax_{i_1,i_2}\{v(i_1, i_2)\text{-}c(i_1)\text{-}c(i_2)\} = argmax_{i_1,i_2}\{pi_1 + (1-p)i_2\text{-}i_1^2\text{-}i_2^2\}$. The solution is $i_1^* = p/2$, i_2^*=(1-p)/2, and the first-best surplus equals $(p^2+(1-p)^2)/4$. Intuitively, the optimal level of investment by a party increases with the productive capacity of this party.

[6] In the case of joint ownership if the parties disagree at the beginning of stage 3 the decision-making will be done by the party with more than 50% of shares (if it is exactly 50% one can assume without loss of generality that the decision-maker is determined randomly).

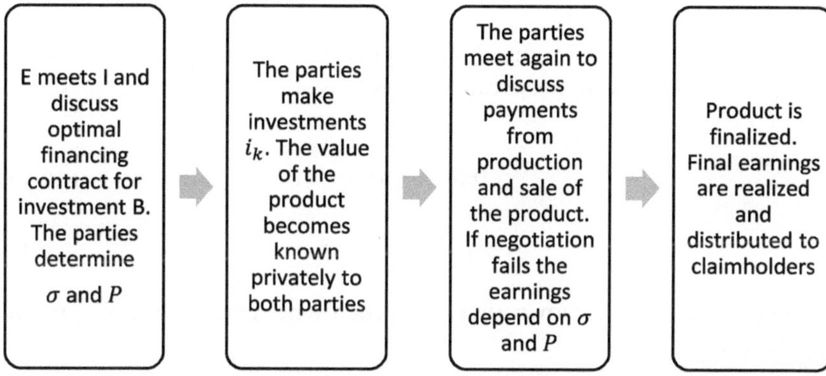

Fig. 6.2 Sequence of events

Proposition 6.4. *If B is sufficiently small, the firm ownership should belong to a more productive party. Joint ownership (equity financing) is never optimal.*

Proof The steps to solve the model in the case when a complete contract that describes i_1 and i_2 is impossible to write are as follows. By backward induction, we first consider stage 3. In stage 3 the parties always cooperate. Intuitively, since no additional surplus is created if the parties do not cooperate, the parties are always better off if they form an agreement in stage 3. The equilibrium in stage 3 depends on the contract signed in stage 1. Firm ownership is relevant because it determines the threat point of the stage 3 bargaining game. If E owns the firm and $P \leq pi_1$, the default payoff of E is $pi_1 - P$ and that of I is P. If the negotiation takes place, the total payoffs will be $pi_1 + (1 - p)i_2$. The total gain from cooperation is $pi_1 + (1 - p)i_2 - pi_1 = (1 - p)i_2$. According to the Nash bargaining solution (see e.g., Osborne, 1994), the parties receive their default payoffs plus half of the gains from cooperation. Thus, the payoffs of E and I respectively will be:

$$0.5(1 - p)i_2 + pi_1 - P \tag{6.12}$$

$$0.5(1 - p)i_2 + P \tag{6.13}$$

If $P > pi_1$, the default payo□ of E is 0 and that of I is pi_1. If the negotiation takes place, the total payoffs will be $pi_1 + (1 - p)i_2$. The total gain from cooperation is $pi_1 + (1 - p)i_2 - pi_1 = (1 - p)i_2$. According to the Nash bargaining solution, the parties receive their default payoffs plus half of the gains from cooperation. The payoffs of E and I respectively will be:

$$0.5(1 - p)i_2 \tag{6.14}$$

$$0.5(1 - p)i_2 + pi_1 \tag{6.15}$$

Similarly, it can be shown that if I is the owner and $P \leq (1 - p)i_2$, the payoffs are:

$$0.5pi_1 + P \tag{6.16}$$

$$0.5pi_1 + (1 - p)i_2 - P \tag{6.17}$$

If P > $(1 - p)i_2$, the payoffs of E and I respectively will be:

$$0.5pi_1 + (1 - p)i_2 \tag{6.18}$$

$$0.5pi_1 \tag{6.19}$$

It is clear from (6.12)–(6.19) that the parties payoffs (resulting from the negotiation in stage 3) increase in their productive skills.

If the case of joint ownership, if the negotiation fails, E's expected utility equals xpi_1 (if $x \geq 1/2$) and that of I is $(1-x)pi_1$. Hence the total expected Payoff will be pi_1. If the negotiation takes place, then the total payoffs will be $pi_1 + (1 - p)i_2$. The total gain from trade is thus $pi_1 + (1 - p)i_2 - pi_1 = (1 - p)i_2$. According to the Nash bargaining solution, E gets half of the gains from trade at date 2. Hence, the payoffs of E and I respectively will be

$$xpi_1 + 0.5(1 - p)i_2 \tag{6.20}$$

$$(1 - x)pi_1 + 0.5(1 - p)i_2 \tag{6.21}$$

Respectively if $x < 1/2$ then the payo□s of E and I respectively will be

$$x(1 - p)i_2 + 0.5pi_1 \tag{6.22}$$

$$(1-x)(1-p)i_2 + 0.5pi_1 \tag{6.23}$$

These formulas show that when joint ownership was established at stage 1, the payoff of a party resulting from negotiation in stage 3 increases in its fraction of ownership.

Stage 2: investments.

Consider the case when E owns the firm. The equilibrium depends on the parties expectations about the outcome of the negotiation in stage 3. The parties chose the level of their investment by comparing the expected payoff from negotiations at the beginning of stage 3 described previously and the cost of investment. We first describe E's choice of effort for a given level of effort by I. From (6.12) and (6.14) E chooses the effort level

$$i_1^{**} = \begin{cases} argmax_{i_1}\{0.5(pi_1 + 0.5(1-p)i_2 + pi_1) - P - i_1^2\}, if\, P \le pi_1 \\ argmax_{i_1}\{0.5(1-p)i_2 - i_1^2\}, if\, P > pi_1 \end{cases}$$

The solution is: $i_1^{**} = p/2$ if

$$\frac{p^2}{4} - P > 0 \tag{6.24}$$

and $i_1^{**} = 0$ otherwise.

From (6.13) and (6.15) I chooses the effort level

$$i_2^{**} = \begin{cases} argmax_{i_2}\{0.5(pi_1 + 0.5(1-p)i_2 + pi_1) - P - i_2^2\}, if\, P \le pi_1 \\ argmax_{i_1}\{0.5(1-p)i_2 - i_2^2\}, if\, P > pi_1 \end{cases}$$

It implies that $i_2^{**} = (1-p)/4$.

It follows from this analysis above that the level of parties' investments increases in their productive skills. A similar analysis of the case when I owns the firm leads to the following. The condition which is similar to (6.24) in this case is:

$$\frac{(1-p)^2}{4} - P > 0 \tag{6.25}$$

The solution is: $i_1^{**} = \frac{p}{4} \text{and} i_2^{**} = \frac{1-p}{2}, if\, P \le \frac{(1-p)^2}{4}$ and 0 otherwise.

Similarly for the case of joint ownership established we get: if $x \geq 1/2$ then $i_1^{**} = \frac{xp}{2}$ and $i_2^{**} = \frac{1-p}{4}$ and if $x < 1/2$ then $i_1^{**} = \frac{p}{4}$ and $i_2^{**} = \frac{(1-x)(1-p)}{2}$.

Stage 1: initial contracting.

The total surplus equals $\pi(\sigma) = pi_1^{**} + (1-p)i_2^{**}\text{-}i_1^{**\,2}\text{-}i_2^{**\,2}$, where i_1^{**} and i_2^{**} are determined previously. The parties will choose an option which provides them with the maximal total surplus. The bargaining power belongs to E and E makes a take-or-leave-it offer to I. I will accept E's offer if his expected payoff is at least B. Since in this case E can always offer a contract that offers I exactly B (since I is not wealth-constrained), an option with maximal total surplus also gives maximal payoff to E.

If E owns the firm and if (6.24) holds, then his default (in case the parties disagree at stage 3) payoff is $\pi_1(\sigma) = pi_1^{**} + (1-p)i_2^{**}\text{-}i_1^{**2}\text{-}i_2^{**2}$ and I payoff is $\pi_1(\sigma) = 0.5(1-p)i_2^{**} - i_2^{**}2 = (1-\text{p})2/16^2$. From previous calculations we have $\pi_1(\sigma) = pi_1^{**} + (1-p)i_2^{**}\text{-}i_1^{**2}\text{-}i_2^{**2}$, $\pi_2(\sigma) = pi_1^{**} + (1-p)i_2^{**}\text{-}i_1^{**2}\text{-}i_2^{**2}$ and

$$\pi(E) = \frac{4p^2 + 3(1-p)^2}{16} \tag{6.26}$$

This contract can be accepted by I if $\pi_2(E) \geq B$. Since the left-hand side is positive it holds when B is sufficiently small. Similarly we get

$$\pi(I) = \frac{3p^2 + 4(1-p)^2}{16} \tag{6.27}$$

$$\pi(J) = \frac{3xp^2 + 4(1-p)^2}{16} \tag{6.28}$$

Proposition 6.4 follows from the comparison of total surpluses for different cases. J is never optimal for any value of $0 < x < 1$ as follows from the comparison of (6.28) with (6.26) and (6.27). Also whether E or I is optimal depends on the value of p. For example if p > ½, E-ownership brings a higher surplus as compared to I-ownership.

The intuition why joint ownership is not optimal is that the default payoff under joint ownership is smaller for E that reduces his effort in stage 2 but it does not affect the payoff of I since the default payoff in the case of disagreement depends only on investment made by E. These results are consistent with what is found in incomplete contract literature, which argues that ownership rights should belong to the more productive party and also with Hart (1995, p. 48) in that joint ownership is not optimal. It is also consistent with spirit of Aghion and Bolton (1992) where debt is the optimal contract.[7] Aghion and Bolton (1992) develops a theory of capital structure choice based on the problem of optimal allocation of corporate control. The analysis starts by assuming that not all actions are available to a manager and not all states of the world are describable (ex ante) or verifiable. This creates a problem of control, as some actions (and states of the world) left out of the initial contract will have to be determined ex post. Aghion and Bolton (1992) argue that a state-contingent control is optimal i.e. if a firm performs well, control goes to the shareholders; otherwise the control passes to the creditors.

Empirical evidence related to incomplete contracts is mixed. The attempts to test the approach directly are not numerous. Kaplan and Stromberg (2003) test the main predictions for US firms and find confirmation. However, their results do not seem to hold for other countries. Not even in Canada, which is the closest neighbor and commercial partner the US and has a similar Anglo-Saxon type of financial system (Cumming, 2006). Nobel Prize winners Maskin and Tirole (1999a, 1999b) discuss the major idea of the property rights approach, which is that some actions are observable but non-contractible. They suggest that observable information could be made verifiable by the use of cleverly designed revelation mechanisms. That is, the contracting parties can agree in advance to play a game where they have the appropriate incentives to truthfully reveal their private information in equilibrium. However, these mechanisms are rarely observed in practice. Aghion et al. (2014) further discuss the robustness of the incomplete contracts/property rights approach and suggest possible avenues for future research.

Questions and Exercises

1. The perfect market concept suggests that the prices of securities should reflect their true value. However, empirical evidence suggests that newly issued shares are often mispriced.

[7] For a survey and more examples of literature that uses incomplete contracts ideas to analyze capital structure related issues see e.g., Bolton (2014) or Hart (2017). We discuss some applications later in the book e.g., in Chapter 8.

2. Many empirical studies find that firms seem to issue new shares only as a last resort and that it is a least preferable choice compared to internal funds and debt. Consider this finding in light of the behavioral finance theories/ideas.
3. A company has 3,000,000 shares outstanding trading at $20 apiece (small and large transactions). This price is expected to remain the same in the short term even if the firm decides to issue or repurchase its own shares. Managers believe (correctly) that the discount rate appropriate for the risk borne is 12% and total cash flows are expected to be $4 million next year and will rise by 4% per year indefinitely. The firm has an investment project that requires $2 million. Discuss a strategy that is beneficial to the current shareholders.
4. A firm has assets-in-place that can generate earnings $R = 100{,}000$ with probability $p_1 = 0.4$. There is a new project available. The cost of the project is $B = 30{,}000$. If the investment is undertaken, the probability increases by 0.4. Initially, the firm has debt (senior) with face value $D = 20{,}000$. Everybody is risk-neutral in this economy. The risk-free interest rate is zero.

   a. Find the NPV of the new project
   b. Will the new project be undertaken?
   c. Now suppose that $D = 60{,}000$. Will the new project be undertaken?
   d. What phenomena are illustrated in this example?
   e. Suppose that the entrepreneur thinks that the new investment will increase the probability of success by 0.6 (while objectively it is 0.4). Describe the likely scenario.
   f. Provide meaningful interpretation of your results in question e).

5. Assume that a firm can choose between two projects, A and B, both costing 40. The firm seeks debt to finance the project. There are two states of nature (bad, good) with equal probability. The risk-free rate is 0.

The earnings in the two states are as follows:

	b (=0.50)	*g* (*P* = 0.5)	*Expected earnings*
Project A	80	80	80
Project B	0	110	55

Everybody is risk-neutral in this economy. The risk-free interest rate is zero.

a. What project has a higher NPV?
b. What project will be chosen if the debt face value is 40?
c. Now suppose that the manager believes that the probability of the good state is 70%. Describe the scenario.
d. What phenomena are illustrated in this example?
e. Is there any equilibrium in this case?

6. Good capital structure policy is an important part of corporate financial policy. It can greatly help firms' managers deal with shareholders.
   a) Critically examine the most relevant, from your point of view, theories that explain a firm's capital structure policy (it should be related to behavioral finance). The description should include the main assumption(s) of the theory, its main idea, its main result(s)/prediction(s) and its main weakness(es).
   b) Present an Excel file with the debt/equity ratio for Google between 2000–2017 and create a chart.
   c) Using data in question (b) provide an example that can illustrate at least two theories described in (a)? Use articles/ news or other information to support your conclusions. Which theory(ies) is the most powerful in your opinion?
7. Analyze the model of Sect. 6.3 assuming that the cost of investment is $c(i_k) = 1/2i_k^2, k \in \{1{,}2\}$ and that $v(i_1, i_2) = 2pi_1 + (1 - p)i_2$

References

Aghion, P., & Bolton, P. (1992). An Incomplete Contracts Approach to Financial Contracting. *Review of Economic Studies, 59*, 473–94.

Aghion, P., Bloom, N., & Van Reenen, J. (2014). Incomplete Contracts and the Internal Organization of Firms. *The Journal of Law, Economics, and Organization, 30*, Issue suppl_1, i37–i63.

Baker, M., & Wurgler, J. (2002). Market Timing and Capital Structure. *Journal of Finance, 57*(1), 1–32.

Baker, M., & Wurgler, J. (2012). Behavioral Corporate Finance: A Current Survey. In G. M. Constantinides, M. Harris, & R. M. Stulz (Eds.), *Handbook of the Economics of Finance* (Vol. 2). Elsevier.

Barros, L. A. B. de C., & Silveira, A. di M. da. (2008). Overconfidence, Managerial Optimism, and the Determinants of Capital Structure. *Brazilian Review of Finance, 6*(3), 293–335.

Bilgehan, T. (2014). Psychological biases and the capital structure decisions: A literature review. *Theoretical and Applied Economics, 21*(12), 123–142.

Blanchard, K. H., Zigarmi, D., & Nelson, R. B. (1993). Situational Leadership After 25 Years: A Retrospective. *Journal of Leadership Studies, 1*(1), 21–36.

Bolton, P., Chen, H., & Wang, N. (2013). Market Timing, Investment, and Risk Management. *Journal of Financial Economics, 109*(1), 40–62.

Bolton, P. (2014). Corporate Finance, Incomplete Contracts, and Corporate Control. *The Journal of Law, Economics, and Organization*, *30*(suppl_1), 64–81.

Breuer W., Quinten, B., & Salzmann, A. (2015). Bank Versus Bond Fi-Nance: A Cultural View of Corporate Debt Financing. In B. Christiansen (Ed.), *Handbook of Research on Global Business Opportuities* (Ch 14, pp. 289–315).

Bukalska, E. (2019). Testing trade-off theory and pecking order theory under managerial overconfidence. *International Journal of Management and Economics, 55*(2), 99–117.

Cao, C., & Mauer, D. (2010). *The Effect of Corporate Culture on Capital Structure Policy* (Working Paper).

Cronqvist, H., Low, A., & Nilsson, M. (2009). *Persistence in Firm Policies, Firm Origin, and Corporate Culture: Evidence from Corporate Spin-offs*, (Working Paper). Available at SSRN. http://ssrn.com/abstract=954791.

Cumming, D. J. (2006). Adverse Selection and Capital Structure: Evidence from Venture Capital. *Entrepreneurship Theory and Practice, 30*, 155–184.

De Long, J., Shleifer, A., Summers, L., & Waldmann, R. (1989). Noise Trader Risk in Financial Markets. *The Journal of Political Economy, 98*(4), 703–738.

Fairchild, R. (2005). The Effect of Managerial Overconfidence, Asymmetric Information, and Moral Hazard on Capital Structure Decisions. *ICFAI Journal of Behavioral Finance, 2*(4).

Fairchild, R. (2010). Behavioural Corporate Finance: Existing Research and Future Directions. *International Journal of Behavioural Accounting and Finance, 1*(4), 277–293.

Fischer, S., & Merton, R. (1984). Macroeconomics and Finance: The Role of the Stock Market. *Carnegie-Rochester Conference Series on Public Policy, 21*, 57–108.

Graham, J., & Harvey, C. (2001). The Theory and Practice of Corporate Finance: Evidence from the Field. *Journal of Financial Economics, 60*, 187–243.

Griffin, D., & Tversky, A. (1992). The Weighing of Evidence and the Determinants of Confidence. *Cognitive Psychology, 24*(3), 411–435.

Grossman, S., & Hart, O. (1986). The Cost and Benefits of Ownership: A Theory of Vertical and Lateral Integration. *Journal of Political Economy, 94*, 691–719.

Griffin, D., & Li, K. (2009). *National Culture and Capital Structure Decisions: Evidence from Foreign Joint Ventures in China* (Working Paper).

Hackbarth, D. (2008). Managerial Traits and Capital Structure Decisions. *Journal of Financial and Quantitative Analysis, 43*, 843–881.

Hart, O., & Moore, J. (1990). Property Rights and the Nature of the Firm. *Journal of Political Economy, 98*, 1119–1158.

Hart, O. (1995). *Firms, Contracts and Financial Structure*. Clarendon Press.

Hart, O. (2017). Incomplete Contracts and Control. *The American Economic Review, 107*(7), 1731–1752.

Heaton, J. (2002). Managerial Optimism and Corporate Finance. *Financial Management, 31*(2), 33–45.

Hermalin, B. (2001). Economics and Corporate Culture. In C. L. Cooper, S. Cartwright, & P. C. Earley (Eds.), *The International Handbook of Organizational Culture and Climate*. John Wiley & Sons.

Hilgen, M. (2014). *The Impact of Cultural Clusters on Capital Structure Decisions: Evidence from European Retailers* (Working Paper).

Izhakian, Y., Yermack, D., & Zender, J. (2021). Ambiguity and the Tradeoff Theory of Capital Structure. *Management Science, 68*(6), 4090–4111.

Ji, X., & Miglo, A. (2019). *Capital Structure Choice Under Asymmetric Information and Overconfident Managers* (SSRN Working Paper).

Kaplan, S. N., & Stromberg, P. (2003). Financial Contracting Theory Meets the Real World: An Empirical Analysis of Venture Capital Contracts. *Review of Economic Studies, 70*, 281–315.

Kreps, D. (1990). Corporate Culture and Economic Theory. In J. E. Alt, & K. A. Shepsle (Ed.), *Perspectives in Positive Political Economy* (90–143). Cambridge University Press.

Larwood, L., & Whittaker, W. (1977). Managerial Myopia: Self-Serving Biases in Organizational Planning. *Journal of Applied Psychology, 62*(2), 194–198.

Lemmon, M., & Zender, J. (2010). Debt Capacity and Tests of Capital Structure Theories. *Journal of Financial and Quantitative Analysis, 45*(05), 1161–1187.

Lemmon, M. L., Roberts, M. R., & Zender, J. F. (2008). Back to the Beginning: Persistence and the Cross-Section of Corporate Capital Structure. *The Journal of Finance, 63*, 1575–1608.

Lowry, M., Michaely, R., & Volkova, E. (2017). Initial Public Offerings: A Synthesis of the Literature and Directions for Future Research. *Foundations and Trends in Finance, 11*(3–4), 154–320.

Malmendier, U., Tate, G., & Yanv, J. (2011). Overconfidence and EarlyLife Experiences: The Effect of Managerial Traits on Corporate Financial Policies. *Journal of Finance, 66*(5), 1687–1733.

March, J., & Shapira, Z. (1987). Managerial Perspectives on Risk and Risk Taking. *Management Science, 33*(11), 1404–1418.

Maskin, E., & Tirole, J. (1999). Incomplete Contracts: Where Do We Stand? *Econometrica, 67*(4), 741–781.

Maskin, E., & Tirole, J. (1999). Unforeseen Contingencies and Incomplete Contracts. *Review of Economic Studies, 66*, 83–114.

Miglo, A. (2024a). *Capital Structure and Firm Performance: An Analysis of Impact of Asymmetric Information and Behavioral Biases* (Working Paper).

Modigliani, F., & Miller, M. (1958). The Cost of Capital, Corporation Finance and the Theory of Investment. *American Economic Review, 48*(3), 261–297.

Morck, R., Shleifer, A., Vishny, R. W., Shapiro, M., & Poterba, J. M. (1990). The Stock Market and Investment: Is the Market a Sideshow? *Brookings Papers on Economic Activity, 1990*(2), 157–215.

Osborne, M. (1994). *A Course in Game Theory*. MIT Press.

Reyes, J., Miranda, M., & Vera-Martínez, J. (2019). Capital Structure Construct: A New Approach to Behavioral Finance. *Investment Management and Financial Innovations, 16*(4), 86–97.

Shefrin, H. (2001). Behavioral Corporate Finance. *Journal of Applied Corporate Finance, 14*(3), 113–126.

Stein, J. (1996). Rational Capital Budgeting in an Irrational World. *The Journal of Business, 69*(4), 429–455.

Vivian, A., & Xu, B. (2018). Time-Varying Managerial Overconfidence and Pecking Order Preference. *Review of Quantitative Finance and Accounting, 50*, 799–835.

PART II

Advanced Topics

This part covers such topics as capital structure choice and firms' performance, capital structure and corporate governance, capital structure of small companies and start-up companies, FinTech developments related to capital structure, corporate financing versus project financing, and others.

CHAPTER 7

Capital Structure Choice and Firm's "Quality"

7.1 Interesting Problem

One of the most interesting questions for me throughout the years has been what capital structure choice can say about a firm's quality. Do "good" firms issue shares rather than bonds or vice versa? If there is no strict rule then are there any average correlations between capital structure choice and a firm's quality?

As we discussed in Chapter 3, according to the "pecking-order theory of capital structure", equity should only be used as a last resort by firms who need capital for their investments. Good-quality firms especially should not issue equity to avoid underpricing. Yet, in a December 2015 article, Shira Ovide mentioned an issue of shares by the seemingly very successful company Atlassian.[1] Atlassian made good efforts to increase its share price prior to its IPO with the first-day after IPO trading prices even higher. At the same time, Ovide mentioned that although Atlassian was currently showing signs of success, its profitable business model might not

[1] Ovide (December 10, 2015).

Supplementary Information The online version contains supplementary material available at https://doi.org/10.1007/978-3-031-85459-0_7.

A. Miglo, *Capital Structure in the Modern World*, https://doi.org/10.1007/978-3-031-85459-0_7

work as well in the future. Another topic that is discussed in the article is the situation with start-up IPOs in general in 2015.

Many ideas/topics from the article mentioned above will be discussed in this chapter. Why do successful firms issue shares even though the traditional theory does not favor it? What information is signaled by the firm to market participants when it discusses the issuance of shares? Finally, when do firms prefer to issue shares?

In his 2012 article, Michael Sivy discusses several interesting ideas related to IPOs.[2] One is that an IPO by a firm may signal bad news. Therefore firms sell shares at the moment when they think the market's perception of the company before any bad news comes out. This can be true even for successful companies. Another point is that an IPO can signal information about the future of the market or the future of the economy. Sivy mentioned that firms could sell shares to avoid possible downturns in the economy. As an example, hospital-management company HCA Holdings went ahead with an offering in 2011 because of a variety of uncertainties about health care reform and future tax policy. Sivy also discusses if the famous Facebook IPO could send similar negative signals about the market's future. The experts that advise potential issuers employ many of the world's top economists. Often they have access to knowledge that is unavailable to most market participants. There is no guarantee, of course, that advisers know where the stock market and the economy are going. But they possess better information than most investors.

In December 2015 article, John Ficenec describes an issue of bonds by Entertainment 1.[3] The company was built on the sales of the hugely successful children's cartoon character Peppa Pig. The first warning sign was the exit of one of their major supporting investment groups Marwyn in July of 2015. The next issue was the surprise rights issue in September when the company asked investors to find almost £200 m to fund the buyout of the Peppa Pig rights. The final straw was a poorly communicated issue of £285 m bonds in early December. It was very unclear to investors why an expensive debt was needed. The negative free cash flow and net debt levels rising to £264 m at the end of September put investors at risk. An interesting point of Ficenec's article is that a bond issue does

[2] Sivy (May 30, 2012).

[3] Ficenec (December 21, 2015).

not necessarily signal good news as would be predicted by early capital structure theories, for example by standard trade-off theory discussed in Chapter 2.

This chapter analyzes the link between capital structure and a firm's quality. In most cases, the firm's quality is measured by its operating performance. As mentioned above it is important to look at the link between capital structure and not only the current operating performance but future performance as well. Also note that this question is probably one of the most difficult in capital structure theory at least among basic theories. For example, as was mentioned in Chapter 2, traditional trade-off theory predicts a positive correlation between debt and profitability, which is not quite what empirical evidence shows.

7.2 The Role of Asymmetric Information

In Chapter 3 we learned about the "Pecking-order theory" (POT) that was put forth by Myers and Majluf (1984). According to the theory, firms will use internal funds, if available, to finance profitable projects. If internal funds are not available they will issue debt. Equity is dominated by internal funds and debt in POT. Low-quality firms will use equity as much as internal funds but high-quality firms will prefer internal funds. If high-quality firms issue equity they will be undervalued by investors because of their lack of information. Similarly, equity is dominated by debt. Suppose that firms can finance projects with risk-free debt. Then the high-quality firm can issue debt to avoid any mispricing. If debt issued by the firm is risky, the situation does not change appreciably. The same holds if the firm has available assets-in-place. Hence a "pecking order" emerges: internal funds, debt, and equity (Myers & Majluf, 1984). The authors state (Myers & Majluf, 1984, p. 208): "In our model, the firm never issues equity. If it issues and invests it always issues debt." As we mentioned in Chapter 3 (also see Miglo, 2011), the empirical evidence is mixed about whether or not firms follow POT.

In the pecking-order model, good-quality firms have to use internal funds to avoid adverse selection problems and loss of value. These firms cannot signal their quality by changing their capital structure. The signalling theory of capital structure offers models in which capital structure serves as a signal of private information (Leland & Pyle, 1977; Ross, 1977). Usually in these models, the market reaction to debt issues is positive. However, as we mentioned in Chapter 3, empirical evidence is mixed regarding the predictions of signaling theory about firms' operating performances after issuing equity. Long-term underperformance of firms issuing equity compared to non-issuing firms (Jain & Kini, 1994; Loughran & Ritter, 1997) seems to be consistent with the spirit of signaling theory while the better operating performance of firms issuing equity before or shortly after the issue compared to non-issuing firms does not support the theory. According to Jain and Kini (1994, Fig. 7.1), and Pereira and Sousa (2015) the operating return on assets is higher for IPO firms in the first years after the issue and the operating cash flow on assets is higher in year "0" (immediately after the issue). In Loughran and Ritter (1997), profit margins are higher in years 0 and + 1, although there is different evidence about operating returns. In Mikkelson et al., (1997), IPO firms have higher performances in year 0. Shah (1994) reports that business risk falls after leverage-increasing exchange offers but rises after leverage-decreasing exchange offers.

A rich set of new predictions arises when a dynamic environment is analyzed. Hennessy et al. (2010) examine investment and financing decisions in a model with repeated signaling. They show that good firms can separate themselves from bad firms by changing their investment policy. For example, by accelerating investments (and reducing the values of the projects at the time of the investments) good firms can avoid being mimicked by other firms. They also show that equity can be better than debt. Halov (2006) proposes a model that considers a firm without internal funds where the choice of security depends not only on the

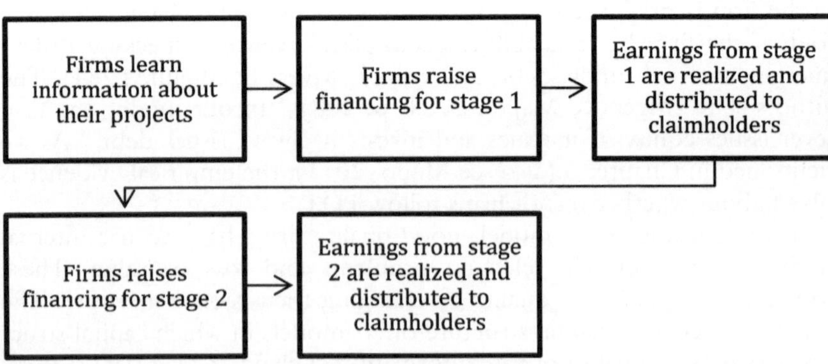

Fig. 7.1 Sequence of events

current adverse selection cost of security but also on its future cost. Halov finds that future adverse selection costs negatively affect the debt component of new external financing and positively affect the cash reserves of the firm. He explains why companies may at times prefer equity to debt. Morellec and Shürnoff (2011) develop a dynamic model of corporate investment and financing decisions and show that information asymmetries may not translate into a financing hierarchy or pecking order over securities.

Miglo (2007, 2017) suggests that multi-stage investments and long-term asymmetric information can affect corporate capital structure. In contrast to the standard POT, firms may issue equity as a signal.[4] He also analyzes the link between the debt-equity choice and the performance of the company following the issue (short-term versus long-term). The following illustrates the idea.

Consider a model with asymmetric information that focuses on a firm's performance profile over time and its effect on capital structure. Suppose a firm considers equity financing for a two-period investment project with cost C_t in period t, $t = 1, 2$. In each period the project may be successful or unsuccessful. In the latter case, the cash flow equals 1 and in the former case the cash flow equals 0. A firm's insiders have private information about the probability of success in each stage. The firms are of two types, type g and type b, with respective probabilities of success p_{gt} and p_{bt} at stage t. Type g has a higher overall value: $p_{g1} + p_{g2} > p_{b1} + p_{b2}$. The NPV of the investment in stage t for type j is $p_{jt} - C_t$, $j = g, b$. The sequence of events is as follows.

The focus of our analysis is on the firm's choice of financing for stage 1. The big question is whether the firm with the higher value will issue equity contrary to the prediction of the standard POT? Hence the focus of our analysis is on the separating equilibrium where the higher valued firm issues equity. In a separating equilibrium, all uncertainties about a firm's type are resolved in stage 1, which means that the financing choice in stage 2 is based on perfect information. For simplicity, suppose that a firm issues debt for stage 2 with face value D. We get:

$$p_{g2}D = C_2 \tag{7.1}$$

[4] See also Miglo and Zenkevich (2006) and Miglo (2012).

At stage 1, investors require an s_1 fraction of equity such that:

$$s_1 p_{g1} + s_1 p_{g2}(1 - D) = C_1 \tag{7.2}$$

Now consider the payoff of the shareholders of b in case b decides to mimic g, which equals $(1 - s_1)p_{b1} + (1 - s_1)p_{b2}(1 - D)$. If a signaling equilibrium exists, the shareholders' payoff for type b will be $p_{b1} + p_{b2} - C_1 - C_2$ (the present value of b).[5] Thus, a separating equilibrium exists if

$$(1 - s_1)p_{b1} + (1 - s_1)p_{b2}(1 - D) < p_{b1} + p_{b2} - C_1 - C_2 \tag{7.3}$$

In order to analyze this equation, let us denote the total expected cash flow for type j over both periods to be $v_j = p_{j1} + p_{j2}$. Also let r_j denote the rate of earnings growth (p_{j2}/p_{j1}). The probabilities of success at each stage are then:

$$p_{j1} = \frac{v_j}{1 + r_j} \textit{ and } p_{j2} = \frac{v_j r_j}{1 + r_j} \tag{7.4}$$

Equation (7.3) can be rewritten as.

$$\left(1 - \frac{C_1}{v_g - C_2}\right)\left(\frac{v_b}{1 + r_b} + \frac{v_b r_b}{1 + r_b}\left(1 - \frac{C_2(1 + r_g)}{v_g r_g}\right)\right) < v_b - C_1 - C_2 \tag{7.5}$$

Miglo (2012) argues that this equation holds and a separating equilibrium, where g issues equity, exists if and only if the difference between the firms' values is sufficiently small, and the difference between the rates of earnings growth is sufficiently high. It should also be true if $p_{g1} > p_{b1}$ and $p_{g2} < p_{b2}$. As an example suppose that $v_g = v_b$. Equation (7.5) becomes $p_{g2} < p_{b2}$.

Proposition 7.1. *A separating equilibrium exists when the extent of the asymmetric information is sufficiently small regarding the firms' total values and sufficiently large regarding the firms' earnings profile over time.*

[5] In signaling models it is usually not a problem for a low-value type of firms find a strategy that can not be mimicked by a high-value type. It can be some kind of debt with covenants for example where the payoffs depend on firm's total earnings over two periods. Since g has higher total value it would not be interested in mimicking b.

Proof. Given v_b and r_b, the amount of earnings that firm b can get by mimicking firm g (the left side of inequality (7.5)) depends on the fraction of equity sold at stage 1, which equals $\frac{C_1}{v_g - C_2}$ and the face value of debt at stage 2, which equals $\frac{C_2(1+r_g)}{v_g r_g}$. Given r_g, the fraction of equity sold at stage 1 and the face value of debt at stage 2 both decrease with v_g. On the other hand, given v_g, the fraction of equity sold at stage 1 does not depend on r_g and the face value of debt at stage 2 decreases with r_g because $\frac{\partial\left(\frac{C_2(1+r_g)}{v_g r_g}\right)}{\partial r_g} < 0$. So in order to reduce the incentive for b to mimic g, both v_g and r_g need to be as small as possible. Since $v_g > v_b$, the minimal incentive case is when v_g is close to v_b and when r_g is as small as possible compared to r_b.

The pecking-order model arises as a special case here. Suppose $p_{g1} = p_{g2}$ and $p_{b1} = p_{b2}$. Then Eq. (7.5) becomes $v_g < v_b$. This does not hold. Hence a separating equilibrium does not exist.[6] The result is not surprising because the rates of growth are identical for every type of firm ($p_{g2}/p_{g1} = p_{b2}/p_{b1} = 1$) and Proposition 7.1 predicts that a separating equilibrium can only exists if the difference between firms' rates of growth is large enough. In this case, however, the firms' rates of growth are identical and the firms only differ in their overall values. Thus the case is one-dimensional like the classical POT case. More generally, a separating equilibrium will never exist and POT holds if $p_{g1} > p_{b1}$ and $p_{g2} > p_{b2}$. Also, POT holds if one considers a one-stage investment with short-term (one stage) private information. This is the case with $c_2 = p_{j2} = 0$.[7]

On an intuitive level, Proposition 7.1 is straightforward. First, it is well known that in a separating equilibrium each financing strategy is chosen by the worst possible type of firm for that strategy (from the investor's viewpoint).[8] So if type g decides to issue equity in equilibrium and has high earnings over two periods, with higher second-period earnings, other firms would find it attractive to mimic this strategy. High total earnings would imply a high share price at stage 1 and high second-period earnings

[6] Cooney and Kalay (1993) demonstrate that POT can fail if projects have negative NPV.

[7] In Goswami, Noe and Rebello (1995) a firm receives earnings for two periods and private information is long-term but investment is one-staged.

[8] Brennan and Kraus (1987).

would imply a low face value of debt at stage 2. Proposition 7.1 makes sure that it does not happen and a separating equilibrium exists.

Firm's performance after issue The above analysis implies that the adverse selection cost of equity is negatively related to the rate of earnings growth for firm g and negatively related to its total value. For any firm, the incentive to issue equity diminishes when the firm's value increases or its rate of earnings growth increases, because it increases the chances of being mimicked by other firms and thus increases the cost of issuing equity.

Example 7.1. Consider the following example that is based on the model described above and the sequence of events as in Fig. 7.1. Let $p_{g1} = 0.8$, $p_{g2} = 0.3$, $p_{b1} = 0.2$, $p_{b2} = 0.85$ and $C_t = 0.2$, $t = 1, 2$.

Suppose g issues equity at stage 1 and issues debt at stage 2. We have: $0.3D = 0.2$. Hence $D = 2/3$. At stage 1 investors require a fraction of equity s_1 such that: $s_1 0.8 + s_1 0.3(1 - 2/3) = 0.2$. Therefore $s_1 = 2/9$. The payoff of the shareholders of b, in case b decides to mimic g, equals $\frac{7}{9} * 0.2 + \frac{7}{9} * 0.85(1 - \frac{2}{3}) = \frac{203}{540}$. If a signaling equilibrium exists, the shareholders' payoff for type b is $p_{b1} + p_{b2} - C_1 - C_2 = 0.65$ (the present value of). Thus, a separating equilibrium exists where the firm type with a higher value issues equity because $203/540 < 0.65$ and bb has no incentive to mimic g.

To further illustrate Proposition 7.1 consider the same example but this time assume that $p_{g1} = 0.3$, $p_{g2} = 0.8$. Now we have: $0.8D = 0.2$. Hence $D = 1/4$. At stage 1 investors require a fraction of equity s_1 such that: $s_1 0.3 + s_1 0.8(1 - 1/4) = 0.2$. Therefore $s_1 = 2/9$ (Note that s_1 is the same as it is in the previous case because the total value of the type g firm remains the same and as was mentioned before the share price at stage 1 depends only on the total value of the firm). The payoff of the shareholders of b, in case b decides to mimic g, equals $\frac{7}{9} * 0.2 + \frac{7}{9} * 0.85 * (1 - \frac{1}{4}) = \frac{469}{720}$. If a signaling equilibrium exists, the shareholders' payoff for type b is 0.65 like in the previous case. Thus, a separating equilibrium does not exist where the firm type with higher value issues equity because $\frac{469}{720} > 0.65$ and b has an incentive to mimic g.

Ultimately, the main result of the above analysis is the link between the capital structure choice and the firm's performance after the issue. A separating equilibrium, where only high-value firms issue equity, implies that firms issuing equity have better operating performance at the moment of issue or soon after the issue. These firms also have a lower operating performance in the long run.

We mentioned previously that the results presented above are consistent with early works like Jain and Kini (1994). Note the following works in recent research. Pereira and Sousa (2015) study the post-IPO operating performances of a sample of 555 European firms that went public between 1995 and 2006. They found a decline in post-issue operating performances of IPO firms. Firms located in emerging European countries performed even worse after the IPO than firms located in developed European countries. They also find that operating performances, in absolute terms, are higher for IPO firms prior to the IPO and in some cases immediately after the IPO.

Eldomiaty and Mohamed (2009) examine the links between firms' debt financing structures and operating performances. The results show that in medium-debt firms, both short-term debt and long-term debt help adjust the firms' performance measures to a target level. In low-debt firms, long-term debt in particular has a negative effect on operating income/sales. In general, a relatively high correlation between debt financing and operating performance is found.

Jiahui (2015) analyzes the link between the capital structure and the firm's performance for small and medium-sized companies in China. The results show that capital structure and corporation performance have an interactive relationship and capital structure, growth ability, equity concentration, and board and corporation scale will significantly influence corporation performance. Profitability, growth ability, debt-paying ability, collateral value of assets, and enterprise scale will significantly influence capital structure. Profitability is negatively correlated with debt and growth is positively correlated with debt.

An interesting new direction of research is the performance of IPO firms involved in MA activities.[9] These firms are growing as opposed to firms who are targets and use IPOs as exit strategies. Bessler and Zimmerman (2011) find that MA IPOs outperformed exit IPOs. MA IPOs also have more leverage (see Celikyurt et al., 2010) after the IPO since they need cash resources for merger activities. These results are consistent with the idea that higher debt signals better performance in the long-term.

[9] MA: mergers and acquisitions.

Among recent research notes Larrain et al. (2022) find that the performance of IPO firms improves after an IPO. This contrasts the traditional perceptions that equity is a negative signal but is consistent with some ideas in this section that an equity issue can signal an increase in a firm's short-term performance. Larrain et al. (2022) also study the connections between their findings and firm commercialization strategy. Also note Miglo (2017) argues that up-front equity financing can mitigate asymmetric information problems about the timing of earnings. Hence Miglo (2017) combines asymmetric information about the timing of earnings and moral hazard problem that puts significant costs on firms that use up-front equity financing. It is found that under some conditions a separating equilibrium where some profitable firms issue equity can exist.

7.3 Capital Structure, Market Timing, and Business Cycle

As discussed in previous chapter the market timing theory of capital structure (MT) suggests that the decision to issue equity depends on stock market performance (Baker & Wurgler, 2002; Korajczyk et al., 1992; Lucas & McDonald, 1990). Financial managers prefer to issue shares when prices are relatively high. When the stock market is not doing well, firms do not issue equity. Since the equity market performance often moves in unison with the economy as a whole, an alternative interpretation of MT is that when the economy is bad, firms do not issue equity. When the economy is average, some firms will issue equity. When the economy is booming, equity issues are large. Therefore there is a positive relationship between equity issues and the business cycle. Miglo (2011) noticed that empirical evidence often provides support for MT (see, for example, Choe et al. (1993) and Baker and Wurgler (2002)).

An interesting question is whether investors overpay for shares or not. As was discussed in Chapter 6, some researchers argue that investors tend to be excessively optimistic during new issues of shares. Other researchers prefer "rational investor" arguments. In recent research, note the following. Bolton et al. (2013) combine the firm's precautionary cash hoarding and market timing motives. Firms value financial slack and build cash reserves to mitigate financial constraints. The finitely lived favorable financing condition induces them to rationally time the equity market. This market timing motive may cause investments to decrease (and the marginal value of cash to increase) in financial slack, and may lead a financially constrained firm to gamble.

To illustrate the basic idea about the connection between capital structure and macroeconomic conditions, consider the following simple model with asymmetric information in the spirit of the standard POT.[10] A firm has an investment project. It has some assets-in-place that generate earnings A. To finance the new project, the firm needs to raise B. The cash flow of the firm is $A + R$ if the investment is made ($R > B$), and A if it is not. There are two types of firms. For type 1, $A = A_1 + m$ and for type 2, $A = A_2 + m$, $A_2 > A_1$. The publicly available parameter m depends on the macroeconomic situation. As usual, we assume that everybody is risk-neutral and the risk-free interest rate is zero. The sequence of events is presented (Fig. 7.2).

Suppose the market believes that the fraction of type 1 firms among firms issuing equity is x. The investors' expected return should be equal to the investment cost. This implies that $B = \alpha(xA_1 + (1 - x)A_2 + m + R)$, where α is the fraction of equity requested by investors. We have

$$\alpha = \frac{B}{xA_1 + (1 - x)A_2 + m + R}$$

The earnings of initial shareholders are:

$$(1 - \alpha)(A + R) \tag{7.6}$$

Type 1 will issue shares regardless of the value of x. To see this, let's compare (7.6) for type 1 and earnings for type 1 if no new investment is made that is $A_1 + m$. (7.6) is greater if $R > \frac{B(A_1+m+R)}{xA_1+(1-x)A_2+m+R}$. It always

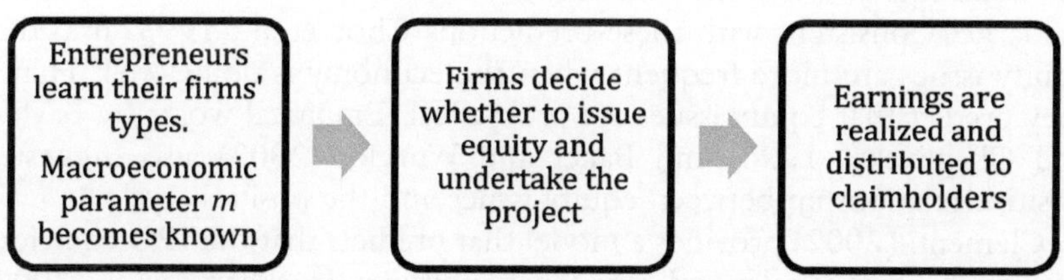

Fig. 7.2 Sequence of events

[10] See also Tirole (2006, Ch. 6).

holds because $R > B$ and $A_2 > A_1$. Consider the incentives for type 2. It's optimal choice depends on $R > \frac{B(A_2+m+R)}{xA_1+(1-x)A_2+m+R}$. Since $A_2 > A_1$, this condition depends on m. It is more likely to hold if m increases. This leads to the following proposition.

Proposition 7.2. *Equity issues are procyclical.*

The analysis of the basic model reveals the following ideas. Low-quality firms always issue equity and undertake investments. The incentives for high-quality firms depend on the macroeconomic situation. If the economy is in contraction (low m), high-quality firms prefer not to issue new equity, whereas if the economy is growing they will certainly issue new equity. Thus, equity issues are procyclical.

Example 7.2. To finance the new project, the firm needs to raise $B = 0.16$. For type 1, $A = 0.2 + m$ and for type 2, $A = 0.5 + m$. The publicly available parameter m depends on the macroeconomic situation. Also $R = 0.2$.

Suppose that the fraction of type 1 firms issuing equity is 0.5. Consider a pooling equilibrium where both firms issue equity. We have

$$\alpha = \frac{0.16}{0.5 * 0.2 + 0.5 * 0.5 + m + 0.2} = \frac{0.16}{0.55 + m}$$

Consider the incentives for type 2 firms. Their optimal choice depends on $0.2 > \frac{0.16(0.7+m)}{0.55+m}$. This condition depends on m. It holds if $m > \frac{0.02}{0.04} = 0.5. m > \frac{0.02}{0.04} = 0.5$.

The model predicts that when the economy is bad (m is low), firms do not issue equity. When the economy is booming (m is high), equity issues are large. Consistent with these predictions Choe et al. (1993) find that equity issues are more frequent when the economy is doing well. Hence they predict that equity issues are procyclical. Empirical works by Bayless and Chaplinsky (1996) and Baker and Wurgler (2002) also suggest a positive relationship between equity issues and the business cycle.

Clementi (2002) provides a model that predicts that the IPO coincides with an increase in sales and capital expenditures. Hackbarth et al. (2006) find that for their base parameters, the value-maximizing leverage ratio is higher in a recession than in a boom. Hence, Hackbarth et al's (2006) model predicts that debt is counter-cyclical. In Bhamra et al. (2010) the risk-free rate of return vary procyclically and the optimal market leverage ratio evolves procyclically over the business cycle. In related work, Chen (2010) reaches the same conclusion of pro-cyclical market leverage dynamics. Halling et al. (2015) show that, on average, target leverage ratios evolve counter-cyclically. These counter-cyclical dynamics are robust to different subsamples of firms, data samples, empirical models of leverage, and definitions of leverage. As was previously mentioned Miglo and Zenkevich (2006) analyze the effect of asymmetric information about the timing of earnings on capital structure and argue that a separating equilibrium where some firms issue equity exists. Further, they argue that a separating equilibrium exists when the economy is growing.[11] When the economy is stagnating, the equilibrium is pooling with debt.

De Angelo et al. (2010) analyze whether SEO (seasoned equity offerings)[12] decisions are better explained by timing opportunities or by the lifecycle theory, where firms sell stock primarily in the early stages of their lifecycle, when growth opportunities exceed internally generated cash flow. It is found that both timing and lifecycle theories have a significant influence, with the lifecycle effect being quantitatively stronger, but neither adequately explains SEO decisions.

Share Price and Equity Issue A higher m implies a higher share price. Let n denote the initial number of shares outstanding and let Δn_t denote the number of shares issued by type a in period t in case a separating equilibrium exists. Let p be the share price in period 1. From the previous example we know that $s_1 = \frac{B}{xA_1+(1-x)A_2+m+R}$. By definition it is also equal to $\frac{\Delta n_1}{n+\Delta n_1}$. Also $p\Delta n_1 = B$. Solving these equations we find

$$p = \frac{xA_1 + (1-x)A_2 + m + R}{n} \tag{7.7}$$

From the previous section we know that issuing equity is more likely when m is large. From (7.7) it follows that equity issues are more likely when the share price is high.

[11] See also Miglo (2017).

[12] A seasoned equity is a sale of additional shares by a company that is already publicly traded. This is opposite to IPO when the firm issues equity for the first time.

Another interpretation of this result looks at stock returns before the equity issue. If the arrival of growth opportunities occurs independent of price history, then firms issuing equity will have average performances before the issue. Firms with a low share price will have above-average performances as they wait for the price to improve before they issue equity. Thus, on average, positive abnormal returns precede equity issues. The evidence confirms this prediction (Korajczyk et al., 1990; Loughran & Ritter, 1995).

Many MT predictions seem to be consistent across different countries. For example, Chichti and Bougatef (2010) investigate the relevance of market timing considerations on the debt-equity choice using a panel of Tunisian and French listed firms. Consistent with the market timing theory, they find that firms tend to issue equity when their market valuations are relatively high and after a market performance improvement. The impact of equity market timing on capital structure persists beyond eight years. Dong et al. (2012) study market timing and pecking order in a sample of debt and equity issues and share repurchases of Canadian firms from 1998 to 2007. They find evidence that firms issue (repurchase) equity when their shares are overvalued (undervalued) and that overvalued issuers earn lower post-announcement long-run returns only when the firms are not financially constrained. Similarly, they find that firms prefer debt to equity financing only when they are not overvalued. These findings highlight an interaction between market timing and pecking-order effects. Setyawan and Frensidy (2013) find that the market to book ratio has a negative impact on market leverage for Indonesian IPO firms, which is consistent with MT. On the other hand, Khanna et al. (2015) analyze MT for Indian firms and find that firms rely more on profitability than MT when issuing equity. Among more recent research note Alkan (2022) first calculates equity mispricing using 155 anomalies and finds that US firms are 59% more likely to issue equity when they are overvalued and 28% more likely to repurchase shares when they are undervalued.

Questions and Exercises

1. Firms issuing equity usually underperform compared non-issuing firms in the long run.
2. Signaling theory usually suggests that debt issues is a good signal of firm's operating performance while empirical evidence finds negative correlation between debt and profitability.
3. Multistage investment and long-term asymmetric information can explain why higher quality firms can be interested in issuing equity.
4. Consider a setup from Sect. 7.2. Suppose a firm considers equity financing for a two-period investment project with a cost 0.1 in period 1, 2. In each period the project may be successful or unsuccessful. In the latter case the cash flow equals 1 and in the former case, the cash flow equals 0. A firm's insiders have private information about the probability of success in each stage. The firms are of two types, type a and type b, with respective probabilities of success in period 1 and 2 as follows:

   $p_{a1} = 0.7$, $p_{a2} = 0.25$ p_{gt}, $p_{b1} = 0.1$ and $p_{b2} = 0.8$.
   Describe signaling equilibrium.

5. Consider a setup from Sect. 7.3. To finance the new project, the firm needs to raise $B = 0.1$. For type 1, $A = 0.1 + m$ and for type 2, $A = 0.3 + m$. The publicly available parameter m depends on the macroeconomic situation. Also $R = 0.12$. Suppose that the fraction of type 1 firms is 0.3. Describe possible equilibria. Provide interpretation.

References

Alkan. (2022). *Market Timing in Corporate Finance Decisions: Evidence from Stock Market Anomalies* (working paper). https://wpcarey.asu.edu/sites/default/files/2022-10/Market%20Timing%20in%20Corporate%20Finance%20Decisions%20-%20Evidence%20From%20Stock%20Market%20Anomalies.pdf

Baker, M., & Wurgler, J. (2002). Market Timing and Capital Structure. *Journal of Finance, 57*, 1–32.

Bayless, M., & Chaplinsky, S. (1996). Is There a Window of Opportunity for Seasoned Equity Issuance? *Journal of Finance, 51*, 253–278.

Bessler, W., & Zimmermann, J. (2011). Acquisition Activities of Initial Public Offerings in Europe: An Analysis of Exit and Growth Strategies. Midwest Finance Association 2012 Annual Meetings Paper. Available at SSRN: http://ssrn.com/abstract=1929060

Bhamra, H., Kuehn, L., & Strebulaev, I. (2010). The Aggregate Dynamics of Capital Structure and Macroeconomic Risk. *The Review of Financial Studies, 23*(12), 4187–4241.

Bolton, P., Chen, H., & Wang, N. (2013). Market Timing, Investment, and Risk Management. *Journal of Financial Economics, 109*(1), 40–62.

Brennan, M., & Kraus, A. (1987). Efficient Financing under Information Asymmetry. *Journal of Finance, 42*(5), 1225–1243.

Celikyurt, U., Sevilir, M., & Shivdasani, A. (2010). Going Public to Acquire? The Acquisition Motive in IPOs. *Journal of Financial Economics, 96*(3), 345–363.

Chen, H. (2010). Macroeconomic Conditions and the Puzzles of Credit Spreads and Capital Structure. *Journal of Finance, 65*(6), 2171–2212.

Chichti, J., & Bougatef, K. (2010). Equity Market Timing and Capital Structure: Evidence from Tunisia and France. *International Journal of Business and Management, 5*(10), 167–177.

Choe, H., Masulis, R., & Nanda, V. (1993). Common Stock Offerings Across the Business Cycle. *Journal of Empirical Finance, 1*, 1–29.

Clementi, G. (2002). IPOs and the Growth of Firms, NYU Stern 2004 Working Paper No. 04–23. Available at SSRN: http://ssrn.com/abstract=314277

Cooney, J., & Kalay, A. (1993). Positive Information from Equity Issue Announcements. *Journal of Financial Economics, 33*, 149–172.

DeAngelo, H., DeAngelo, L., & Stulz, R. (2010). Seasoned Equity Offerings, Market Timing, and the Corporate Lifecycle. *Journal of Financial Economics, 95*, 275–295.

Dong, M., Loncarski, I., Horst, J. ter., & Veld, C. (2012). What Drives Security Issuance Decisions: Market Timing, Pecking Order, or Both? *Financial Management, 41*(3), 637–663.

Eldomiaty, T., & Mohamed, E. (2009). Is Debt Governance Structure Relevant to Firm Operating Performance in Egypt?A Dynamic Approach. *International Journal of Accounting and Finance, 1*, 216–249.

Ficenec, J. (2015, December 21). Questor's Biggest Investment Mistakes of 2015. *The Telegraph, Questor*. http://www.telegraph.co.uk/finance/markets/questor/12059106/Questors-biggest-investment-mistakes-of-2015.html

Goswami, G., Noe, T., & Rebello, M. (1995). Debt Financing under Asymmetric Information. *Journal of Finance, 50*, 633–659.

Graham, J., & Harvey, C. (2001). The Theory and Practice of Corporate Finance: Evidence from the Field. *Journal of Financial Economics, 60*, 187–243.

Hackbarth, D., Miaob, J., & Morellec, E. (2006). Capital Structure, Credit Risk, and Macroeconomic Conditions. *Journal of Financial Economics, 82*, 519–550.

Halling, M., Yu, J., & Zechner, J. (2015). Leverage Dynamics over the Business Cycle, AFA 2012 Chicago Meetings Paper. Available at SSRN: http://ssrn.com/abstract=1762289

Halov, N. (2006). *Dynamics of Asymmetric Information and Capital Structure* (Working Paper). New York University.

Hennessy, C., Livdan, D., & Miranda, B. (2010). Repeated Signaling and Firm Dynamics Signal. *Review of Financial Studies, 23*, 1981–2023.

Jain, B., & Kini, O. (1994). The Post-Issue Operating Performance of IPO Firms. *Journal of Finance, 49*(5), 1699–1726.

Jiahui, M. (2015). Relationship Between Capital Structure and Firm Performance Evidence from Growth Enterprise Market in China. *Management Science and Engineering, 9*(1), 45–49.

Khanna, S., Srivastava, A., & Medury, Y. (2015). Is Equity Market Timing the Sole Criteria for Capital Structure Decisions? An Insight from Indian Firms, *Indian Journal of Finance, 9* (10), 48–64.

Korajczyk, R., Lucas, D., & McDonald, R. (1990), Understanding Stock Price Behavior Around the Time of Equity Issues. In R. Glenn Hubbard (Ed.), *Asymmetric Information, Corporate Finance, and Investment* (pp. 257–278). University of Chicago Press.

Korajczyk, R., Lucas, D., & McDonald, R. (1992). Equity Issues with Time-Varying Asymmetric Information. *Journal of Financial and Quantitative Analysis, 27*, 397–417.

Larrain, B., Phillips, G., Sertsios, G., & Urzua, F. (2022). *The Effects of Going Public on Firm Profitability and Strategy* (Tuck School of Business Working Paper No. 3830690). Available at SSRN: https://ssrn.com/abstract=3830690

Leland, H., & Pyle, D. (1977). Information Asymmetries, Financial Structure, and Financial Intermediation. *Journal of Finance, 32*, 371–378.

Loughran, T., & Ritter, J. (1995). The New Issues Puzzle. *Journal of Finance, 50*, 23–51.

Loughran, T., & Ritter, J. (1997). The Operating Performance of Firms Conducting Seasoned Equity Offerings. *Journal of Finance, 52*, 1823–1850.

Lucas, D., & McDonald, R. (1990). Equity Issues and Stock Price Dynamics. *Journal of Finance, 45*, 1019–1043.

Miglo, A. (2007). Debt-Equity Choice as a Signal of Earnings Profile over Time. *Quarterly Review of Economics and Finance, 47*(1), 69–93.

Miglo, A. (2011). Trade-off, Pecking Order, Signaling and Market Timing Models. In H. K. Baker & G. S. Martin (Eds.), *Capital Structure and Corporate Financing Decisions: Theory, Evidence, and Practice* (pp. 171–190). Wiley, Ch. 10.

Miglo, A. (2012). Multi-stage Investment, Long-Term Asymmetric Information and Pecking Order Revisited. *Journal of Current Issues in Finance, Business and Economics, 4*(4), 331–348.

Miglo, A. (2017). Timing of Earnings and Capital Structure. *The North American Journal of Economics and Finance (Elsevier), 40* (issue C), 1–15.

Miglo, A., & Zenkevich, N. (2006). Non-Hierarchical Signalling: Two-Stage Financing Game. *International Journal of Mathematics, Game Theory and Algebra, 15*(3), 257–273.

Mikkelson, W., Partch, M., & Shah, K. (1997). Ownership and Operating Performance of Companies that Go Public. *Journal of Financial Economics, 44*, 281–307.

Morellec, E., & Schürhoff, N. (2011). Corporate Investment and Financing under Asymmetric Information. *Journal of Financial Economics, 99*(2), 262–288.

Myers, S., & Majluf, N. (1984). Corporate Financing and Investment Decisions When Firms Have Information That Investors do not have. *Journal of Financial Economics, 13*, 187–221.

Ovide, S. (2015, December 10). A Robust IPO, but no Signal. *Bloomberg Gadfly*. http://www.bloomberg.com/gadfly/articles/2015-12-10/atlassian-bucks-trend-but-is-poor-barometer-for-tech-ipos

Pereira, T., & Sousa, M. (2015). Is there Still a Berlin Wall in the Post-Issue Operating Performance of European IPOs? Available at SSRN: http://ssrn.com/abstract=2347535

Ross, S. (1977). The Determination of Financial Structure: The Incentive Signaling Approach. *Bell Journal of Economics, 8*, 23–40.

Shah, K. (1994). The Nature of Information Conveyed by Pure Capital Structure Changes. *Journal of Financial Economics, 36*, 89–126.

Sivy, M. (2012, May 30). Does Facebook's Floundering IPO Signal a Market Top? *Time*. http://business.time.com/2012/05/30/does-facebooks-floundering-ipo-signal-a-market-top/

Tirole, J. (2006). *The Theory of Corporate Finance*. Princeton University Press.

CHAPTER 8

Capital Structure and Corporate Governance

8.1 Corporate Governance

Corporate governance broadly refers to the mechanisms, processes, and relations by which corporations are controlled and directed.[1] As we know, corporations are owned by their shareholders whose objective is usually to maximize the value of their investments. However, in a typical corporation, relationships between interested parties often involve asymmetric information and moral hazard problems. Corporate governance is often seen as a mechanism that insures that corporations act in the interests of their shareholders. This chapter covers several topics related to corporate governance: managerial incentives, links between levels of debt and managerial effort, the free cash flow theory, control rights allocation, earnings management, links between capital structure and earnings manipulation, and international variations of corporate governance systems.

[1] For a review see, for example, Becht et al. (2003).

Supplementary Information The online version contains supplementary material available at https://doi.org/10.1007/978-3-031-85459-0_8.

This chapter is coauthored with Victor Miglo.

A. Miglo, *Capital Structure in the Modern World*,
https://doi.org/10.1007/978-3-031-85459-0_8

Capital structure affects relationships between interested parties in a corporation. In Chapters 4 and 5 we focused on shareholder-creditor agency problems. We begin this chapter by analyzing the shareholder-manager conflict and how capital structure can help resolve it. The topic of managerial incentives is very popular in corporate finance literature including academics, news, and magazines. The list of possible problems is very long and contains, among others, earnings manipulations, inefficient levels of effort, "empire-building," information manipulation, etc. Although managerial incentives had been analyzed by theorists for a long time, they became particularly relevant in the early 2000s due to the high number of corporate scandals including some cases that became famous worldwide such as Enron, WorldCom, etc.

Financial contracts are very complex because a lot of information in the business world is hard to verify, as we discussed in Chapter 3, and lots of contingencies are difficult, if not impossible, to specify and enforce. An interesting example is the story of Nortel. It was a multinational telecommunications and data networking equipment manufacturer. At its height, Nortel accounted for more than a third of the total valuation of all the companies listed on the Toronto Stock Exchange (TSX).[2] In late October 2003, Nortel announced that it intended to restate approximately $900 million worth of liabilities carried on its previously reported balance sheet as of June 30, 2003, following a comprehensive internal review of these liabilities. A dozen of the company's most senior executives returned $8.6 million of bonuses they were paid based on the erroneous accounting. Investigators ultimately found about $3 billion in revenue had been booked improperly in 1998, 1999, and 2000.[3] In 2007 both the U.S. Securities and Exchange Commission and the Ontario Securities Commission pressed charges against the former senior financial officials of Nortel for fudging the company's revenue.[4] Finally, In June 2009, the company announced it would cease operations and sell off all of its business units.[5]

Richard Milne, in his November 2015 article, analyzes the situation when Volkswagen (VW) was hit with an emission system problem

[2] Hasselback and Tedesco (September 27, 2014).

[3] http://buzzspotr.com/accounting-scandal-at-nortel/.

[4] Erman (March 13, 2007).

[5] Gillies (June 20, 2009).

scandal.[6] The article points out that the pattern of overspending in good times could potentially be one of the problems of the company. VW's administrative costs had almost tripled since 2007. In both 1993 and 2005 the German carmaker faced scandals and almost non-existent profit margins thanks to overspending. Capital structure may affect the company's decisions related to spending/cuts. Large amounts of debt put a significant pressure on management and create an incentive to cut spendings.[7]

These two stories represent examples of two important aspects of shareholder-manager conflicts: information manipulation and cash overuse. In this chapter we will look at these situations as well as many others more closely. Special focus will be on the role of capital structure in creating/resolving shareholders-manager conflicts.

8.2 Financing Strategy and Managerial Incentives. Free Cash Flow Theory

In this section, we focus on the role of debt contracts in corporate governance. How does leverage affect the level of investment? Consider a model of a firm where the firm manager's decisions are explained by a trade-off between the threat of losing his job due to bankruptcy and the perks from shirking (Grossman & Hart, 1982; Jensen, 1986). The basic setup consists of two periods; in the first period, the firm issues debt (with face value D) and equity to raise B to invest. After the funds are received, the manager decides how they are spent. More specifically, the manager should choose between two projects. Project j generates non-negative earnings R_j, $j = 1, 2$. R_j is distributed according to the distribution function F_j. If project j is chosen, the manager's non-cash/private benefit is m_j. These benefits can include providing jobs to family members, investments in friends' companies, establishing new personal connections, etc. By assumption, R_1 first-order dominates R_2. However, $m_2 > m_1$. The manager's official benefits are approximately equal for these projects. For the sake of simplicity we assume that they are negligibly small. A possible interpretation of these assumptions is that Project 2 does not have the same value for the firm as Project 1 does but it extends the amount of

6 Milne (November 20, 2015).

7 Bryant et al. (October 13, 2015).

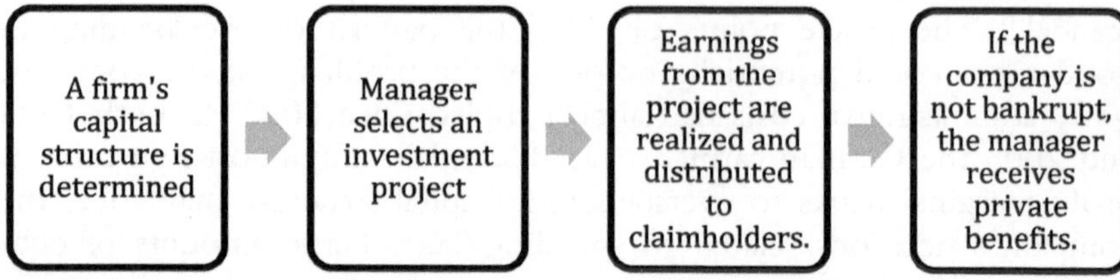

Fig. 8.1 Sequence of events

resources under the manager's control. This phenomenon is often called "empire-building". Also, bankruptcy is very costly for the manager! If the firm is bankrupt the manager's total benefit is zero. For example, the manager loses his job, his reputation, etc. The sequence of events is presented (Fig. 8.1).

Proposition 8.1. *Under equity financing, the manager will choose the inefficient project. Debt financing may, in some cases, improve managerial incentives.*

Since Project 1 first-order dominates Project 2, the expected earnings and the NPV of Project 1 are greater than those of Project 2. So from the firm's point of view, the manager should choose Projcct 1. The manager's expected payoff if project j is chosen, equals $m_j(1 - F_j(D))$. Note that the expression in brackets shows the probability of "no bankruptcy" for company j or that $R_j \geq D$. $D = 0$. implies $F_j(D) = 0$. In this case, the manager's expected payoff if project j is chosen, equals m_j. The manager chooses Project 2 since $m_2 > m_1$.

If $D > 0$, several situations may exist where the manager will choose Project 1. For example, if the difference between m_1 and m_2 is sufficiently small, $m_1(1-F_1(D)) > m_2(1-F_2(D))$ because Project 1 first-order dominates Project 2 implying $F_2(D) > F_1(D)$. Another example is a situation where $R_1^{max} > D > R_2^{max}$ (R_j^{max} is the maximal R_j with positive density). In this case $m_2(1 - F_2(D)) = 0$ and the manager chooses Project 1.

conclusion, the usage of debt financing can be used to mitigate the tendency for "empire-building." Jensen (1986, 1989) argued that debt financing is an important way to resolve agency problems between managers and investors. It would limit managerial discretion by minimizing the "free cash flow" available to managers and thus provide protection to investors. Sometimes in the literature this idea is referred to as the "debt and discipline" theory.[8]

As we know, using debt as the major source of financing incurs substantial costs of financial distress. Firms may face direct bankruptcy costs or indirect costs in the form of debt overhang or asset substitution (see Chapters 4–5). To reduce the risk of financial distress, it may be desirable to have the firm rely partly on equity financing. Also, the role of debtholders differs between countries. Countries where debt regulation is subject to political intervention and lobbying have weaker bases for using debt as a commitment device. Some research suggests that this was the case in the United States in the early 2000s. For more analysis of this issue see Franks and Sussman (2005) and Berglöf and Rosenthal (1999).

DeMarzo and Fishman (2007) consider a dynamic model where a firm's manager can divert the firm's cash flow. It is shown that the optimal mechanism can be implemented by combining equity, long-term debt, and a line of credit.

Zheng (2013) analyzes the effect of a firm's capital structure on managerial incentives and controlling the free cash flow agency problem and compares it to incentives provided by compensation contracts. It was found that debt and executive stock options act as substitutes in attenuating a firm's free cash flow problem. It was also found that firms trade-off the adjustment of their capital structure and compensation structure to control overinvestment.

Edmans (2011) suggests that the option to terminate a manager early minimizes the investors' losses if the manager is unskilled. It also deters a skilled manager from undertaking efficient long-term projects that risk low short-term earnings. This paper demonstrates how risky debt can overcome this tension. Leverage concentrates equityholders' stakes, inducing them to learn the cause of low earnings. Unlike traditional theories, a non-paying manager is not automatically fired. The firm is liquidated only if the cause of the weak earnings is low managerial skill.

Morellec et al. (2012) combine a dynamic trade-off theory with moral hazard (free cash) and argue that one can obtain capital structure dynamics consistent with the data. In particular, they find that the model needs an average agency cost of 1.5% of equity value to resolve

[8] See, for example, Kale et al. (2015).

the low-leverage puzzle mentioned in Chapter 5. Miglo (2020) combines free cash flow problems with flexibility ideas. The model helps to explain the zero-debt puzzle as well as to explain why zero-debt firms often pay higher dividends compared to other firms. In addition, the model predicts that firms with zero-debt policy should be influenced by free cash flow considerations more than by bankruptcy cost considerations. Also the choice of zero-debt policy can be used by high-quality firms to signal their quality. This is in contrast to most traditional signalling literature such as Leland and Pyle (1977), for example, where debt serves as a signal of quality. The model can explain why the probability of selecting the zero-debt policy is positively correlated with profitability and investment size and negatively correlated with the tax rate. It also predicts that firms that are farther away from their target capital structures are less likely to select the zero-debt policy compared to firms that are close to their target levels.

DeMarzo and Sannikov (2006) study the optimal contract in a cash flow diversion model. They use a continuous time framework and argue that an optimal contract can be implemented as a mix of long-term debt, a credit line, and equity. Biais et al. (2007) show that the contract of DeMarzo and Sannikov (2006) arises in the limit of discrete-time models as the agent's actions become more frequent.

8.3 Costly Effort, Capital Structure, and Managerial Incentives

Jensen and Meckling (1976) argue that when the decision-maker's effort is costly, then under equity financing the decision-maker should control 100% of the equity in order to mitigate moral hazard problems. If the decision-maker controls less than 100% of equity, there will be a distortion in the effort because the decision-maker bears 100% of his effort's cost and receives less than 100% of the benefits. Innes (1990) further shows that debt financing can improve the manager's effort.

Consider a firm fully financed with equity. The firm's founder/manager/entrepreneur (E) is risk-neutral. The firm's expected first-period earnings r depend on E's effort $e \in [0, 1]$. For simplicity we assume that the expected value of r equals e or $Er = e$. The cost of effort is e^2.

E will choose the level of effort where his marginal revenue equals his marginal cost. Since his individual marginal revenue is below the firm's marginal revenue, the chosen level of effort is less than first-best.

Proposition 8.2. *If the manager owns less than 100% of equity, the level of effort is below the first-best level.*

Formally, the first-best effort maximizes the firm's value: $e - e^2$. Socially optimal $e^* = 1/2$. However, E will maximize $ke - e^2$, where k is the fraction of equity that belongs to E. Optimal $e' = k/2$. For any < 1, $e' < e^*$.

Now we consider an example that illustrates that debt can be a better contract. Suppose that earnings can have 3 values (all with equal probabilities): 0, e and $2e$. One can see that $Er = e$. Suppose that the firm has an investment project with cost $b = 1/8$. If the firm is financed with equity the manager's choice of effort is $e' = k/2$.

Figure 8.2 illustrates the optimal effort under equity financing. The manager's profit is then $k^2/4$. To find the optimal contract, we have to find the value of k that will maximize the entrepreneur's profit under the condition that the investor's expected profit is not less than b. This condition is $e(1 - k) = k(1 - k)/2 \geq 1/8$. The left side of this inequality reaches its maximum at $k = 1/2$. In this case I's expected payoff is 1/8. E's expected payoff is $k^2/4$. It increases when k increases. Hence the optimal k is the largest value of k that satisfies I's budget constraint, i.e., 1/2. Optimal $e' = 1/4$ and E's expected payoff is 1/16.

Now consider debt financing. Two cases are possible. 1) $e < D$. In this case the manager maximizes $1/3 * (2e - D) - e^2$. So optimal $e = 1/3$. The manager's payoff is $1/9 - D/3$. 2) $e > D$. In this case the manager maximizes $1/3(e - D) + 1/3(2e - D) - e^2$. So optimal $e = 1/2$. The manager's payoff is $1/4 - 2D/3$. By comparing manager's payoffs in each case we find that if $D < 5/12$ the optimal $e = 1/2$ and otherwise $e = 1/3$. Now to find D note that the investor's payoff should be greater than b. So in the second case $D = 3/2b$. It is possible only if $b < 5/18$ that is our case indeed. So the firm can be financed with debt with face value 3/16 and the manager's profit is 1/8 in this case.

One can see that under debt financing the manager chooses optimal $e = 1/2$. Innes shows that debt can be optimal if the distribution function for the firm's earnings follows the MLRP condition,[9] the manager is risk neutral and the contracts are non-decreasing.

Among other papers note the following. Dybvig and Zender (1991) combine a firm's managerial problems including managerial costly effort

[9] See Holmstrom (1979).

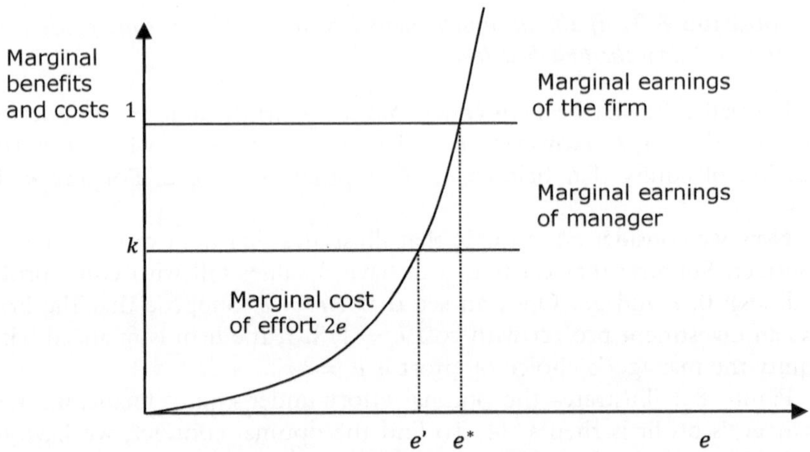

Fig. 8.2 Optimal effort under equity financing

with asymmetric information and argue that such a setup may lead to capital structure irrelevance in some cases although the negative market reaction to firm equity issues should still be observed. Berkovitch et al. (2000) investigate the interaction between financial structure and managerial compensation. A three-period model is considered. In period 0, a manager is hired. In period 1, the manager takes actions that determine the firm's future earnings. The authors argue that it also makes the firm more dependent on his ability. For example, the manager selects workers, organizes production, chooses the firm's strategy in the product market, etc. After observing signals about the firm's future earnings, shareholders may replace the manager. When the firm is leveraged, replacing a manager whose ability is known with a new manager whose ability is unknown shifts value from the debtholders to the shareholders (similar to the asset substitution effect from Chapter 4). Consequently, risky debt credibly commits the shareholders to an overly aggressive replacement policy, and this may motivate the manager to exert more effort ex ante in order to promote his chances to keep his job.

Some research points out that, in many cases, a manager's contract looks like an inside debt (pension plans for example) that may align the interests of managers and outside debtholders (Anantharaman et al., 2014; Sundaram & Yermack, 2007). Some of these contracts are unfunded and unsecured, while others are funded and secured to some extent, and they may be invested in equity and withdrawn flexibly pre-retirement. Special arrangements in executive debt-like compensation could hence weaken, or even nullify, any incentive-alignment effect.

Dewatripont et al. (2003) develop an agency model with a risk-averse entrepreneur and observable but unverifiable effort, and renegotiable contracts. Within this class of contracts/equilibria, regardless of who has the renegotiating bargaining power, debt and convertible debt maximize the entrepreneur's incentives to exert effort.

Mu et al. (2017) consider a dynamic model where the firm's output depends on the manager's efforts. They derive some results for the value of debt, credit spread, default threshold, and for optimal capital structure. The numerical results indicate that the firm issues more debt with higher coupon ex ante and defaults earlier ex post than without managerial moral hazard.

8.4 Earnings Manipulation

Corporate scandals over the last 10–20 years have raised heated debates regarding the manipulation of earnings (EM) by firm insiders. Some issues in this area are related to the links between capital structure and a firm's incentives to engage in EM.

It was documented in the literature that firms manage their earnings prior to their IPOs (window-dressing). IPO firms manipulate earnings using accrual earnings management around IPOs and this manipulation leads to lower post-IPO stock performances (Teoh et al., 1998a, 1998b; Gramlich & Sorensen 2004). Similar observations were made for SEOs (DuCharme et al., 2001; Rangan, 1998).

Secondly, it was also found that managers manage earnings more actively (empirical studies document a discontinuity in earnings management estimations) when firms have to achieve a "zero-earnings" threshold (Burgstahler & Dichev, 1997; Degeorge et al., 1999). It is especially important for leveraged firms since failure to achieve this threshold can lead to bankruptcy.

It was also found that managers of firms who provide large stock options to their employees are more willing to engage in EM. Some evidence is consistent with executives influencing the grant date stock price through timing, i.e., by accelerating the release of negative information before scheduled grant dates and delaying the release of positive information after scheduled grant dates (Aboody & Kasznik, 2000; Yermack, 1997). Another way that managers can influence the grant date stock price is ex post timing of the grant date itself, or backdating. Bebchuk et al. (2006) find evidence of opportunistic timing of director grants largely related to backdating.

In the aftermath of the accounting scandals at Enron and Worldcom Sarbanes–Oxley Act (2002) eliminated insiders' discretion in several standards and choices. Other regulations were also created including The International Accounting Standard Board in Germany, the Deutsche Standardisierungsrut, and some others.

Earnings manipulation exists because earnings verification is costly. Earlier theoretical literature related to problems of earnings verification suggested that debt is an optimal contract and that under this contract a truthful revelation of earnings will be delivered by the firm (Gale & Hellwig, 1985; Townsend, 1979).[10] If this can solve the problem of earnings reporting why do problems still exist? On one hand, relying on debt financing is risky and increases potential bankruptcy costs. Another interesting issue is the difference between accounting misreporting and real earnings manipulations.[11] Graham et al. (2005) show that accounting misreporting declined after the Sarbanes–Oxley Act, while real earnings manipulations increased. They also find that 3/4 of firms are involved in earnings manipulations (in their opinion it is a lower bound). In their survey, the authors asked financial managers the following question: "Imagine a hypothetical scenario. Near the end of the quarter, it looks like your company might come in below the desired earnings target. Which of the following choices might your company make?" It was found that firms are more willing to be engaged in real actions (for example, "decrease discretionary spending including R&D, advertising, etc." or "delay starting a new project even if this entails a small sacrifice in value") than in accounting actions (for example "alter accounting assumptions" (e.g., allowances)).

In contrast to earnings being misreported, which in most cases represents accounting fraud, real earnings manipulation is often considered

[10] More discussion about this idea is provided in Chapter 11.

[11] See, for example, Roychowdhury (2006).

in literature as a transfer of funds between periods. This transfer does not create any social value (in contrast to productive effort) and is usually costly. Some typical examples include recognition of sales not yet shipped, allowance of bad debt, delays in maintenance expenditures, delayed approvals of important decisions, and inefficient discount policies. Certain methods are possibly optimal economic actions in certain economic circumstances. However, if managers engage in these activities more extensively than what is considered normal, given their economic circumstances with the objective of beating some thresholds that increase the value of claims belonging to them and destroy the firm's value, they are engaging in EM.

Degeorge et al. (1999) present a theoretical model involving EM by a manager with a bonus-like contract. The authors show that the manager's incentive to manipulate earnings depends on the values of the latent (pre-managed) earnings, the manager's bonus, and the magnitude of the social loss from the EM. The manager's decision also relies on whether predictions of future profits are certain or risky.

Miglo (2010) develops a model where EM is a part of the equilibrium relationships between firms' insiders and outsiders. It is shown that values of firms that manipulate earnings can be higher than those of firms that do not manipulate earnings. Also, the model suggests that debt can provide better incentive than equity.

To see the idea, consider a setup that is similar to those we considered previously. This time the firm has to make an investment $b > 0$. The firm needs external financing from an outside investor (I). If the investment is made, the firm generates earnings R_1 at period 1 and R_2 at period 2. R_1 depends on E's effort $e \in [0, 1]$. R_1 equals 1 with probability e and 0 otherwise. This implies that $ER_1 = e$. The cost of effort is e^2. E can be involved in EM after observing intermediate earnings R_1^0 and R_2^0. So if $R_1^0 = 0$ and E uses EM, the final first-period earnings $R_1 = R_1^0 + s$ and the second-period earnings $R_2 = R_2^0 + s - c$, where c is the cost of the EM.

Under equity financing, E has no interest in EM since it does not change E's fraction of earnings nor does it change who controls the company in period 2. As we saw in previous examples, optimal $e' = k/2$ and it is below the socially optimal level of effort. Under debt financing, E will use EM ($s = D$) if $R_1^0 = 0$. Otherwise, E loses control of the firm and gets nothing in the second period. If $R_1^0 = 1$, earnings will not be manipulated since any changes in second-period earnings for E will just mirror the change in period 1 (opposite signs) minus the cost of EM.

If $R_1^0 = 0$, E gets $s - D + R_2^0 - s - c$. If $R_1^0 = 1$, E gets $1 - D + R_2^0$.

E.'s payoff is $e(1 - D + R_2^0) + (1 - e)(R_2^0 - D - c) - e^2$. Optimal e equals $e'' = (1 + c)/2$.

If c is sufficiently small and b is sufficiently large (making k relatively small), e'' will be closer to the optimal level of effort ½ than e'. This means that the firm's value will be higher in this case. Furthermore, if EM is impossible, the outcome will be worse. If $R_1^0 = 0$, E gets 0. If $R_1^0 = 1$, E gets $1 - D + R_2^0$. E's payoff is $e(1 - D + R_2^0) - e^2$. Optimal e equals $e''' = (1 - D + R_2^0)/2$.

Figure 8.3 illustrates that if $c < 1$, E's level of effort is closer to the socially optimal level and provides a better social surplus than the case without any EM.

This analysis also shows that Innes' (1990) result can hold even if the manager is subject to a double moral hazard problem: production effort and earnings manipulation.

An et al. (2016) examine the effect of earnings management on financial leverage and how this relation is influenced by institutional

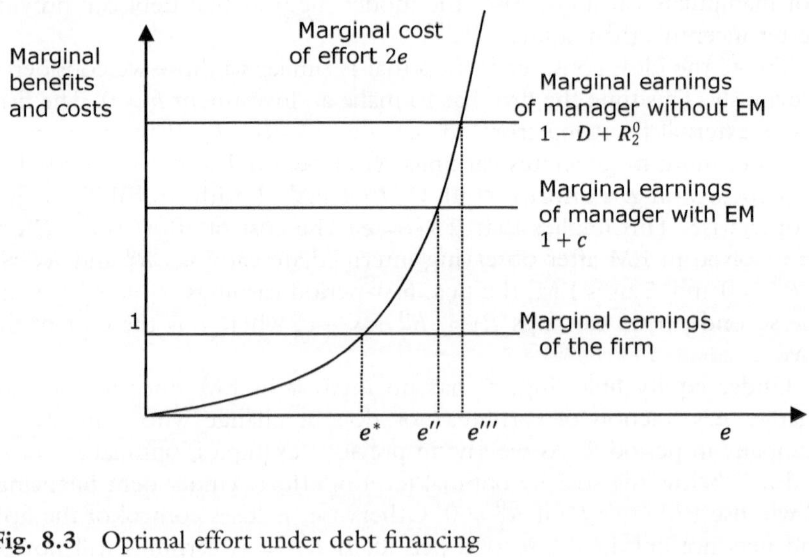

Fig. 8.3 Optimal effort under debt financing

environments by employing a large panel of 25,798 firms across 37 countries spanning the years 1989 to 2009. It was found that firms with high-earnings management activities are associated with high corporate leverage.

Gunny (2010) examines real earnings manipulation in firms that meet two earnings benchmarks (zero and last year's earnings). The results indicate that real activities manipulations of expenses on R&D, SG&A,[12] and production are positively associated with firms just meeting the earnings benchmarks. Also, it was found that firm-years reflecting real earnings manipulation to just meet earnings benchmarks had higher subsequent firm performances (compared to firm-years that do not engage in earnings manipulation and miss or just meet the earnings benchmarks).

Cohen and Zarowin (2010) examine earnings management behavior around SEOs, focusing on both real activities and accrual-based manipulation. They document that firms use real, as well as accrual-based, earnings management tools around SEOs.

Alhadab et al. (2013) find that IPO firms engage in real and accrual earnings management during the IPO and that big audit firms constrain discretionary expenses-based and accrual-based manipulations. Also they find that the presence of high-quality auditors is not sufficient to constrain all forms of earnings management. For example, IPO firms undertake sales-based manipulation in order to manage earnings upward at the end of the IPO year.

Adeneye and Kammoun (2022) examine the impact of real earnings management on the capital structure of listed firms across ASEAN countries using the fixed effects panel data estimator for the period 2014–2019 and find that real earnings manipulation has a significant positive effect on leverage.

8.5 Other Works

Capital Structure and Employees/Bargaining Issues

Matsa (2010) analyzes the strategic use of debt financing to improve a firm's bargaining position with an important supplier—organized labor. Because maintaining high levels of corporate liquidity can encourage

[12] R&D: research and development, and SG&A: selling, general, and administrative expenses.

workers to raise their wage demands, a firm with external finance constraints has an incentive to use the cash flow demands of debt service to improve its bargaining position with workers. It is shown that strategic incentives from union bargaining appear to have a substantial impact on corporate financing decisions.

Chang (1992) analyzes a model, where investors can force a value enhancing restructuring that is costly for employees in bankruptcy. Issuing more debt makes bankruptcy, and the associated restructuring, more likely. Optimal leverage is determined by maximizing firm value subject to this trade-off. In a related paper, Chang (1993) focuses on the interaction between payout policy, capital structure, and compensation contracts. Managers are induced to pay dividends through their compensation contracts; bankruptcy serves as an opportunity for investors to get information on the optimal payout level and hence to restructure the firm. When the right amount of debt is issued *ex ante*, bankruptcy occurs in states where new information about the optimal payout level is likely to be available.

Baldwin (1983) models a firm in which employees can appropriate the return to capital after capital costs have been sunk. Issuing a sufficient amount of debt may mitigate this holdup problem, but bankruptcy is assumed to be costly for workers. Perotti and Spier (1993) emphasize a similar role of debt. In their model equityholders may issue junior debt, thereby creating an underinvestment incentive. This can then be used to obtain wage concessions from employees to restore incentives to invest. Subramanian (2002) also analyzes a firm where the employee makes capital structure and investment decisions, taking his personal bankruptcy costs and risk aversion into account. In each period, the employee's income is derived from a bargaining process with the equityholders.

Berk et al. (2010) derive a firm's optimal capital structure and managerial compensation contract when employees are averse to bearing their own human capital risk, while equity holders can diversify this risk away. An important new empirical prediction is that firms with more leverage should pay higher wages.

Shareholders-Based vs. Stakeholders-Based Corporate Governance and Capital Structure

Some researchers argue that there are 2 major types of corporate governance systems: a shareholders-based (dominant in such countries as the

United States, Canada, Australia, etc.) and stakeholders-based (dominant in such countries as Germany, Japan, etc.).[13] Under the former the firm primarily acts in the interest of shareholders; its main objective is to maximize the value of shareholders' shares; the ownership structure is greatly diversified; a large proportion of share ownership belongs to private individuals. Further as argued, e.g., in Ungureanu (2012), the shareholders-based corporate governance system is often associated with a market-based system of raising funds. It is also often associated with countries where capital markets for both equity and debt are well developed and the sources of financing are well diversified. Under stakeholders-based (also called corporatist model) the interests of shareholders as well as other interested groups are taken into account, i.e., managers, employees of the firm, their customers, the state, business partners with whom the firm cooperates, etc. In countries with this type of corporate governance a bank-based system of raising funds often dominates. For example in Germany, firms raise in some years about 80% of external funding from banks while this number does not typically exceed 30% in the United States for example.[14] Further in these countries banks often own significant fractions of ownership in businesses. In an interesting article, Jilian Birkinshaw (February 20, 2017) compares governance systems in two large international corporations: Kraft Heinz and Unilever.

Among articles comparing the effect of different corporate governance systems on capital structure note the following. Ezeani et al. (2023) analyze the effects of board characteristics on the capital structure for firms in shareholder and stakeholder-oriented corporate governance environments. They find that firms in shareholder corporate governance environments use leverage to benefit shareholders by reducing managers' perquisite consumption. Firms in a stakeholder-oriented environment do not consider the stock market their primary source of finance since banks play a significant role in providing external finance. In this model, firms resolve agency conflicts by involving various stakeholders in the monitoring process. Barroso et al. (2018) find that the varying effects of corporate governance mechanisms on agency conflict have implications for leverage. This implies a negative relationship between board characteristics and leverage. Morellec et al. (2012) document a positive relationship

[13] See, e.g., La Porta et al. (1997), Barroso et al. (2018) or Ball et al. (2000).

[14] See Eakins and Mishkin (2018) or Hackethal and Schmidt (2004).

between board characteristics and leverage in the shareholder-oriented environment. Ezeani et al. (2023) find a negative relationship between board gender diversity and leverage, implying that women's presence on board reduces firms' use of debt irrespective of the corporate governance system. Board independence, board size, and board meeting are also negatively associated with leverage in France and Germany. However, a positive relationship is found between board independence, board size, and leverage among UK firms.

Imperfect Contracts and Capital Structure

The connections between stakeholders' (potential stakeholders') power and capital structure choice and management have been underexplored. Even though one aspect of these connections is well known (e.g., issuing more shares reduces the number of shares/votes of existing shareholders and so reduces their power) as practice shows different aspects of power can be related to the capital structure problem. The above-mentioned number of shares represents a formal measure of stakeholder power in a firm but is not related to other aspects. In some high-profile cases, the destiny of some firms depends on legal battles/court decisions which can be affected by different abilities of different firm stakeholders to win them/negotiate with judges/defend the firm patents, etc., as in the case of Enron, Tesla, or some legal battles related to Trump businesses.[15] In some cases some stakeholders get an advantage over other stakeholders because of better ability to negotiate different questions with other stakeholders involved (note, e.g., the ownership "battles" of Microsoft or Facebook).[16] So a difference exists between formal and real authority of different stakeholders involved.[17]

Miglo (2024) assumes that in contrast to the traditional incomplete contracts approach, contracts are imperfect. It means that the enforcement of even feasible contracts is not guaranteed. For example, a party who owns an amount of money to another party can claim that it has been already returned say indirectly in the form of a value-creating activity

[15] See, e.g., Quinn (2017) or https://www.law.berkeley.edu/files/Tesla_Motors_IP_Open_Innovation_and_the_Carbon_Crisis_-_Matthew_Rimmer.pdf.

[16] See, e.g., Gavil and First (2014) or https://www.immagic.com/eLibrary/ARCHIVES/GENERAL/IMM/I110708F.pdf.

[17] See Aghion and Tirloe (1997).

for the firm. The basic ground for that will be, as mentioned before, that the control of activities in early stages of product development is very difficult/impossible. If the parties disagree, the issue will be resolved in the court of law (we call it "external" fight), where a different set of skills may prevail in terms of likelihood of winning the case.[18] Similarly in the case of joint ownership, the parties can disagree on major issues including new projects, earnings distribution, hiring key personnel to the extent that even without formal transfer of shares, one party can emerge as a major winner (we call such a disagreement "internal" fight with an example being a shareholders' meeting). It's been mentioned in the literature that the development and execution of contractual relationships is often not only driven by differences in productive skills of parties but by their fighting (lobbying capacities, political power, military power, etc.) skills (Grossman and Kim (1995), Grossman (2001), Muthoo (2004), Skaperdas (1992), Skaperdas and Syropoulos (1997)). The agents' power or the set of skills required to win fights described above can be quite different than traditional production skills.[19] Miglo (2024) argues that debt financing becomes more probable with an improvement in the productive skills of the more productive party and/or a decrease in its internal fighting skills. The levels of effort (investments) depend on future renegotiations concerning the division of the surplus from cooperation. The ownership of the firm and the type of financing affects the renegotiation outcome because it determines the residual default payments. In case of debt financing, the party who owns the firm typically provides a higher effort because it expects a higher surplus in the renegotiation (given the nature of debt financing in that it is less sensitive to changes in firm's value compared to equity) so higher effort has a stronger impact on the owner's earnings compared to equity financing. On the other hand, in

[18] The regulation of intellectual property has being expanding dramatically in many countries in last 25 years (see, for example, Lianos (2017)). A lot of issues still remain uncertain, there are a lot of court cases including high profile cases such as Microsoft and Oracle/Google (https://www.wsj.com/articles/oracle-wins-court-ruling-against-google-in-long-running-copyright-case-1522164091) and competition authorities are actively working on developing new strategies and regulations and this area (see, for example, http://trade.ec.europa.eu/doclib/docs/2014/july/tradoc_152643.pdf.

[19] To some extent, this development is in the spirit of Hart (2017) that suggests that the current state of incomplete contracts is pretty "messy" and new developments are required. One approach in that paper was dropping agents rationality. In our paper the agents remain rational.

the case of equity financing, renegotiations related to the surplus will be based on the results of a potential internal fight. Comparing this situation with debt financing, intuitively, the incentive of the owner will be reduced if its internal fighting skills are not very strong. Third, debt/equity ratio increases with the owner's external fighting skills. In order to balance the investor participation constraint, an increase in the investor's external fighting skills (and respectively, rise of probability for the investor to win an external fight) should lead to a decrease in the value of the debt value negotiated initially. These results have a number of empirical predictions. The model predicts, for example, that firms with strong external power should have high debt/equity ratio. Although this prediction has not been tested directly it seems to be consistent with the observation that industries with high external power like banking (recall that banks negotiated large bailouts in 2007–2009) or insurance companies have high debt/equity ratios. Oppositely firms with small external but high internal power have a small debt/equity ratio. Start-up firms for example have high internal power since the founder is usually the main manager and has a lot of power (no separation between management and control), etc. Also countries with relatively strong creditors' rights (i.e., smaller external fighting power of firm owners) have less debt (see, for example, Cho et al., 2014).

Questions and Exercises

1. Consider a situation where a firm issues debt (with face value D) and equity to raise $B = 2$ to invest. After funds are received the manager should choose among two projects. Project j generates non-negative earnings R_j, $j = 1, 2$. R_j is uniformly distributed. The support for R_1 is [0.5] and for R_2 is [0.3]. If Proejct 2 is chosen, the manager's non-cash or private benefit equals 0.5 and if Project 1 is chosen it equals 0.2. Official manager's benefits are equal to zero for either project. If the firm is bankrupt the manager's total benefit is zero. For example, the manager loses job, reputation, etc.

   a. Show that under equity financing, the manager will choose an inefficient project.

b. Find the condition under which debt financing can improve managerial incentives. What is the minimal face value of debt that satisfies this condition?
c. What is the real value of debt found in the previous question?
d. What fraction of investment will be financed by equity and by debt?

2. Consider a firm totally financed with equity. The firm's founder/manager/entrepreneur (E) is risk-neutral. Also the firm has an investment project with cost $b = 1/4$. The project's expected first-period earnings r depend on E's effort $e \in [0, 1]$. The cost of effort is $2e^2$. Suppose that earnings can have 3 values (all with equal probabilities): 0, $2e$, and $4e$.

   a. Find the first-best level of manager's effort.
   b. Find the manager's effort and optimal contract for the manager under equity financing.
   c. Consider debt financing. Same question.
   d. What is the optimal financing strategy?

3. Consider a firm that has to make an investment that costs 19/32. The firm's owner/entrepreneur (E) needs external financing from an outside investor (I). E and I are risk-neutral. If the investment is made, the firm generates earnings R_1 in period 1 and R_2 in period 2. R_1 equals 1 with probability e and 0 otherwise. The cost of effort is e^2. I cannot observe e. E can be involved in EM after observing intermediate earnings R_1^0 and R_2^0. So if $R_1^0 = 0$ and E uses EM, the final first-period earnings $R_1 = R_1^0 + s$ and the second-period earnings $R_2 = R_2^0 + s - c$, where $c = 1/8$ is the cost of EM. Show that financing with short-term debt and some degree of earnings manipulation can be better than financing with equity.
4. Discuss the intuition behind the rule of marginal revenues discussed in Sect. 8.5.
5. Under corporatist (German) corporate governance the interests of shareholders as well as other interested groups are taken into account, i.e., managers, employees of the firm, the state, and also business partners who the firm cooperates with.
6. Usually bank loans is a more important financing source for firms in Germany than for firms in the United States.

7. Japanese and German banks hold substantial equity stakes in commercial firms.

References

Aboody, D., & Kasznik, R. (2000). CEO Stock Option Awards and The Timing of Corporate Voluntary Disclosures. *Journal of Accounting and Economics, 29*, 73–100.

Adeneye, Y., & Kammoun, I. (2022). Real Earnings Management and Capital Structure: Does Environmental, Social and Governance (ESG) Performance Matter? *Cogent Business & Management, 9*(1), 130134.

Aghion, P., & Tirole, J. (1997). Formal and Real Authority in Organizations. *The Journal of Political Economy, 105*(1), 1–29.

Alhadab, M., Clacher, I., & Keasey, K. (2013). Effects of Audit Quality on Real and Accrual Earnings Management and Subsequent Return Performance: Evidence from IPOs. Available at SSRN: http://ssrn.com/abstract=2225409

Anantharaman, D., Fang, V., & Gong, G. (2014). Inside Debt and the Design of Corporate Debt Contracts. *Management Science, 60*(5), 1260–1280.

An, Z., Li, D., & Yu, J. (2016). Earnings Management, Capital Structure, and the Role of Institutional Environments. *Journal of Banking and Finance, 68*, 131–152.

Baldwin, C. (1983). Productivity and Labor Unions: An Application of the Theory of Self-enforcing Contracts. *Journal of Business, 56*, 155–185.

Ball, R., Kothari, S., & Robin, A. (2000). The Effect of International Institutional Factors on Properties of Accounting Earnings. *Journal of Accounting and Economics, 29*(1), 1–51.

Barroso, R., Ben Ali, C., & Lesage, C. (2018). Blockholders' Ownership and Audit Fees: The Impact of the Corporate Governance Model. *The European Accounting Review, 27*(1), 149–172.

Bebchuk, L. A., Grinstein, Y., & Peyer, U. (2006). Lucky Directors, Harvard Law and Economics Discussion Paper No. 573.

Becht, M., Bolton, P., & Roell, A. (2003), Corporate Governance and Control. In G. M. Constantinides, M. Harris & R. Stulz (Eds.), *Handbook of the Economics of Finance*, Elsevier (1 ed., (1), Ch. 1, pp. 1–109).

Berglöf, E., & Rosenthal, H. (1999). *The Political Economy of American Bankruptcy: The Evidence from Roll Call Voting, 1800–1978*. Mimeo (Princeton University).

Berk, J., Stanton, R., & Zechner, J. (2010). Human Capital, Bankruptcy, and Capital Structure. *Journal of Finance, 65*(3), 891–926.

Berkovitch, E., Israel, H., & Spiegel, Y. (2000). Managerial Compensation and Capital Structure. *Journal of Economics & Management Strategy, 9*(4), 549–584.

Biais, B., Mariotti, T., Plantin, G., & Rochet, J.-C. (2007). Dynamic Security Design: Convergence to Continuous Time and Asset Pricing Implications. *The Review of Economic Studies, 74*(2), 345–390.

Birkinshaw, J., (2017, February 20). Kraft Heinz Vs. Unilever: A Contest Between Two Models Of Capitalism. *Forbes*. https://www.forbes.com/sites/lbsbusinessstrategyreview/2017/02/20/kraft-heinz-versus-unilever-a-contest-between-two-models-of-capitalism/

Bryant, C., Milne, R., & Sharman, A. (2015, October 13). Volkswagen Starts to Cut Investment after Emissions Scandal. *FT*, http://www.ft.com/intl/cms/s/0/ab3de3aa-6db6-11e5-aca9-d87542bf8673.html#axzz43qbJkUSc

Burgstahler, D., & Dichev, I. (1997). Earnings Management to Avoid Earnings Decreases and Losses. *Journal of Accounting and Economics, 24*(2), 99–126.

Chang, C. (1992). Capital Structure as an Optimal Contract Between Employees and Investors. *Journal of Finance, 47*(3), 1141–1158.

Chang, C. (1993). Payout Policy, Capital Structure, and Compensation Contracts When Managers Value Control. *Review of Financial Studies, 6*, 911–933.

Cho, S., El Ghoul, S., Guedhami, O., & Suh, J. (2014). Creditor Rights and Capital Structure: Evidence from International Data. *Journal of Corporate Finance, 25*, 40–60.

Cohen, D., & Zarowin, P. (2010). Accrual-based and Real Earnings Management Activities around Seasoned Equity Offerings. *Journal of Accounting and Economics, 50*(1), 2–19.

Degeorge, F., Patel, J., & Zeckhauser, R. (1999). Earnings Management to Exceed Thresholds. *The Journal of Business, 72*(1), 1–33.

DeMarzo, P., & Fishman, M. (2007). Optimal Long-Term Financial Contracting. *The Review of Financial Studies, 20*(5), 2079–2128.

DeMarzo, P., & Sannikov, Y. (2006). Optimal Security Design and Dynamic Capital Structure in a Continuous-Time Agency Model. *Journal of Finance, 61*(6), 2681–2724.

Dewatripont, M., Legros, P., & Matthews, S. (2003). Moral Hazard and Capital Structure Dynamics. *Journal of the European Economic Associtation, 1*(4), 890–930.

DuCharme, L., Malatesta, P., & Sefcik, S. (2001). Earnings Management: IPO Valuation and Subsequent Performance. *Journal of Accounting, Auditing & Finance, 16*, 369–396.

Dybvig, P., & Zender, J. (1991). Capital Structure and Dividend Irrelevance with Asymmetric Information. *The Review of Financial Studies, 4*(1), 201–219.

Eakins, S., & Mishkin, F. (2018). *Financial Markets and Institutions* (9th ed.). Pearson.

Edmans, A. (2011). Short-Term Termination without Deterring Long-Term Investment: A Theory of Debt and Buyouts. *Journal of Financial Economics, 102*(1), 81–101.

Erman, B. (2007, March 13). Ex-Nortel CEO John Roth says he's Cleared. *The Globe and Mail* (Toronto), http://www.theglobeandmail.com/report-on-business/ex-nortel-ceo-john-roth-says-hes-cleared/article1357907/

Ezeani, E., Kwabi, F., Salem, R., Usman, M., Alqatamin, R., & Kostov, P. (2023). Corporate Board and Dynamics of Capital Structure: Evidence from UK, France and Germany. *International Journal of Finance & Economics, 28*(3), 3281–3298.

Franks, J. R., & Sussman, O. (2005). Financial Innovations and Corporate Insolvency. *Journal of Financial Intermediation, 14*(3), 283–317.

Gale, D., & Hellwig, M. (1985). Incentive-Compatible Debt Contracts: The One-Period Problem. *Review of Economic Studies, 52*, 647–663.

Gavil, A. I., & First, H. (2014). *The Microsoft Antitrust Cases: Competition Policy for the Twenty-First Century*. The MIT Press, Cambridge, Massachusetts.

Gillies, R. (2009, June 20). Nortel to Sell Itself off in Pieces. *PhysOrg. AP*, http://phys.org/news/2009-06-nortel-pieces.html

Graham, J., Harvey, C., & Rajgopal, S. (2005). The Economic Implications of Corporate Financial Reporting. *Journal of Accounting and Economics, 40*, 3–73.

Gramlich, J. D., & Sorensen, O. (2004). Voluntary Management Earnings Forecasts and Discretionary Accruals: Evidence from Danish IPOs. *European Accounting Review, 13*, 235–259.

Grossman, S., & Hart, O. (1982). Corporate Financial Structure and Managerial Incentives. *J* (pp. 107–140). University of Chicago Press.

Grossman, H. (2001). The Creation of Effective Property Rights. *American Economic Review, 91*, 347–352.

Grossman, H., & Kim, M. (1995). Sword or Plowshares? A Theory of the Security of Claims to Property. *Journal of Political Economy, 103*, 1275–1288.

Gunny, K. (2010). The Relation Between Earnings Management Using Real Activities Manipulation and Future Performance: Evidence from Meeting Earnings Benchmarks. *Contemporary Accounting Research, 27*(3), 855–888.

Hackethal, A., & Schmidt, R. (2004). Financing Patterns: Measurement Concepts and Empirical Results, Working Paper Series: Finance & Accounting, No. 125, Johann Wolfgang Goethe-Universität Frankfurt am Main, Fachbereich Wirtschaftswissenschaften, Frankfurt a. M., https://nbn-resolving.de/urn:nbn:de:hebis:30-16667

Hart, O. (2017). Incomplete Contracts and Control. *The American Economic Review, 107*(7), 1731–1752.

Hasselback, D., & Tedesco, T. (2014, September 27). The Fate of Once-Mighty Nortel's Last Billions Lies in the Hands of Two Men. *financial-post.com*. National Post. http://business.financialpost.com/legal-post/the-fate-of-once-mighty-nortels-last-billions-lies-in-the-hands-of-two-men

Holmstrom, B. (1979). Moral Hazard and Observability. *Bell Journal of Economics, 10*, 74–91.

Innes, R. (1990). Limited Liability and Incentive Contracting with Ex-ante Action Choices. *Journal of Economic Theory, 52*(1), 45–67.

Jensen, M. (1986). Agency Costs of Free Cash Flow, Corporate Finance, and Takeovers. *American Economic Review, 76*, 323–329.

Jensen, M. (1989). The Eclipse of the Public Corporation. *Harvard Business Review, 67*, 61–74.

Jensen, M., & Meckling, W. (1976). Theory of the Firm: Managerial Behavior, Agency Costs and Ownership Structure. *Journal of Financial Economics, 3*, 305–360.

Kale, J., Ryan, H., & Wang, L. (2015). Outside Employment Opportunities, Employee Productivity, and Debt Discipline. Available at SSRN: http://ssrn.com/abstract=1022067

La Porta, R., Lopez-de-Silanes, F., Shleifer, A., & Vishny, R. (1997). Legal Determinants of External Finance. *The Journal of Finance, 52*(3), 1131–50.

Leland, H. E., & Pyle, D. (1977). Information Asymmetries, Financial Structure, and Financial Intermediation. *Journal of Finance, 32*(2), 371–378.

Lianos, I. (2017). Competition Law and Intellectual Property (IP) Rights: Analysis, Cases and Materials. Chapter 13 in Ioannis Lianos & Valentine Korah with Paolo Siciliani, Competition Law. Available at SSRN: https://ssrn.com/abstract=2863814 or https://doi.org/10.2139/ssrn.2863814

Matsa, D. (2010). Capital Structure as a Strategic Variable: Evidence from Collective Bargaining. *The Journal of Finance, 65*(3), 1197–1232.

Miglo, A. (2010). Capital Structure and Earnings Manipulation. *Journal of Economics and Business, 62*(5), 367–382.

Miglo, A. (2020). Zero-Debt Policy Under Asymmetric Information, Flexibility and Tax Considerations. *Journal of Risk and Financial Management, 13*(12), 296. https://doi.org/10.3390/jrfm13120296

Miglo, A. (2024). Imperfect Contracts, Power and Capital Structure, working paper, SSRN.

Milne, R. (2015, November 20). Volkswagen Brand Choked by Cost and Complexity. *Financial Times*. http://www.ft.com/cms/s/0/e2afceba-8ec8-11e5-94a4-639039952d45.html#axzz43qbJkUSc

Morellec, E., Nikolov, B., & Schürhoff, N. (2012). Corporate Governance and Capital Structure Dynamics. *The Journal of Finance, 67*(3), 803–848.

Mu, C., Wang, A., & Yang, J. (2017). Optimal Capital Structure with Moral Hazard. *International Review of Economics and Finance, 48*, 326–338.

Muthoo, A. (2004). A Model of Origins of Basic Property Rights. *Games and Economic Behavior, 49*, 288–312.

Perotti, E., & Spier, K. (1993). Capital Structure as a Bargaining Tool: The Role of Leverage in Contract Renegotiation. *American Economic Review, 83*, 1131–1141.

Rangan, S. (1998). Earnings Management and the Performance of Seasoned Equity Offerings. *Journal of Financial Economics, 50*, 101–122.

Roychowdhury, S. (2006). Earnings Management through Real Activities Manipulation. *Journal of Accounting and Economics, 42*(3), 335–370.

Quinn, P. S. (2017). Head-of-State-Owned Enterprise Immunity. *Vanderbilt Journal of Transnational Law, 50*(4), 1065–[ii].

Skaperdas, S. (1992). Cooperation, Conflict, and Power in the Absence of Property Rights. *American Economic Review, 82*(4), 720–39.

Skaperdas, S., & Syropoulos, C. (1997). The Distribution of Income in the Presence of Appropriate Activities. *Economica, 64*, 101–17.

Subramanian, A. (2002). *Managerial Flexibility, Agency Costs, and Optimal Capital Structure* (Working paper). Georgia Institute of Technology.

Sundaram, R., & Yermack, D. (2007). Pay me Later: Inside Debt and its Role in Managerial Compensation. *Journal of Finance, 62*(4), 1551–1588.

Teoh, S., Welch, I., & Wong, T. (1998). Earnings Management and the Long-Run Market Performance of Initial Public Offerings. *The Journal of Finance, 53*, 1935–1974.

Teoh, S., Wong, T., & Rao, G. (1998). Are Accruals During Initial Public Offerings Opportunistic? *Review of Accounting Studies, 3*(1–2), 209–221.

Townsend, R. M. (1979). Optimal Contracts and Competitive Markets with Costly State Verification. *Journal of Economic Theory, 21*, 265–293.

Ungureanu, M., (2012), Models And Practices Of Corporate Governance Worldwide, CES Working Papers, Centre for European Studies, Alexandru Ioan Cuza University, 4(3a), 625–635.

Yermack, D. (1997). Good Timing: CEO Stock Option Awards and Company News Announcements. *Journal of Finance, 50*(2), 449–476.

Zheng, M. (2013). Empirical Research of the Impact of Capital Structure on Agency Cost of Chinese Listed Companies. *International Journal of Economics and Finance, 5*(10), 118–12.

CHAPTER 9

Capital Structure of Start-Up Firms and Small Firms

9.1 Life Cycle Theory of Capital Structure

An interesting idea is to look at the importance of different factors affecting the capital structure choice at different stages of a firm's development (so-called "life cycle theory" of capital structure).[1] Figure 9.1 illustrates some ideas. For example, start-up firms usually do not have much profit, so the tax advantage of debt (Chapter 2) is not as important as it is for a mature firm. Start-up firms do not usually require strong incentives for managers (Chapter 8) since there is no large separation between ownership and management like in big public corporations. This leads to the idea that mature firms value debt more than start-up firms do.

Among factors affecting the capital structure choice in the early stages of a firm's development are flexibility (firms can lose flexibility if they have too much debt (debt overhang)—Chapter 5), asymmetric information (Chapter 3), costly managerial effort (Chapter 8) and asset substitution (Chapter 5). The extent of asymmetric information is large for start-up

[1] See, for example, Damodaran (2003).

Supplementary Information The online version contains supplementary material available at https://doi.org/10.1007/978-3-031-85459-0_9.

A. Miglo, *Capital Structure in the Modern World*,
https://doi.org/10.1007/978-3-031-85459-0_9

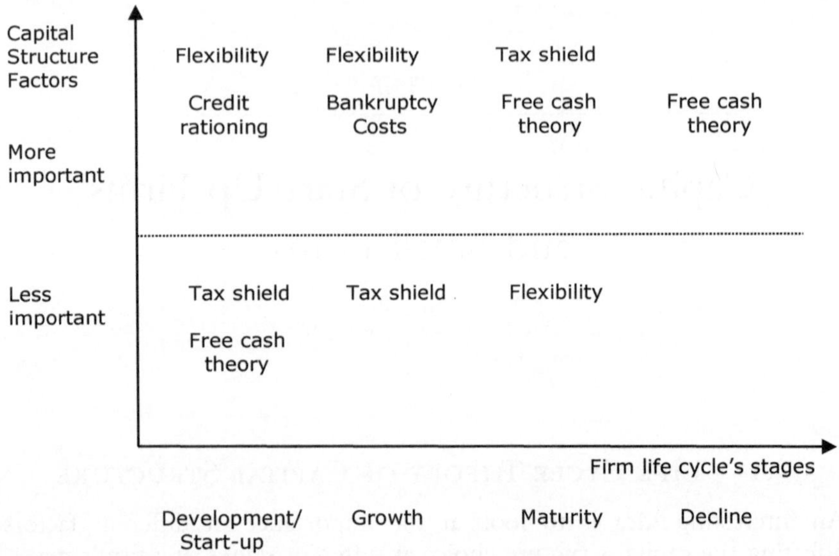

Fig. 9.1 Capital structure ideas across a firm's life cycle

firms especially for start-up innovative firms. It results in difficulties in raising bank financing and in issuing shares publicly. Since these firms have a lot of choice, the asset substitution problem is important but only if the firm has a lot of debt. Nevertheless, the credit rationing phenomenon is very important for these firms. Although it was explained with the asset substitution effect it can also be explained with asymmetric information between lenders and borrowers.[2]

Most factors point to the preference of equity over debt for start-up firms. For many years it was used as an explanation for why start-up firms often use the capital of their firms' founders and managers or "sweet" equity from friends and relatives and why they have difficulties using bank financing.[3] Closer analyses of start-up entrepreneurial firms, however, reveal that many firms use convertible securities for financing.

[2] See, for example, Stiglitz and Weiss (1981) and Freixas and Rochet (1999).

[3] In the spirit of life cycle idea of capital structure DeHan (2014) for example found that radically innovative firms at the beginning of the innovation life cycle will be rather using equity than firms at the end of the life cycle with less innovative activity.

Jacob Demitt, in a December 2015 article, described an $8 million financing for a start-up Textio via series A funding.[4] It was led by Emergence Capital, one of the top software-as-a-service investors, known for backing companies like Salesforce, Box and Yammer. Textio was founded in 2014, after one of their founders Snyder conducted research on gender bias in performance reviews in the tech industry. Snyder is a linguistics expert who previously worked at Amazon and Microsoft's Bing unit. Co-founder and CTO Jensen Harris, meanwhile, spent 16 years at Microsoft including stints running the user experience teams for Outlook, Office and Windows. The key to Textio's offering is the use of artificial intelligence to sift through job postings and make recommendations for edits based on what kind of language is going to appeal—or scare away—certain demographics. For instance, if you use words like "manage a team" or "proven track record," Texio says you're going to get more male applicants. Phrases like "passion for learning" and "develop a team," meanwhile, will attract more women. Wikipedia describes Series A Preferred Stock was offered during the seed or early stage round. Preferred stock is often convertible into common stock in certain cases such as an IPO or the sale of the company. Further in this chapter we will consider a model that illustrates why a start-up firm may be interested in using convertible securities.

Another issue in the financing of start-up and small firms is the revival of debt financing. Debt financing for start-up and small companies is subject to credit rationing as we discussed in Chapter 4. Until recently, experts thought that debt was not a major source of financing for start-up firms and instead paid more attention to entrepreneurs own funds, venture funds and angels financing. In recent years the situation seems to have been changing. We will consider later why debt financing is important for start-up firms and what the usage of debt signals about the firm's quality.[5]

[4] Demitt (2015, December 16).

[5] For a review of literature related to financing of small and start-up firms see e.g., Abdulsaleh and Worthington (2013), Kumar et al. (2020) or Miglo (2022a, 2022b).

9.2 Capital Structure of Venture Firms

Venture capital (VC) differs from other forms of finance because the venture capitalist often provides management and commercial expertise along with funds. The founder of a small firm has many functions in managing the enterprise. In the growth enterprise, assistance may be needed in management.

VC is usually provided to high-risk ventures that provide potentially higher returns than other investments. The company receives management assistance through its development and often further injections of funds until maturity, which is when the investor anticipates a capital gain from the sale of the firm. This may take several years depending on where the venture capitalist enters the firm's growth cycle.

Below we develop a model that is able to generate predictions regarding the optimal financing structure for venture firms, in particular, the usage of convertible securities.

Consider a firm that has to make an investment$b = 5/16$. The firm's owner/entrepreneur (E) needs external financing from an outside investor (I). In exchange for the investment I expects to receive 1/8 in period 1 and 3/16 (net of effort cost) in period 2. E and I are risk-neutral. If the investment is made, the firm generates earnings R_1 in period 1 and R_2 in period 2. R_1 depends on E's effort $e \in [0,1]$. Similar to the case from Chapter 7, R_1 can have 3 values (all with equal probabilities): 0, e and $2e$. It implies $ER_1 = e$. The cost of effort is e^2. R_2 depends on E's effort $e_1 \in [0,1]$ and I's effort $e_2 \in [0,1]$. R_2 can also have 3 values (all with equal probabilities): 0, $e_1 + e_2$ and $2(e_1 + e_2)$. This implies $ER_2 = e_1 + e_2$. The cost of efforts are $e_i^2, i = 1,2$. . The interpretation of this condition is that in period 1 (start-up stage) the firm's success mostly depends on the entrepreneur's effort while in the second stage both the entrepreneur and the investor can contribute to the firm's success. The investor's contribution may consist of management expertise, as we discussed previously, or fundraising help. It will be shown that financing with convertible debt or convertible preferred equity can be better than financing with equity or debt.

The sequence of events is as follows (Fig. 9.2):

Period 1. The first-best effort maximizes the firm's value: $e - e^2$. Socially optimal $e^* = 1/2$. In the case of equity financing E will maximize $ke - e^2$, where k is the fraction of equity that belongs to E. Optimal $e\prime = k/2$. For any < 1, $e\prime < e^*$.

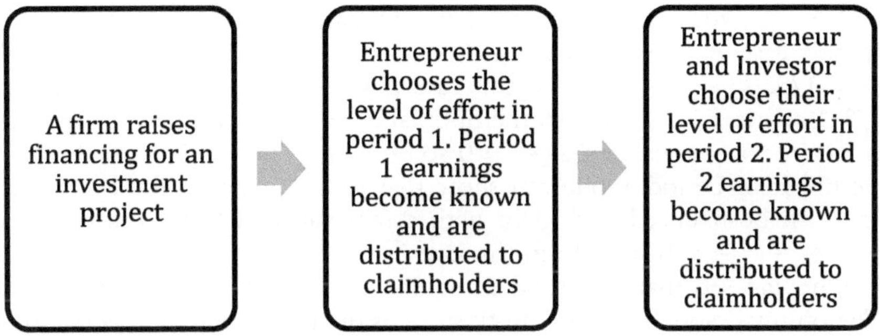

Fig. 9.2 Sequence of events

E's profit is then $k^2/4$. To find the optimal contract, we have to find k that will maximize E's profit under the condition that the investor's expected profit is not less than b. This condition is $e(1-k) = k(1-k)/2 \geq 1/8$. The left side of the inequality reaches its maximum when $k = 1/2$. In this case, I's expected payoff is 1/8. E's expected payoff is $k^2/4$. It is increasing on k. Hence the optimal k is the largest value of k that satisfies I's budget constraint, i.e. 1/2. The optimal $e = 1/4$ and E's expected payoff is 1/16.

Now consider debt financing. Two cases are possible. 1) $e < D$. In this case the manager maximizes $1/3 * (2e - D) - e^2$. So the optimal $e = 1/3$. E's expected payoff is $1/9 - 1/3D$. 2) $e > D$. In this case the manager maximizes $1/3(e - D) + 1/3(2e - D) - e^2$. So the optimal $e = 1/2$. E's expected payoff is $1/4 - 2/3D$. By comparing the manager's payoffs in each case we find that if $D < 5/12$ the optimal $e = 1/2$ and otherwise $e = 1/3$. Now to find D, note that the investor's payoff should be greater than b. So in the second case $D = 3/2b$. It is possible only if $b < 5/18$, which is our case. So the firm can be financed with debt with face value 3/16. The manager's profit, in this case, is 1/8.

Period 2. The first-best effort maximizes the firm's value: $e_1 + e_2 - e_1^2 - e_2^2$. Hence, socially optimal $e_1^* = e_2^* = 1/2$. Under equity financing, E has a fraction k of the firm's equity. So E will maximize $k(e_1 + e_2) - e_1^2$. Optimal $e_1\prime = k/2$. Similarly we find $e_2\prime = (1-k)/2$.

I's payoff equals $(1-k)(e_1 + e_2) - e_2^2 = \frac{1-k}{2} - \frac{(1-k)^2}{4}$. If $k = 1/2$, it equals 3/16. E's payoff also equals 3/16.

Now consider debt financing. Two cases are possible. 1) $e_1 + e_2 < D$. In this case E maximizes $1/3 * (2(e_1 + e_2) - D) - e_1^2$. So the optimal $e_1 = 1/3$. 2) $e_1 + e_2 > D$. In this case E maximizes $1/3(e_1 + e_2 - D) + 1/3(2(e_1 + e_2) - D) - e_1^2$. So the optimal $e_1 = 1/2$. In this case I's payoff is $2/3D$. So D equals 3/32. $e_2 = 0$ so $e_1 + e_2 > D$. Similarly to the way we did it in Period 1 one can show that case 2 is better for E. So the firm can be financed with debt with a face value of 9/32. E's profit is $e_1 + e_2 - e_1^2 - 3/16 = 1/16$ in this case.

One can see that in period 2, equity is a better financing structure. The optimal capital structure in this case is debt financing in period 1 and equity financing in period 2. It can also be interpreted as a convertible debt or convertible preferred equity that is converted into common equity in period 2.

Empirical literature in this field generally confirms that the entrepreneur has more control when the business is performing relatively well while the degree of control is significantly reduced in favor of venture capitalists when the opposite occurs. This literature also stresses that, while in real financial contracts the allocation of cash flow rights plays an important role, the parties involved usually make separate determinations for the allocations of various kinds of property rights. These rights include residual cash flow rights, liquidation rights, board rights, etc. Moreover, there are significant quantitative differences between the percentages of different rights allotted to the parties.[6]

Among papers that explain why, in many cases, investors hold convertible securities and not simply debt note Berglof (1994), Kalay and Zender (1997), Gompers (1998), Schmidt (2003), Cornelli and Yoscha (2003), Hellmann (2006) and Winton and Yerramilli (2008).

As was found in Kaplan and Stromberg (2003), convertible preferred shares were used in 170 rounds and convertible preferred participating shares were used in 82 rounds.[7] These two are the most popular types of securities used in combination with VC. In the early stages of a firm, when

[6] See, for instance, Kaplan and Stromberg (2003) and Elfenbein and Lerner (2003) with regard to venture capital contracts and Gilson (1990) for corporate contracts.

[7] Convertible preferred stock: preferred stock that can be converted at the shareholder's discretion into common stock. Participating convertible preferred stock: A type of preferred stock that gives the holder the right to receive dividends equal to the normally specified rate that preferred dividends receive as well as an additional dividend based on some predetermined condition.

risk is high, preferred shares (as opposite to common shares) can mitigate risk for investors by promising a fixed dividend that does not depend on the amount of profit. It may also be a flexible option for the firm since in the event of insufficient profits the dividend can be cumulative, i.e., paid in later years. It also reduces the risk for investors because preferred shares have priority to common shares in case of liquidation. Convertible preferred shares on the other hand allow investors to convert shares into common shares if business is developing successfully.

Cumming (2005) analyzes VC in United States and finds that the results are consistent with the proposition that convertible preferred equity is the optimal form of VC finance. It also presents new evidence from 208 US VC financings of Canadian entrepreneurial firms. In contrast to VC investments in US entrepreneurial firms, US venture capitalists finance Canadian entrepreneurial firms with a variety of forms of finance. The differences are attributable to the importance of institutional determinants of venture capitalist capital structures within the United States and abroad. Among other things, the data indicates that US venture capitalists often do not choose convertible preferred shares in the absence of tax considerations in favor of that financing vehicle.

Among recent articles about venture capital, consider Tian (2011). It shows that VC investors located farther away from an entrepreneurial firm tend to finance the firm using a larger number of financing rounds, shorter durations between successive rounds, and investing a smaller amount in each round. However, VC investors' propensity to stage is independent of whether the firm is located in a close community. It also finds that VC staging positively affects the entrepreneurial firm's operating performance in the initial public offering (IPO) year, and post-IPO survival rate, but only if the firm is located far away from the VC investor.

Talmor and Cuny (2005) analyze the choice between milestone financing and round financing when VC commits to future rounds up front. When the role of a venture capitalist's effort is small, the incentivization of the entrepreneur dominates the contractual relationship, and round financing is preferred to milestone financing. When it is the role of entrepreneurial effort that is small, however, the need for contract flexibility dominates, and milestone financing is preferred to round financing.

Häussler, Harhoff, and Mueller (2014) develop a model where certification serves as a signal about the quality of entrepreneurial firms. They derive and empirically test several hypotheses using a sample of British and

German companies that seek VC. They find that patent applications—as signals from ventures—are positively related to VC financing. Moreover, applications trigger institutionalized processes at the patent office, which can generate valuable technological and commercial information via search reports, citations and opposition procedures and thus affect VC financing. The results highlight the role of signaling, but additional information about venture quality is generated via an institutionalized certification process.

Another recent trend in the financing of start-up firms is crowdfunding. Crowdfunding is the practice of funding a start-up company or a project by raising funds from a large number of people ("crowd"). It is usually performed online.[8] The concept can also be executed through mail-order subscriptions, benefit events, and other methods. More discussions about crowdfunding and other financing methods related to the development of FinTech is provided in Chapter 12.[9]

Finally note that although straight outside equity is usually not the significant source of financing for small and start-up firms (see e.g., Berger & Udell, 1998), some entrepreneurs still use it and some types of investors (e.g., angel investors) prefer this type of investment.[10] To justify the usage of straight equity for small and start-up businesses, most of ideas considered in previous chapters can usually be applied. In addition note papers that specifically analyze the choice between straight equity and other forms of financing for start-up and venture firms see e.g., de Bettignies and Brander (2007).

9.3 Debt financing for Small Businesses

Capital structure is one of the most important topics of corporate finance. The vast majority of research has been focused on large public companies. In recent years, however, the capital structure of small companies, especially start-ups, has been a quickly growing area of research.[11]

[8] See, for example, Schwienbacher and Larralde (2012).

[9] For a review of crowdfunding literature see e.g., Moritz and Brock (2014), Miglo (2022b).

[10] For an analysis of angel financing or the choice between angel financing and venture capital see e.g., Hellmann and Thiele (2014) and Chemmanur and Chen (2014).

[11] For a detailed discussion of reasons for that and the role of Kauffmann foundation see, for example, Robb and Robinson (2012) and Cole and Sokolyk (2014).

One of the issues that has been receiving a lot of attention is the usage of debt by small companies (Cole & Sokolyk, 2014; Robb & Robinson, 2012). Some authors argue that recent findings about the importance of outside (formal) debt for small companies are contradictory to common opinion that small businesses, especially start-ups, rely heavily on internal finance including the owner's equity and funds from relatives and friends (Robb & Robinson, 2012). Robb and Robinson (2012) also find that the usage of outside debt by a start-up firm is indicative of its success a few years after its creation. In particular, they find that firms that use outside debt have better growth and have better chances of survival compared to firms that do not use outside debt. Below we present a model where entrepreneurs have a choice between outside debt, inside debt and the owner's equity to finance their start-up firms.

Consider a set of entrepreneurs, indexed with j, with investment projects available. The projects require the same amount of external financing equal to 1. In the case of success, a project generates a cash flow F_j and a cash flow of zero otherwise. The probability of success is p_j. There are three types of financing available for the project. Full financing for the project can be obtained via outside debt (OD). It is assumed that each entrepreneur has collateral valued 1. Alternatively, the entrepreneur can use inside debt (ID). Here, an entrepreneur borrows an amount $\beta, \beta \leq 1$ from a friend or relative. If the project succeeds, the earnings are βF_j. Finally, the entrepreneur can use inside equity (IE).[12] An entrepreneur has an amount α available to finance the firm, $\alpha < \beta$. If the project succeeds, the earnings are αF_j. F_j and p_j are private information for each entrepreneur. Entrepreneurs and investors are risk-neutral.

In this model, the entrepreneurs' choices of financing for their start-up firms are based on the following trade-off. Entrepreneurs who do not use OD face greater financial constraints during the first years of their businesses. On the other hand the providers of OD have more experience in enforcing debt payments compared to the providers of ID. Asymmetric information between the entrepreneurs and the capital providers plays a very important role in start-up firms, which affects the details of negotiations including interest rates on loans and collateral. Robb and Robinson (2012) mentioned that outside debt providers,

[12] Outside equity is ruled out. It does constitute a relatively small fraction of small firms' capital structure. Seven times as many firms report outside debt as report outside equity (Robb & Robinson, 2012).

like banks, are more experienced in terms of controlling collaterals and enforcing debt contracts (both for firms with unlimited liability and firms with limited liability) compared to friends and relatives. Even if the firm is formally created as a firm with limited liability, financing start-ups often circumvents limited liability and requires personal guarantees from entrepreneurs. Often entrepreneurs own levered equity in their firms. They borrow on their own behalf and then invest in their start-up firms. If the firm fails, the entrepreneur can lose a large part of the wealth that he pledged as collateral.

We argue that in equilibrium entrepreneurs with business credit have higher success rates and greater revenues than other firms. This is consistent with empirical evidence.

Choice of Financing

We have the following set of equations that determine an equilibrium. The choice between ID (the face value is D) and IE is given by:

$$p_j(\beta F_j - D) = \alpha p_j F_j - \alpha \tag{9.1}$$

The left side of (9.1) shows the entrepreneur's expected earnings for ID. The probability of success is multiplied by the net earnings in the case of success. The right side shows the entrepreneur's expected earnings for IE. The firm's expected revenues are reduced by the amount of the initial investment. Equation (9.1) can be rewritten as:

$$p_j = \frac{-\alpha}{\beta F_j - D - \alpha F_j} \tag{9.2}$$

For marginal entrepreneurs (marginal entrepreneurs' projects satisfy (9.2)) we have: $\frac{\partial p_j}{\partial F_j} = \frac{\alpha(\beta-\alpha)}{(\beta F_j - D - \alpha F_j)^2} > 0$. Also: $\frac{\partial^2 p_j}{\partial {F_j}^2} = \frac{2\alpha(\beta-\alpha)^2}{(\beta F_j - D - \alpha F_j)^3} > 0$.

If an entrepreneur's project satisfies (9.1) he is indifferent between ID and IE.

The choice between ID and OD (the face value is $\prime$) is given by:

$$p_j(\beta F_j - D) = p_j(F_j - D\prime) - (1 - p_j)$$

This equation can be rewritten as:

$$p_j = \frac{-1}{\beta F_j - D + D\prime - 1 - F_j} \tag{9.3}$$

We have $\frac{\partial p_j}{\partial F_j} = \frac{-(1-\beta)}{\beta F_j - D + D\prime - 1 - F_j)^2} > 0$ and $\frac{\partial^2 p_j}{\partial F_j{}^2} = \frac{2(1-\beta)^2}{(\beta F_j - D + D\prime - 1 - F_j)^3} > 0$.

Finally, the choice between OD and IE is given by:

$$p_j(F_j - D\prime) - (1 - p_j) = \alpha p_j F_j - \alpha$$

This equation can be rewritten as:

$$p_j = \frac{1-\alpha}{F_j - D\prime + 1 - \alpha F_j} \tag{9.4}$$

We have: $\frac{\partial p_j}{\partial F_j} = \frac{-(1-\alpha)^2}{(F_j - D\prime + 1 - \alpha F_j)^2} > 0$. Also: $\frac{\partial^2 p_j}{\partial F_j{}^2} = \frac{2(1-\alpha)^2}{(F_j - D\prime + 1 - \alpha F_j)^3} > 0$.

The analysis of Eqs. (9.2)–(9.4) reveals that the marginal entrepreneur with $F_j = F^*$ and $p_j = p^*$ is indifferent between every type of financing where

$$F^* = \frac{-D + \alpha D - \alpha D\prime + \alpha}{-\beta + \alpha\beta} \tag{9.5}$$

and

$$p^* = \frac{-\beta + \alpha\beta}{-D + \alpha D + \beta D\prime - \alpha D\prime - \beta + \alpha} \tag{9.6}$$

One can also check that the slope of (9.4) is larger than that of (9.3). Figure 9.3 illustrates the equilibrium decision-making for the entrepreneurs. The thick lines represent Eqs. (9.2), (9.3) and (9.4). Letters IE, OD and ID denote the areas where the entrepreneurs choose the internal equity, the outside debt, or the inside debt respectively.

From Fig. 9.3, entrepreneurs with OD have a higher probability of success for any value of F_j compared to entrepreneurs with IE and ID. Also, entrepreneurs with OD have a higher F_j for any value of p_j compared to entrepreneurs with IE and ID.[13]

[13] The fact that Eqs. (9.2), (9.3) and (9.4) have discontinuities does not affect this result. For example, the line corresponding to Eq. (9.2) has a discontinuity in $F_j =$

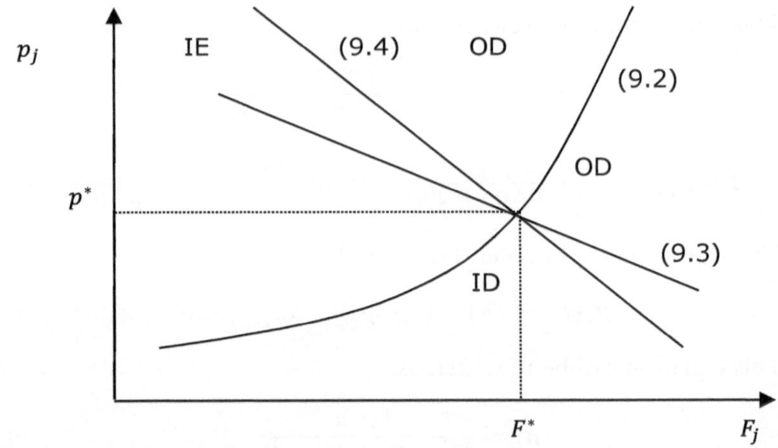

Fig. 9.3 The choice of financing

From recent literature we know that seventy five percent of firms use some type of credit at the firm's start-up.[14] We also know, from empirical literature in the field, that the role of outside debt for start-up firms is underestimated in the theory. The model in this chapter suggests that, in equilibrium, entrepreneurs with business credit have higher success rates and greater revenues than other firms. This is consistent with the empirical evidence. The model also shows that the decision to use debt at the firm's start-up matters for the critical subsequent firm outcomes of survival and growth.

A start-up's first three years in operation are critical to its survival and performance. A better understanding of what types of firms use credit can help policymakers take action to increase the availability of credit to start-up firms, which will potentially lead to the creation of more jobs and faster economic growth. According to the model in this chapter, firms that use outside debt have a better survival potential and more growth opportunities. Also, firms that use internal debt overinvest. So creating more organizations interested in providing loans for start-up firms will

$D/(\beta - \alpha)$. But the continuation of this line after the disconnection lies below $p_j = 0$. So in the area above this line entrepreneurs prefer ID to IE.

[14] Cole and Sokolyk (2014).

reduce the extent of the asymmetric information between entrepreneurs and lenders and potentially reduce distortions in the market for start-up financing (we discussed an example at the beginning of the chapter). Secondly, the government can increase taxes on firms using internal debt. This will reduce overinvestment in this group. This can be a part of a tax reform proposal.

Another takeaway is that good-quality firms prefer debt to internal funds. This is opposite to public companies. The pecking-order theory predicts that firms will prefer internal funds to avoid any asymmetric information problems. This order is different for small firms where collateral, including entrepreneurs' own wealth, plays an important role. These firms are often created with unlimited liability. Using outside debt sends a strong message about a firm's quality.

Several strands of the existing literature discuss related problems. One is the literature on debt financing of privately held firms (see, e.g., Ang [1992], Berger and Udell [1998], Cole [2013], Brav [2009], Ang et al. [2010], Robb and Robinson [2012], Cole [2013]). Secondly, the growing literature that analyzes start-up firms using data from the Kauffman Firm Surveys (see, e.g., Coleman and Robb [2009], Fairlie and Robb [2009], Cole [2011], Coleman and Robb [2012], Robb and Watson [2012], and Robb and Robinson [2012]). Thirdly, capital structure choice literature that is based on asymmetric information (see, e.g., mentioned in Chapter 3, Myers & Majluff [1984]; also DeMeza & Webb [1987] and Boadway & Keen [2005]). Finally, the literature that analyzes the role of unlimited liability in entrepreneurs' decision-making (see, e.g., Becker & Fuest [2007], Miglo [2007]).

Stiglitz and Weiss (1981) and de Meza and Webb (1987) focus on debt financing under asymmetric information. They predict that when intermediaries are unable to distinguish between high- and low-quality new investment projects, they will make an inefficient volume of loans. This may create the possibility of welfare-improving interventions even by a government that is no better informed than the intermediaries themselves. Boadway and Keen (2005) argue that the assumptions are too restrictive in both of those papers (in terms of revenue distributions) which on one hand leads to opposite predictions (too many loans vs. too few loans) and secondly, does not help understand the capital structure choice. Internal funds are not a part of their models. They also lack other features of financing related to small businesses.

There is also literature on the difference between firms with limited liability and unlimited liability. To the best of our knowledge, there is no paper that predicts that either type has a natural advantage in terms of signaling the firm's quality or survival opportunities. Some papers address the issues close to ours. For example, Becker and Fuest (2007) and Miglo (2007) use the asymmetric information framework to explain the link between the limited liability/unlimited liability choice and corporate taxation in situations when entrepreneurs can offset potential losses and when asymmetric information exists regarding projects' qualities.

Cole (2010) looks at data from the 1993, 1998, and 2003 SSBFs to provide evidence about the types of firms that use the different types of credit: trade credit, bank credit, both, or no credit. Only about one in five firms use no credit and finance assets with 100% equity. Robb and Robinson (2012) use data from the Kauffman Firm Surveys to document that newly founded firms rely heavily on formal debt financing rather than on informal funding from friends and family. They document that, contrary to the widely held view about entrepreneurial finance, the largest part of total financial capital comes from outsiders' debt. Cole and Sokolyk (2014) confirm the importance of outside (formal) debt for small companies. Robb and Robinson (2012) also find that firms that use outside debt have better growth and have better chances of survival compared to firms that do not.

Nanda and Phillips (2023) use data from the US Survey of Business Owners and the UK's SME Finance Monitor, and find that about half of small firms do not report any external financing used. Among those that do, bank and credit card-based borrowing account for the largest share of external financing.

Questions and Exercises

1. According to the life cycle theory of capital structure which of the following companies will have a higher debt/equity ratio (all other things remain similar):

   a. start-up firm
   b. mature firm

2. Convertible preferred equity usually gives its holder the right to convert it into a discount bond.

3. Consider a firm that has to make an investment $b = 1/4$. The firm's owner/entrepreneur (E) needs external financing from an outside investor (I). In exchange for the investment I expects to receive 1/4 in period 1 and 3/8 (net of effort cost) in period 2. E and I are risk-neutral. If the investment is made, the firm generates earnings R_1 in period 1 and R_2 in period 2. R_1 depend on E's effort $e \in [0, 1]$. R_1 can have 3 values (all with equal probabilities): 0, $2e$ and $4e$. The cost of effort is $2e^2$. R_2 depends on E's effort $e_1 \in [0,1]$ and I's effort $e_2 \in [0, 1]$. R_2 can also have 3 values (all with equal probabilities): 0, e_1+e_2 and $2(e_1+e_2)$. It implies $ER_2 = e_1+e_2$. The cost of efforts is $e_i^2, i = 1, 2$. Suppose that the investor's claim in each period can have either a form of debt or equity. Show that the outcome exists when the investor holds debt in period 1 and equity in period 2.

   a. Find the first-best in Period 1.
   b. Find optimal contract in the case of equity financing in Period 1.
   c. Now consider debt financing. Same question.
   d. Compare debt and equity financing.
   e–h. Repeat questions a–d for Period 2.
   i. Provide an interpretation of your results.

4. Consider a set of entrepreneurs, indexed by j, with investment projects available. Projects require the same amount of external financing equal to 1. In the case of success a project generates a cash flow F_j and a cash flow of zero otherwise. The probability of success is p_j. There are three types of financing available for the project. A full financing for the project can be obtained with an outside debt (OD). It is assumed that each entrepreneur has collateral, equal to 0.3. Alternatively, the entrepreneur can use an inside debt (ID). Here, an entrepreneur borrows an amount 0.5 from a friend or relative. If the project succeeds, the earnings are βF_j. Finally, the entrepreneur can use inside equity (IE). An entrepreneur has an amount 0.3 available for financing the firm. If the project succeeds, the earnings are $0.3F_j$. F_j and p_j are the private information of each entrepreneur. Entrepreneurs and investors are risk-neutral.

   a. Find equations describing equilibrium. Show them graphically.
   b. On the graph, show the areas of underinvestment and overinvestment. How can tax policy help to mitigate these problems?

References

Abdulsaleh, A., & Worthington, A. (2013). Small and Medium-Sized Enterprises Financing: A Review of Literature. *International Journal of Business and Management, 8*(14), 36–54.

Ang, J. (1992). On the Theory of Finance for Privately Held Firms. *Journal of Small Business Finance, 1*, 185–203.

Ang, J., Cole, R., & Lawson, J. (2010). The Role of Owner in Capital Structure Decisions: An Analysis of Single-Owner Corporations. *Journal of Entrepreneurial Finance, 14*, 1–36.

Becker, J., & Fuest, C. (2007). Why is There Corporate Taxation? The Role of Limited Liability Revisited. *Journal of Economics, 92*, 1–10.

Boadway, R., & Keen, M. (2005). Financing and Taxing New Firms under Asymmetric Information. Queen's University working paper.

Berger, A., & Udell, G. (1998). The Economics of Small Business Finance: The Roles of Private Equity and Debt Markets in the Financial Growth Cycle. *Journal of Banking and Finance, 22*, 613–673.

Berglof, E. (1994). A Control Theory of Venture Capital. *Journal of Law, Economics and Organizations, 10*(2), 247–267.

de Bettignies, J., & Brander, J. (2007). Financing Entrepreneurship: Bank Finance versus Venture Capital. *Journal of Business Venturing, 22*(6), 808–832.

Brav, O. (2009). Access to Capital, Capital Structure, and the Funding of the Firm. *The Journal of Finance, 64*, 263–308.

Chemmanur, T., & Chen, Z. (2014). Venture Capitalists versus Angels: The Dynamics of Private Firm Financing Contracts. *Review of Corporate Finance Studies, 3*, 39–86.

Cole, R. (2010). Bank credit, trade credit or no credit? Evidence from the Surveys of Small Business Finances, U.S. Small Business Administration Research Study No. 365.

Cole, R. (2011). How do firms choose legal form of organization? U.S. Small Business Administration Research Study No. 383.

Cole, R. (2013). What Do We Know About the Capital Structure of Privately Held Firms? Evidence from the Surveys of Small Business Finances. *Financial Management* (Winter), 777–813.

Cole, R., & Sokolyk, T. (2014). Debt Financing, Survival, and Growth of Start-Up Firms. EFM Conference.

Coleman, S., & Robb, A. (2009). A Comparison of New Firm Financing by Gender: Evidence from the Kauffman Firm Survey Data. *Small Business Economics, 33*, 397–411.

Coleman, S., & Robb, A. (2012). Capital Structure Theory and New Technology Firms: Is There a Match? *Management Research Review, 35*(2), 106–120.

Cornelli, F., & Yosha, O. (2003). Stage Financing and the Role of Convertible Securities. *Review of Economic Studies, 70*(242), 1–32.

Cumming, D. (2005). Capital Structure in Venture Finance. *Journal of Corporate Finance, 11*(3), 550–585.

Damodaran, A. (2003). *Corporate Finance: Theory and Practice*. Wiley Series in Finance.

DeHan, C. P. (2014). Capital Structure over the Life Cycle. *Advances in Business Research, 5*, 16–32.

Demitt, J. (2015, December). Textio Raises $8M as Major Tech Companies Use its Tools to Attract More Diverse Job Applicants. *GeekWire*. http://www.geekwire.com/2015/textio-raises-8m-as-most-major-tech-companies-try-its-tools-to-attract-more-diverse-job-applicants/

DeMeza, D., & Webb, D. (1987). Two Much Investment: A Problem of Asymmetric Information. *Quarterly Journal of Economics, 102*, 281–92.

Elfenbein, D., & Lerner, J. (2003). Ownership and Control Rights in Internet Portal Alliances, 1995–1999. *RAND Journal of Economics, 34*(2), 356–369.

Fairlie, R., & Robb, A. (2009). Gender Differences in Business Performance: Evidence from the Characteristics of Business Owners Survey. *Small Business Economics, 33*, 375–395.

Freixas, X., & Rochet, J. (1999). *Microeconomics of Banking*. MIT Press.

Gilson, S. (1990). Bankruptcy, Boards, Banks and Blockholders: Evidence on Changes in Corporate Ownership and Control when Firms Default. *Journal of Financial Economics, 27*, 355–387.

Gompers, P. (1998). An Examination of Convertible Securities in Venture Capital Investments. Harvard Business School.

Häussler, C., Harhoff, D., & Mueller, E. (2014). How Patenting Informs VC Investors–The Case of Biotechnology. *Research Policy, 43*(8), 1286–1298.

Hellmann, T. (2006). Ipo's, Acquisitions and the Use of Convertible Securities in Venture Capital. *Journal of Financial Economics, 81*, 649–67.

Hellmann, T., & Thiele, V. (2014). Friends or Foes? The Interrelationship Between Angel and Venture Capital Markets. *Journal of Financial Economics, 115*, 639–653.

Kalay, A., & Zender, J. (1997). Bankruptcy, Warrants, and State Contingent Changes in the Ownership of Control. *Journal of Financial Intermediation, 6*(4), 347–379.

Kaplan, S., Stromberg, P., & P. (2003). Financial Contracting Theory Meets the Real World: An Empirical Analysis of Venture Capital Contracts. *The Review of Economic Studies, 70*(243), 281–316.

Kumar, S., Sureka, R., & Colombage, S. (2020). Capital Structure of SMEs: A Systematic Literature Review and Bibliometric Analysis. *Management Review Quarterly, 70*, 535–565.

Miglo, A. (2007). A Note on Corporate Taxation, Limited Liability and Asymmetric Information. *Journal of Economics, 92*, 11–19.

Miglo, A. (2022a). Theories of Financing for Entrepreneurial Firms: A Review. *International Review of Entrepreneurship, 20*(2), 301–330.

Miglo, A. (2022b). Theories of Crowdfunding and Token Issues: A Review. *Journal of Risk and Financial Management, 15*(5), 218.

Moritz, A., & Block, J. (2014). Crowdfunding und Crowdinvesting: State-of-the-Art der wissenschaftlichen Literatur, *Zeitschrift für KMU und Entrepreneurship, 62*(1), 57–89. http://ssrn.com/abstract=2274141

Myers, S., & Majluf, N. (1984). Corporate Financing and Investment Decisions When Firms Have Information That Investors Do Not Have. *Journal of Financial Economics, 13*, 187–221.

Nanda, R., & Phillips, G. (2023). Small Firm Financing: Sources, Frictions, and Policy Implications. In B. E. Eckbo, G. Phillips, M. Sorensen (Eds.), *Handbook of the Economics of Corporate Finance, 1*(1), 107–135. North-Holland.

Robb, A. M., & Robinson, D. T. (2012). The Capital Structure Decisions of New Firms. *The Review of Financial Studies, 1*(1), 1–27.

Robb, A. M., & Watson, J. (2012). Gender Differences in Firm Performance: Evidence from New Ventures in the United States. *Journal of Business Venturing, 27*(5), 544–558.

Schwienbacher, A., & Larralde, B. (2012). Alternative Types of Entrepreneurial Finance. In Douglas Cumming (Ed.), *The Oxford Handbook of Entrepreneurial Finance*. Oxford University Press.

Shmidt, K. (2003). Convertible Securities and Venture Capital Finance. *Journal of Finance, 58*(3), 1139–1166.

Stiglitz, J., & Weiss, A. (1981). Credit Rationing in Markets with Imperfect Information. *American Economic Review, 71*, 393–410.

Talmor, E., & Cuny, C. (2005). The Staging of Venture Capital Financing: Milestone vs. Rounds, EFA 2005 Moscow Meetings Paper. http://ssrn.com/abstract=487414

Tian, X. (2011). The Causes and Consequences of Venture Capital Stage Financing. *Journal of Financial Economics, 101*(1), 132–159.

Winton, A., & Yerramilli, V. (2008). Entrepreneurial Finance: Banks versus Venture Capital. *Journal of Financial Economics, 88*(1), 51–79.

CHAPTER 10

Corporate Capital Structure vs. Project Financing

10.1 Introduction

This chapter discusses project finance. From my experience, when speaking about project finance people think about different things. Often they are confused because they don't understand why project finance should be discussed as a separate topic since it is, seemingly, a part of almost every other topic including general topics like investments, net present value, etc. We will learn in this chapter that project financing has a very special meaning in finance and is often related to terms like non-recourse debt, limited-recourse debt, asset-backed securities, and many others. To begin, let us note that project financing has been used in many important projects around the globe including many historical projects. Below we will review some of them.

Lyonett du Moutier (2010) describes the famous Parisian Eiffel Tower construction, which was the world's tallest structure at its completion in 1889. Apparently, a project finance model was used. Public authorities awarded a concession to the project's private sponsor. The sponsor was financing it with equity and limited-recourse debt. Lyonett (2010)

Supplementary Information The online version contains supplementary material available at https://doi.org/10.1007/978-3-031-85459-0_10.

A. Miglo, *Capital Structure in the Modern World*,
https://doi.org/10.1007/978-3-031-85459-0_10

analyzes how specific provisions in the Eiffel Tower project contracts helped reduce agency costs, which are often very substantial in large projects.

The World Bank's Project finance and guarantees group describes on its website (2005) the development of the Nam Theun 2 hydropower project.[1] Since 1995, it has been a top priority for the Government of Laos. Electricité de France of France, Italian-Thai Development Public Company Limited of Thailand, and Electricity Generating Public Company Limited of Thailand sponsored the project. It is the largest ever foreign investment in Laos, the world's largest private sector cross-border power project financing, the largest private sector hydroelectric project financing and one of the largest internationally financed projects in Asia. The project has been structured as a limited-recourse financing which, the article argues, allows for an efficient allocation of multiple risks that are usually involved in large construction projects including completion risk, commercial and political risks, geological risk and risk for timely and within budget completion of the hydro facility with large amounts of associated liabilities.

In a December 2015 article by **Matthew Amlôt** we learned that the National Central Cooling Company PJSC (Tabreed) announced its completion of the signing of an AED 192.5 million long-term limited-recourse project finance facility with Emirates NBD for the district cooling plant it is developing for Dubai Parks and Resorts.[2] Jasim Husain Thabet, Tabreed's Chief Executive Officer, said, "Tabreed's approach to financing new projects is to utilize long term project financing wherever possible which we believe is the best way of financing our assets and maximizing value for all stakeholders. This loan facility with Emirates NBD is a landmark deal as it is amongst the first district cooling transactions completed in the UAE under a limited recourse project finance structure for a Greenfield development."

In 2004, project financing in the United States made up 10 to 15% of total capital investment.[3] In 2007 the total volume of project financing reached 44,476.30 bln. (Gardner & Wright, 2012). According to Corielli,

[1] http://siteresources.worldbank.org/INTGUARANTEES/Resources/Lao_NamTheun2_Note.pdf.

[2] Amlôt (2015, December 16).

[3] Esty (2004).

Gatti, and Steffanoni (2010), the compound annual growth rates across all global markets from 1994 to 2006 were 23% for project finance bank loans and 15% for project finance bond issuances. Such outstanding growing trend is also found by other authors (Kleimeier & Versteeg, 2010). With a rapid growth, project finance became one of the most important sources of finance in the financial market. Even the global financial crisis of 2008 has had a less harmful effect on the market of project finance transactions than on the market of syndicated loans as a whole. To be precise, the global lending volume of syndicated loans decreased by 44% compared to 2007. At the same time, the amount of project finance transactions declined by only 10% and is still signaling promising growth trends (Bonetti et al., 2010).

While project financing has a long history dating back to Roman colonies, the 1980s saw the emergence of project financing as a popular capital structure choice. More recently, it has become a global phenomenon spreading not only to developed countries but to undeveloped countries as well. In 1985, project financing was used in approximately 80 countries. In 2003, this number increased by 75% to 140 countries.[4] According to Standard & Poor's expectations presented at the 20th Annual Project Finance Hot Topics Conference (November 1, 2011), the following 20 years should present a 5 tremendous change in the composition of project finance deals from western countries to transactions located in emerging markets. Among the main reasons for those allocations are increasing privatization processes and the urge for enormous investments into infrastructure development in low-income countries.

Generally speaking, project financing is the financing of a project by a sponsoring firm, where the cash flows of the specific project are designated as the source of funds to repay the loan. The project is incorporated as a separate legal entity, and the assets and cash flows are segregated from those of the sponsoring firm. The firm repays this new entity's debt obligations solely from the cash flow generated by the operation of the project.

In this sense, the debt of a project-financed venture is known as "non-recourse" debt because the creditors have no recourse to the assets of the parent company. If, on the other hand, a firm jointly incorporates the new

[4] Hainz and Kleimeier (2012).

project and issues standard corporate debt to raise the initial investment cost, the lenders will usually have first recourse to any assets generated by the entire company. These are not necessarily attributable to the returns on the new project itself. Non-recourse debt allows the firm's managers to "protect" the remaining assets of the firm because the lender is only entitled to the assets of the project-financed company.

The theories discussed in this chapter differ in their explanation of the use of project financing. They look to agency costs, asymmetric information, or corporate control considerations as the primary reasons to use project financing. The models that focus on agency costs look primarily at how separating the debt claims of old and new creditors leaves shareholders' payoffs unaltered and thus reduces the agency costs of underinvestment or overinvestment. The models that look at asymmetric information look primarily at the lack of information for investors and how project financing may signal information to investors and mitigate the misevaluation of securities issued by the firm.

Existing empirical literature has discovered the following stylized facts (Esty, 2003; Kleimeier & Megginson, 2001): (i) project companies are characterized by high capital expenditures, long loan periods, and uncertain revenue streams; (ii) project companies use very high leverage compared to corporate financed companies; (iii) project companies have very concentrated debt and equity ownership with debt being non-recourse to the sponsoring companies; (iv) project finance requires finance executives to disclose more propriety information than they would have to disclose under corporate finance; (v) structuring a project finance company legally, rather than financing the project as part of the corporate balance sheet, is more expensive and takes much more time.[5]

10.2 Moral Hazard Models

The central concept around which most discussions on the optimality of project financing have been developed is the underinvestment problem. As Myers (1977) argues, it can arise because of, for instance, a debt overhang (see Chapter 5). Theoretical papers that will be discussed in this section show that project financing can both solve underinvestment problems and prevent them from arising.

[5] For a review of project finance related literature see, e.g., Kumar, Srivastava, and Tabash (2021).

Berkovitch and Kim (1990) look at moral hazard problems and examine how project financing works to effectively overcome the under-investment incentives of entrepreneurs. They develop a theoretical model with the primary goal of investigating the effects of seniority rules and restrictive covenants on the incentives associated with risky debt.

Berkovitch and Kim's model is set up as a two-period model. An investment project is undertaken in the first period by issuing debt. A firm's managers will decide whether to accept or reject the new project in the second period. Berkovitch and Kim show the presence of under-investment incentives by examining the effect that the new project will have on the market value of the old debt. When cash flows from a new project accrue to existing creditors, as opposed to shareholders, the market value of the old debt increases. This causes the shareholders to reject the project. By using project financing, the firm separates the new investment from its current assets, as well as the current debt obligations, and removes the underinvestment problem because old creditors do not accrue any benefits and there are no wealth transfers.

The following illustrates Berkovitch and Kim's main insights into project financing. There are two dates ($t = 0, 1$). The interest rate is equal to 0. Suppose a firm owns the following project (project-in-place). At $t = 1$, cash flow from the project depends on the state of nature. In the good state G (that occurs with probability p_1) it equals $R_1 > 0$. In state B (bad state) it equals R_2, $R_1 > R_2$. At $t = 0$, the firm is given the opportunity to make an investment$K$, which generates $C_1 > 0$ in state G and C_2 in state B, $C_1 > C_2$. This investment has a positive NPV, i.e.,

$$p_1 C_1 + (1 - p_1) C_2 - K > 0 \tag{10.1}$$

The firm issued senior debt with total amount D such that

$$R_1 + C_1 > D > R_2 + C_2 \tag{10.2}$$

This means that in the good state the project's payoff exceeds the amount of debt but not in the bad state. The sequence of events is as follows (Fig. 10.1).

Proposition 10.1 *The usage of project financing (non-recourse debt) can solve a debt overhang problem.*

Without the new project the shareholders' expected profit is

$$p_1 (R_1 - D) \tag{10.3}$$

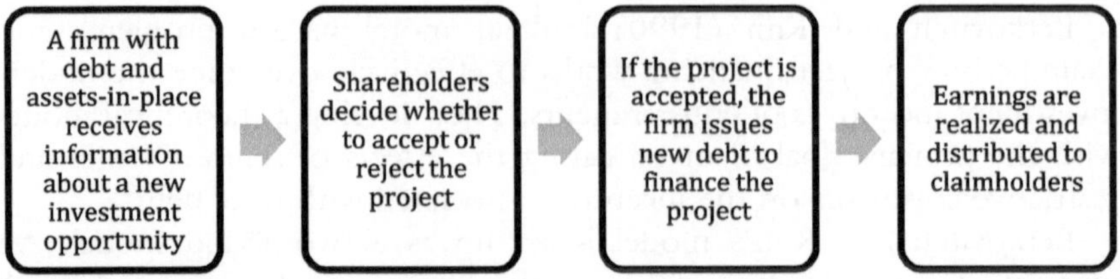

Fig. 10.1 Sequence of events

If the firm invests in the new project, the shareholders' expected profit is: $p_1(R_1 + C_1 - D) - K$. This is equal to the firm's expected cash flow (the total earnings in state G reduced by the payment to the senior creditors multiplied by the probability of success) minus the payment to the new outside investors. Whether the financing of the new project is done using junior debt or equity, the expected payment to the investors should be equal to the cost of the investment. Comparing the shareholders' payoff without the investment and with the investment we find that the firm will invest if $p_1C_1 - K > 0$.

If $p_1C_1 - K < 0$ the new project (even though it has a positive NPV) will not be undertaken. This is similar to the debt overhang problem because the presence of existing risky claims reduces the incentive for existing shareholders to invest in that project because it increases the value of the existing debt and not the value of shares, which is the essence of the debt overhang problem.

Now suppose that the firm uses project financing (non-recourse debt). In this case, the debtholders' payoffs depend only on the returns from the new project and not on the returns from the assets already in place. The face value d can be found from:

$$K = dp_1 + (1 - p_1)C_2 \tag{10.4}$$

If B is realized, the debtholders get the cash flow from the new project (C_2). The shareholders' expected payoff is (note that the shareholders get nothing if B is realized): $p_1(C_1 - d + R_1 - D)$. This is greater than (10.3) because it follows from (10.1) and (10.4) that $d < C_1$. Hence, the shareholders' payoff with the new project is higher than it is without it. So the project will be undertaken and it will be financed with non-recourse debt.

The second situation is based on overinvestment: the shareholder's incentive to invest in negative NPV projects (similar to the asset substitution effect from Chapter 4). Consider the same firm with assets-in-place, as described previously. This time, assume that the firm has a senior debt with a face value

$$D > R_1 \tag{10.5}$$

The new project reduces the probability of G occurring by Δp. Also assume that $C_2 = 0$ and

$$\Delta p R_2 - \Delta p R_1 + (p_1 - \Delta p)C_1 < K \tag{10.6}$$

This implies that the change in the firm's expected earnings (left side of this inequality) is less than the amount of the investment, which means that the new project has a negative NPV.

Proposition 10.2 *The usage of project financing can solve overinvestment problems.*

Suppose that to finance the new project the firm issues a standard subordinated debt. Assuming risk neutrality and a risk-free interest rate of zero, the face value, $d\prime$, of this debt can be found from the following equation: $K = d\prime(p_1 - \Delta p) + (1 - p_1 + \Delta p)(0)$. This means that if G is realized, the new debtholders will receive the face value of the debt; if, however, B is realized, the firm's cash flow will be $R_2 + C_2$, which (as follows from (10.4)) is less than the face value of the senior debt D, leaving the new creditors with nothing.

The shareholders' expected payoff without the new investment is 0. They get nothing even in state G as follows from (10.5). With the new project, it will be $(p_1 - \Delta p)(R_1 + C_1 - D - d\prime)$. In some cases it is positive (see an example below) so, the project can be undertaken even when its NPV is negative.

Now suppose that the firm uses project financing. In this case, the debtholders' payoffs depend only on the returns from the new project and not on the returns from the assets already in place. Since the NPV is negative, the firm will not be able to finance the project.

To summarize our analysis of these two cases. Without the ability to issue non-recourse debt the firm is not able to solve the debt overhang problem. Secondly, by issuing subordinated debt the firm will be able to invest in projects with negative NPVs at the expense of the firm's overall value. Setting a new project as a new independent project and issuing non-recourse debt will eliminate the incentive to invest in projects with negative NPVs. Project financing, or financing with non-recourse, can also help other agency problems related to debt financing. It will also help to solve free cash flow problems or empire-building problems (Chapter 8). This is especially important for large projects with potentially large amounts of cash. It can also help increase managerial incentives (Chapter 8) compared to only equity financing.

Example 10.1 Consider a firm with assets-in-place, an investment opportunity available, and outstanding senior debt with a face value of $D = 5000$. Existing assets can produce: 8000 in state G (good state) with probability 1/2 and 3000 in state B with probability 1/2. The new project requires an initial investment of 1500, and the firm will finance this investment by issuing new debt. A new project's cost is 1500. The new project generates 2200 in state G and 1000 in state B.

First note that the new project has a positive net present value (NPV) because $1/2 * 1000 + 1/2 * 2200 > 1500$. Now suppose that to finance the new project the firm issues a standard subordinated debt. The face value, $d\prime$, of this debt can be found from the following equation:

$$1500 = d\prime * 1/2 + 1/2 * 0$$

Therefore $d\prime = 3000$. The shareholders' expected payoff without the new investment is $1/2*(8000 - D) = 1500$. With the new project, it will be $1/2(8000 + 2200 - D - d\prime) = 1100$. Since the expected payoff without the new project is more than that with the project, it will not be undertaken.

Now suppose that the firm uses project financing (non-recourse debt). The face value d can be found from:

$$1500 = d * 1/2 + 1/2 * 1000$$

Here $d = 2000$. The shareholders' expected payoff is (note that the shareholders get nothing if B is realized): $1/2 * (8000 - D + 2200 - d) = 1600$. This is greater than 1500 (the shareholders' expected payoff without the new investment), and thus the project will be undertaken and it will be financed with non-recourse debt.

Now assume that the firm (with the same initial project) has a senior debt with a face value of $D = 10000$. The new project requires an initial investment of 100. The new project generates 4000 in state G and 0 in state B and it also reduces the probability of G occurring by 30%. Note that the new project has a negative net present value (NPV) because $0.3 * 3{,}000 - 0.3 * 8000 + 0.2 * 4000 < 100$ (see condition (10.6)).

Suppose that to finance the new project the firm issues a standard subordinated debt. The face value, $d\prime$, of this debt can be found from the following equation:

$$100 = d\prime * 0.2 + 0.8 * 0 \tag{10.7}$$

This means that if G is realized, the new debtholders will receive the face value of the debt; if, however, B is realized, the firm's cash flow is $3000 + 1000 = 4000$, which is less than the face value of the senior debt, leaving the new creditors with nothing. From (10.7), $d\prime = 500$.

The shareholders' expected payoff without the new investment is 0. With the new project, it will be $0.2 * (12000 - 10000 - 500) = 300$. Since the expected payoff with the new project is more than that without the project, it will be undertaken.

Now suppose that the firm uses project financing (non-recourse debt). In this case, the debtholders' payoffs depend only on the returns from the new project and not on the returns from the assets already in place. Since the NPV is negative, the firm will not be able to finance the project.

John and John (1991) analyze project financing in the context of the underinvestment problem in the spirit of Myers (1977). They also introduce taxes into consideration. It is shown that a project financing arrangement, where the debt is optimally allocated to the sponsor firm and the new venture, increases the project's value by reducing agency costs and increasing the value of the tax shields (compared to the case of straight debt financing).

There are several ect financing in capital structure and how it has worked to mitigate the moral hazard problem.

For instance, Kensinger and Martin (1988) noted that because of the number of large capital expenditures that businesses are making, moral hazard dilemmas are of paramount concern. Project financing helps reduce agency costs, particularly by reducing underinvestment incentives. Kensinger and Martin (1988) also noted that project finance could play a role in a company's restructuring because it pushes companies toward greater specialization and decentralization. Similarly, project finance has the power to act as a catalyst for a change in the governance of business activities because it allows companies to segregate cash flows from newly adopted projects; this protects both the sponsoring firm and the managers from defaulting on it.

Esty (2003) observes that in the United States, the majority of project-financed ventures can be seen in the natural resource and infrastructural development sectors. Project financing is being used to fund power plants, toll roads, mines, pipelines, telecommunications systems, and developments in the oil and gas sectors. These large investment projects with tangible assets are very susceptible to agency conflicts because of the number of people who are involved. Project companies help deter opportunistic behavior.

Brealey, Cooper, and Habib (1996) also credit the growing importance of project financing in infrastructure to its ability to mitigate some agency problems. With any new investment, contractual and financing arrangements, which project financing can offer, are very important; their importance is magnified in infrastructure projects because of their scope, duration, and implications for so many people.

Hainz and Kleimeier (2006) develop a double moral hazard (an effort by a bank and an effort by a firm) model in which the bank's incentive to mitigate risk is highest with a non-recourse project finance loan, while full-recourse loans are best for the firm. It is suggested that the use of project finance increases with both the political risk of the country in which the project is located and the lender's influence over this political risk exposure. Furthermore, the use of project finance should decrease as the economic health and corporate governance provisions of the borrower's home country improve.

10.3 Asymmetric Information Models

This section demonstrates that project financing can help solve asymmetric information problems in finance. As Chapter 3 argued, asymmetric information between a firm's insiders and outsiders can create several problems for the firm. Good-quality firms may not be able to efficiently signal the quality of their projects and thus their stocks may become undervalued. Also, asymmetric information problems are maybe the reason that firms refuse to invest in projects with positive NPVs.

We first demonstrate that project financing can help high-quality firms signal their quality. Brennan and Kraus (1987) show that an efficient separating equilibrium in a financing game, where firms have private information about their future cash flows, is impossible if cash flows are ordered by the first-order dominance condition. Therefore under every type of equilibria, issuing securities will be costly.

To illustrate the Brennan and Kraus (1987) idea, consider a company that has two projects available, $k = 1, 2$. The cost of project k is b_k. The return of project k is R_{jk}, where j is the firm's type j, $j = h, l$. R_{jk} equals 1 with probability θ_{jk} and equals 0 otherwise.[6] $R_h = R_{h1} + R_{h2}$ first-order dominates R_l, which means that the probability that $R_h = 0$ is less than the probability of $R_l = 0$ and that the probability that the probability that R_h equals 0 or 1 is less than that of R_l. It implies:

$$\theta_{h1}\theta_{h2} > \theta_{l1}\theta_{l2} \tag{10.8}$$

$$(1-\theta_{h1})(1-\theta_{h2}) < (1-\theta_{l1})(1-\theta_{l2}) \tag{10.9}$$

Suppose that the firm can only issue securities contingent on the firm total earnings $R = R_1 + R_2$. So a security is a contract $s_j(R)$, i.e., when the firm's earnings are R, the security holder will get $s_j(R)$, $s_j(R) \geq 0$. Further assume that $s_j(R)$ is non-decreasing:

$$s_j(0) = 0$$

$$s_j(2) = s_j(1) + \varepsilon_j, \varepsilon_j \geq 0 \tag{10.10}$$

(the first condition follows from the entrepreneur's limited liability).

The timing of events in this situation is as follows (Fig. 10.2).

An efficient signaling equilibrium is when every type of firm receives its first-best value in equilibrium and no firm has any incentive to deviate from its equilibrium strategy or mimic another type.

Brennan and Kraus (1987, p. 1227) assume that a firm's cash flow is indivisible. Below we show that when cash flow is divided into two parts (two projects) and firms are allowed to issue securities with the projects' contingent payoffs rather than only with total cash flows contingent payoffs, a separation may exist even if the firm's total cash flows are ordered by the first-order dominance condition. Possible interpretations

[6] Next chapter deals with security design problem so a more general assumption will be considered.

Fig. 10.2 Sequence of events

are project financing or financing with non-recourse debt, issuing asset-backed securities and firms' spin-offs. In all of these cases the firm creates securities that represent claims on specific projects (assets).

Proposition 10.3 *If the firm can only use corporate financing an efficient signaling equilibrium does not exist; if the firm uses project financing, a signaling equilibrium can exist.*

Proof The proof of the first part is based on Brennan and Kraus (1987) (see problem 5 at the end of this chapter). Consider the second part. Assume that the firm can use project financing. The contracts are as follows: the creditors of Project k get d_k if Project k is successful and 0 otherwise.

The investor budget constraint for type j and Project k is: $d_{jk}\theta_{kj} = b_k$. Hence,

$$d_{jk} = b_k/\theta_{kj} \tag{10.11}$$

The non-deviation condition for l (i.e., the condition for which type l will choose not to mimic type h) can be written as

$$(1 - d_{h1})\theta_{l1} + (1 - d_{h2})\theta_{l2} \leq (1 - d_{l1})\theta_{l1} + (1 - d_{l2})\theta_{l2}$$

Taking into account (10.11) it becomes:

$$(1 - b_1/\theta_{1h})\theta_{l1} + (1 - b_2/\theta_{2h})\theta_{l2} \leq (1 - b_1/\theta_{1l})\theta_{l1} + (1 - b_2/\theta_{2l})\theta_{l2}$$

After simplifications we get:

$$b_1(1 - \frac{\theta_{l1}}{\theta_{h1}}) \leq b_2(1 - \frac{\theta_{l2}}{\theta_{h2}}) \tag{10.12}$$

If this condition is satisfied, a separating equilibrium may exist where the high profitable type signals its quality by using project financing.

Obviously if $\theta_{h1} > \theta_{l1}$ and $\theta_{l2} < \theta_{h2}$, condition (10.12) fails. However, if $\theta_{h1} > \theta_{l1}$ and $\theta_{l2} > \theta_{h2}$ or $\theta_{h1} < \theta_{l1}$ and $\theta_{l2} < \theta_{h2}$, it may work. Note that the latter does not necessarily contradict (10.8) and (10.9).

Example 10.2 Suppose that $\theta_{h1} = 0.7$, $\theta_{h2} = 0.3$, $\theta_{l1} = 0.2$ and $\theta_{l2} = 0.6$ and $b_1 = b_1 = 0.2$. One can check that R_h first-order dominates R_l because conditions (10.8) and (10.9) hold. From (10.10): $d_{h1} = 2/7$, $d_{h2} = 2/3$, $d_{l1} = 1$ and $d_{l2} = 1/3$. The non-deviation condition for l (i.e., the condition for which type l will choose not to mimic type h) can be written as

$$(1 - 2/7) * 0.2 + (1 - 2/3) * 0.6 \leq (1 - 1) * 0.2 + (1 - 1/3) * 0.6$$

After simplifications we get $5/35 \leq 6/30$ which holds.

In fact, condition (10.12) suggests a large variety of possible strategies for type h to signal its type when it performs better than l in only one project. See Miglo (2010) for more anlaysis.

Many consider Myers and Majluf (1984) to have pioneered asymmetric information models. According to Myers and Majluf (1984), underinvestment occurs because of asymmetric information about the value of assets-in-place and the consideration of the investment project. When insiders know more about the true value of a firm than outside investors, potential creditors must rely on market signals to assess a firm's value. Therefore, if investors know less than insiders about the true value of the firm's assets-in-place, equity may be mispriced.

In their model, Myers and Majluf (1984) show how outside investors will value a firm's shares as the average of two (or more) possible values. There is a return distribution for these shares that is common knowledge to all potential investors. Because of this averaging, "bad" firms will have overpriced shares and "good" firms will have underpriced shares. Therefore, in equilibrium, only bad firms will choose to issue equity. Creditors are assumed to be rational players and realize this. Asymmetric information, in this instance, has a negative implication for the good type of firm because they will prefer to not invest in positive net present value projects than be subject to the underpricing of their shares.

We now proceed with a quick example of their model (see Chapter 3 for more details). Suppose there are two firms with an investment opportunity available. The project costs \$60 and will bring earnings of \$70. The value of their assets-in-place is initially either \$150 or \$40. Management will know the true state of the firm, but the outside market will not. They will only know that there is a 50% chance of either. One can show (analogously to Chapter 3) that an equilibrium where both firms issue shares and undertake the new project does not exist. Only the low-value firm will invest because the payoff from investing is higher than from not investing. For this firm, the shares are overpriced and management will obviously choose to invest in the growth opportunity. The high-value firm, on the other hand, will choose to not invest.

Indeed suppose that an equilibrium exists where both firms issue equity to finance the new project. Let α be the fraction of equity sold to the new investor. The new investor's expected earnings should cover the investment cost: $\alpha * (70 + 0.5 * (40 + 150)) = 60$. It implies that $\alpha = 12/31$. The earnings of the high-value firm shareholders then equal: $(1 - \alpha) * (70 + 150) = 134\frac{26}{31}$. Since it is smaller than 150, the shareholders will not be interested in issuing shares for the new project.

This exemplifies the adverse selection problem. Because of asymmetric information, firms with higher values will pass on positive return projects. The result holds if, instead of issuing equity, firms were allowed to issue standard corporate debt.

The underinvestment problem could be avoided if the firm were to have the ability to issue riskless debt (this assumption is often unrealistic). While Myers and Majluf (1984) do not actually study the implications of project financing, they do "hint" that the underinvestment problem can be resolved by a spin-off of its assets-in-place into a separately incorporated company.[7] In the example above, both types of firms may issue non-recourse debt with face value 60, which would solve the underinvestment problem. The new investor will finance the new project with non-recourse debt. The face value of debt will be 60. . Earnings from the new project (which equal 70) will cover the amount of debt. Furthermore, one can show that in some cases the same insight holds if one considers asymmetric information about the amount of earnings from the new investment and not about the value of assets-in-place as in the above example.

An interesting question is why projects that are financed with non-recourse debt often have a high degree of risk and why the amount

[7] Myers and Majluf (1984, p. 22).

of investment is usually very large. Miglo (2010) considers different scenarios where firms choose between non-recourse debt and conventional debt. To illustrate the idea, consider a model similar to the one described above (where θ_{kj} is the probability of success of project j for a type k firm) but now assume that the firm will use corporate financing (regular debt with recourse with face value D) for the first project and non-recourse debt for the second project (face value d). If the first project is successful, the investors are paid in full. If it fails and the second project succeeds, two situations are possible. If $1-D \geq d$ the investors of Project 1 are paid in full, otherwise they get $1-d$. For the second project, investors are paid in full if the second project is successful and get nothing otherwise.

The promised payment for Project 2 is $d = b_2/\theta_{h2}$. Let $P_k(x)$ be the probability that the total cash flow of firm k equals x. For example, we have $P_h(0) = (1-\theta_{h1})(1-\theta_{h2})$.

If $1 \geq \frac{b_1}{1-P_h(0)} + \frac{b_2}{\theta_{h2}}$ then $D = \frac{b_1}{1-P_h(0)}$. In this case the investors (firm h) of both projects are paid in full if the firm's earnings equal either 1 or 2 (but not 0). If l mimics h, its payoff is: $P_l(2)(2-D-d) + P_l(1)(1-D-d)$. This should not be greater than it's equilibrium value $\theta_{l1} + \theta_{l1} - b_1 - b_2$. The non-deviation constraint for l is then:

$$b_1(1 - \frac{1-P_l(0)}{1-P_h(0)}) \leq b_2(1 - \frac{\theta_{l2}}{\theta_{h2}}) \tag{10.13}$$

If we consider the case when $\theta_{h1} < \theta_{l1}$ and $\theta_{l2} < \theta_{h2}$ then condition (10.13) can be interpreted as follows. The likelihood that this condition is satisfied (and successful utilization of project finance by firm h) increases with an increase in the amount of investment in Project 2 (b_2) maintaining that b_1 is sufficiently small. Secondly, if θ_{l2} is sufficiently smaller than θ_{h2} and/or if $1-P_l(0)$ is sufficiently close to $1-P_h(0)$. This means that a separating equilibrium exists when the asymmetry regarding the firm's overall quality (probability of default in both projects) is sufficiently small while the asymmetry regarding the project, for which the firm issues project-contingent securities, is large. A similar condition can be obtained for the case $1 < \frac{b_1}{1-P_h(0)} + \frac{b_2}{\theta_{h2}}$.

Example 10.3 Suppose that $\theta_{h1} = 0.3$, $\theta_{h2} = 0.6$, $\theta_{l1} = 0.6$ and $\theta_{l2} = 0.2$ and $b_1 = 0.1$ and $b_2 = 0.4$. One can check that R_h first-order dominates R_l because conditions (10.8) and (10.9) above hold.

As follows from our previous analysis: $d = b_2/\theta_{h2}$. So $d = 2/3$. Also $D = \frac{b_1}{1-P_h(0)} = \frac{b_1}{1-(1-\theta_{h1})(1-\theta_{h2})} = 5/36$. The non-deviation condition for l (i.e., the condition for which type l will choose not to mimic type h) can be written as $(1-2/3-5/36)0.6 + (1-2/3)0.2 \leq 0.2$. After simplifications we get $11/60 \leq 0$ which holds.

One can also see that h cannot do it the other way around,i.e., use project financing for Project 1. We have:$d = b_1/\theta_{h1}$. So $d = 1/3$ and $D = \frac{b_2}{1-P_h(0)} = 5/9$. The non-deviation condition for l (i.e., the condition for which type l will choose not to mimic type$h$) can be written as$(1-1/3-5/9)*0.2+(1-2/3)*0.6 \leq 0.2$. After simplifications we get $2/9 \leq 0.2$ which does not hold.

One interpretation of these results is project financing or financing by non-recourse debt. Project financing differs from corporate financing in two ways: (1) the creditors do not have a claim to the profit from other projects if the project fails while corporate financing gives this right to the investors and; (2) it typically has priority on the cash flows from the project over any corporate claims. The case described in the beginning of Sect. 3 can thus be interpreted as financing both projects with non-recourse debt. The second case can be seen as financing Project 2 with non-recourse debt and financing Project 1 with standard corporate debt when the creditors' payoffs depend on the firm's total earnings (after the Project 2 creditors are paid) and are not attached uniquely to the earnings from Project 1).

From (10.13), the existence of a separating equilibrium is probable when the amount of investment financed by non-recourse debt is sufficiently large with regard to the corporate investment and the uncertainty regarding the performance of projects financed by non-recourse debt is greater than that of projects financed by corporate debt. Also, as follows from (10.13), the uncertainty regarding the performance of projects financed by non-recourse debt is greater than that of projects financed by corporate debt. There exists some evidence consistent with the spirit of the above predictions. Brealey et al. (1996), Esty (2003, 2004), McGuinty (1981), and Nevitt (1979) argue that non-recourse debt is typically used for financing large, capital-intensive, projects and that the leverage ratio of project companies is typically larger than that of parent companies. Also, this is consistent with the evidence that project financing is usually used for financing risky projects (see for instance: Esty, 2004;

Flybjerg et al., 2002; McGuinty, 1981; Merrow et al., 1988; Miller & Lezard, 2000; Nevitt, 1979).

Shah and Thakor (1987) analyze optimal financing in the presence of corporate taxation. In their model, projects have the same mean of return, the owners have private information about risk and investors may acquire (costly) information about the parameters of a firm's risks. If the benefits from information production are relatively big, project financing is optimal because the cost of screening a separately incorporated project is low. Alternatively, project financing can result in higher leverage and provide greater tax benefits. This is because, under corporate financing, leverage is below the optimal level. In the absence of bankruptcy costs, the first-best financing method is "pure" debt. However, firms reduce leverage in order to provide a credible signal about risk.

Similarly, the results of this section can be applied to asset-backed securities. Suppose that the firm issues *ABS* to finance the first project. If the project fails then the creditors (or the holders of *ABS*) do not have any legal rights of recourse to the assets of the firm. In addition, there exists bankruptcy remoteness condition. If the parent company fails it cannot use the assets of the project company. Therefore, formally, this debt is analogous to the case of non-recourse debt issued for both projects in the model. *ABS* are now used by many corporations as a financing method. The standard explanation in existing literature is that these securities exist primarily for regulatory reasons (for instance, banks trying to avoid minimal capital requirements). However, recent empirical literature (Calomiris and Mason, 2004) argues that securitization seems to be motivated more by reasons related to efficient contracting.

Finally note that Schipper and Smith (1983) found that 72 out of 93 firms in their sample of spin-offs involved parent companies and subsidiaries with different industry memberships (cross-industry spin-offs). The financing strategies discussed in this paper can be interpreted as a spin-off because they contain financing by non-recourse debt and the creation of an independent company respectively. The likelihood that firms in separate industries have divergent performance (see comments for condition (10.9)) is higher than it is for firms in the same industry. Thus, Schipper and Smith's (1983) results are consistent with the spirit of the present paper.

10.4 Other Models

The paper written by Chemmanur and John (1996) looks at managerial considerations and the threat of a takeover as incentives for the use of project financing. They assume that retaining control of a firm provides the greatest benefit to entrepreneurs and that they will make their capital structure decisions keeping this in mind. For instance, if a firm's current manager was to issue equity to raise funds, there is a possibility that the majority of it will be purchased by another market participant; which jeopardizes the manager's position as the controller. However, by issuing only corporate debt, the firm accrues the bankruptcy costs associated with high debt levels. Therefore, entrepreneurs will always aim to maximize the present value of their control benefits and the security benefits from lower debt levels. Non-recourse debt will allow him to minimize overall debt levels and reduce bankruptcy costs. Whether project financing will be preferred to normal debt depends on the value of the control benefits and their degrees of risk.

In the previous two sections of this paper, the models reviewed either discussed project financing as a solution to agency costs or as a solution to asymmetric information. Habib and Johnsen (1999), however, combine these two and look at how non-recourse secured debt, when combined with ex ante debt contracts, can solve agency costs in spite of information asymmetries. More specifically, they examine the role that non-recourse secured debt plays in ensuring the optimal allocation of ownership over secured physical assets across various possible states of the world. In this case, with non-recourse secured debt, if the borrower defaults, the lender/issuer can seize the collateral, but the lender's recovery is limited only to this collateral.

Habib and Johnsen (1999) apply the results of their model to aircraft financing in order to demonstrate the benefits of non-recourse debt over those of ex post bargaining. They choose to look at the aircraft financing industry because it is made up of a large variety of financing contracts and, more importantly, the industry is subject to exogenous shocks such as wars or industry deregulation and these affect the state of the world. This creates the need for possible/frequent redeployment and also creates an investment environment with relatively high risk. The implication of Habib and Johnsen's (1999) model is that the redeployment value of a firm's assets should have an important influence on its optimal capital structure. This helps explain why some firms have virtually no debt while others have quite a lot. While there are many other considerations behind a firm's capital structure choice, this model helps shed some more light on the subject. It shows how the structure of project financing contracts can help reduce agency costs and moral hazard dilemmas that plague firms even when there are informational asymmetries between entrepreneurs and creditors.

As mentioned, project financing uses a complex series of contracts to "distribute the different risks presented by a project among the various parties involved in the project."[8] They are created to dictate the management's response to any number of issues. The large number of contracts clearly reduces agency costs because there is less worry that the managers will not be acting in the best interests of the firm as a whole. With corporate debt, there are a number of problems with creating contracts to specify actions of shareholders and managers in response to market stimuli. As Brealey, Cooper, and Habib (1999) note, there are simply too many circumstances to consider.

It is very important that these contracts anticipate what may happen and provide a solution. Some of the risks that a project finance company may be subjected to include technological risk, construction risk, and completion risks, inflation risk, environmental risk, regulatory risk, and political and country risk. For example, the telecom sector showed a decline in 2006 likely due to the technological acceleration and development in the sector.[9] The contracts are necessary to properly allocate the risks to the counterparty best able to control and manage them. This is another one of the primary reasons why firm managers will choose to separately incorporate a new investment with project financing.

Marty and Voisins (2007) noted that since the shareholders may be likely to sell off their stake well before the expiring date of the concession, a professional evaluation of the project-financed companies at different stages of the project's life seems increasingly important.

Kleimeier and Versteeg (2010) argue that project finance is designed to reduce transaction costs arising from a lack of information on possible investments and capital allocation, insufficient monitoring and enforcement of corporate governance, risk management, and the inability to mobilize and pool savings. Their empirical analysis of 90 countries, from

[8] Brealey et al. (1996, p. 28).

[9] Gatti (2023).

1991 to 2005, confirms that project finance is a strong driver of economic growth in low-income countries with high transaction costs.

Gatti et al. (2013) study negotiations of financial packages between sponsors and lenders and their costs. It was found that lenders indeed rely on the network of contracts as a mechanism to control agency costs and project risks. This network of nonfinancial contracts limits the managerial discretion of project sponsors, to make cash flows better verifiable for lenders, and to reduce the negative impact of unexpected events on project cash flows. It was also found that lenders are reluctant to reduce the price of the credit if sponsors are involved as project counterparties in the relevant contracts.

In Lyonett du Moutier (2010), a positive agency theory model is built through a detailed analysis of property rights exchanged in the transactions needed to build the Eiffel Tower. The analysis of the original financial documents and contracts of the Tower reveals how specific provisions in the contracts combined to reduce agency costs all around. Thus a model derived from positive agency theory may help us better understand modern project finance.

Hainz and Kleimeier (2012) analyze the design of loan contracts for financing projects in countries with high political risk. They argue that non-recourse project finance loans and the participation of development banks in the loan syndicate help mitigate political risk. Their results also show that if political risk is higher, then project finance loans are more likely to be used, and development banks are more likely to participate in the syndicate.

Steffen (2018) mentions that a strong increase of project finance/non-recourse debt is observed in power generation projects. Further the paper analyzes project financing in renewable energy projects and suggests that debt overhang is the most dominant factor driving project finance.

Questions and Exercises

1. Non-recourse debt can be used to solve a debt overhang problem.
2. The main difference between non-recourse debt and secured debt is that the riskiness of secured debt is firm-specific while the riskiness of non-recourse debt is project-specific.
3. Consider a firm with assets-in-place, an investment opportunity available, and outstanding senior debt with a face value $D = 8000$.

Existing assets can produce: 20000 in state G (good state) with probability 1/2, 2000 in state B with probability 1/2. The new project requires an investment of 3000, and the firm will finance this investment by issuing new debt. The new project generates 5000 in state G and 2000 in state B.

a. Find the NPV of new project.
b. Suppose that to finance the new project the firm issues a standard subordinated debt. Will the new project be undertaken?
c. Now suppose that the firm uses project financing (non-recourse debt). Same question.
d. Now assume that the firm has a senior debt with a face value $D = 15000$. The new project requires an initial investment of 1000. The new project generates 4000 in state G and 0 in state B and it also reduces the probability of G occurring by 10%.

   Find the NPV of the new project.
e. Suppose that to finance the new project the firm issues a standard subordinated debt. Will the new project be undertaken?
f. Now suppose that the firm uses project financing (non-recourse debt). Same question.

4. The economy consists of two different types of firms. Each firm has two projects: they produce 1 if they are successful and 0 otherwise. The probability of success for firm j, $j = 1,2$ and project k, $k = 1,2$ is given by θ_{jk}. We have $\theta_{11} = 0.75$, $\theta_{12} = 0.25$, $\theta_{22} = 0.6$, $\theta_{21} = 0.25$. Both projects require an investment 0.2. Outside investors don't know the type of the firm (there is 50% of each type of firms in this economy) but they can observe the interest rate for each contract signed by each firm.

   a. Discuss if a separating equilibrium is possible where type 1 uses corporate debt (one contract).
   b. Analyze the situation where both firms use project financing for each project.

5. Prove the first part of Proposition 10.3 for the case with 2 projects as described in the text.

References

Amlôt, M. (2015, December 16). Tabreed finalises AED 192.5m loan facility for district cooling plant for Dubai Parks and Resorts. *CPI Financials.* http://www.cpifinancial.net/news/post/34011/tabreed-finalises-aed-192-5m-loan-facility-for-district-cooling-plant-for-dubai-parks-and-Resorts

Berkovitch, E., & Kim, E. (1990). Financial Contracting and Leverage Induced Over and Under Investment Incentives. *The Journal of Finance, 3*, 765–794.

Bonetti V., Caselli S., & Gatti, S. (2010). Offtaking Agreements and How They Impact the Cost of Funding for Project Deals. A Clinical Case Study of the Quezon Power Ltd Co. *Review of Financial Economics, 19*(2), 60–71.

Brealey, R., Cooper, I., & Habib, M. (1996). Using Project Finance to Fund Infrastructure Investments. *Journal of Applies Corporate Finance, 9*, 25–38.

Brennan, M., & Kraus, A. (1987). Efficient Financing Under Information Asymmetry. *Journal of Finance, 42*(5), 1225–1243.

Calomiris, C., & Mason, J. (2004). Credit Card Securitization and Regulatory Arbitrage. *Journal of Financial Services Research, 26*, 5–27.

Chemmanur, T., & John, K. (1996). Optimal Incorporation, Structure of Debt Contacts and Limited-Recourse Project Financing. *Journal of Financial Intermediation, 5*, 372–408.

Corielli, F., Gatti, S., & Steffanoni, A. (2010). Risk Shifting Through Nonfinancial Contracts. Effects on Loan Spreads and Capital Structure of Project Finance Deals. *Journal of Money, Credit and Banking, 42*(7), 1295–1320.

Esty, B. (2003). The Economic Motivations for Using Project Finance, Working paper, Harvard Business School.

Esty, B. (2004). Why Study Large Projects? An Introduction to Research on Project Finance. *European Financial Management, 10*, 213–224.

Flyvbjerg, B., Holm, M., & Buhl, S. (2002). Underestimating Costs in Public Works Projects. *Journal of the American Planning Association, 68*, 279–295.

Gardner, D., & Wright, J. (2012). Project Finance. In Tony Rhodes (Ed.), *Encyclopedia of Debt Finance*, 2nd ed., Ch. 13. Euromoney Learning Solution.

Gatti, S. (2023). *Project Finance in Theory and Practice*, 4th ed. Academic Press.

Gatti, S., Kleimeier, S., Megginson, W. L., & Steffanoni, A. (2013). Arranger Certification in Project Finance. *Financial Management*, Spring, 1–40.

Habib, M. A., & Johnsen, D. B. (1999). The Financing and Redeployment of Specific Assets. *The Journal of Finance, 2*, 693–720.

Hainz, C., & Kleimeier, S. (2012). Political Risk, Project Finance, and the Participation of Development Banks in Syndicated Lending. *Journal of Financial Intermediation, 21*(2), 287–314.

Hainz, C., & Kleimeier, S. (2006). Project Finance as a Risk Management Tool in International Syndicated Lending Discussion Paper No. 183 GESY.

John, K., & John, T. (1991). Optimality of Project Financing: Theory and Empirical Implications in Finance and Accounting. *Review of Quantitative Finance and Accounting, 1*, 51–74.

Kensinger, J., & Martin, J. (1988). Project financing: Raising Money the Old Fashioned Way. *Journal of Applied Corporate Finance, 3*, 69–81.

Kleimeier, S., & Megginson, W. (2001). An Empirical Analysis of Limited Recourse Project Finance, Working paper, University of Oklahoma.

Kleimeier, S., & Versteeg, R. (2010). Project Finance as a Driver of Economic Growth in Low-Income Countries. *Review of Financial Economics, 19*(2), 49–59.

Kumar, A., Srivastava, V., & Tabash, M. (2021). Infrastructure Project Finance: A Systematic Literature Review and Directions for Future Research. *Qualitative Research in Financial Markets, 13*(3), 295–327.

Lyonnet du Moutier, M. (2010). Financing the Eiffel Tower: Project Finance and Agency Theory. *Journal of Applied Finance, 20*(1), 127–141.

Marty, F., & Voisins, A. (2007). The Role of Financial Intermediaries in UK Private Finance Initiatives, Working Paper.

McGuinty, T. (1981). *Project Organization and Finance*. The Cliveland-Cliffs Iron Company.

Merrow, E., McDonnell, L., & Arguden, R. (1988). Understanding the Outcomes of Megaprojects: a Quantitative Analysis of Very Large Civilian Projects. RAND Corporation publication series #R-3560-PSSP.

Miglo, A. (2010). Project Financing versus Corporate Financing Under Asymmetric Information. *Journal of Business and Economics Research, 8*(8), 27–43.

Miller, R., & Lessard, D. (2000). *The Strategic Management of Large Engineering Projects*. MIT Press.

Myers, S. C. (1977). Determinants of Corporate Borrowing. *Journal of Financial Economics, 5*, 147–175.

Myers, S., & Majluf, N. (1984). Corporate Financing and Investment Decisions When Firms Have Information that Investors Do not Have. *Journal of Financial Economics, 13*, 187–221.

Nevitt, P. (1979). *Project Financing*. Euromoney Publications.

Schipper, K., & Smith, A. (1983). Effects of Recontracting on Shareholder Wealth: The Case of Voluntary Spinoffs. *Journal of Financial Economics, 12*, 437–467.

Shah, S., & Thakor, A. (1987). Optimal Capital Structure and Project Financing. *Journal of Economic Theory, 42*, 209–243.

Steffen, B. (2018). The Importance of Project Finance for Renewable Energy Projects. *Energy Economics, 69*, 280–294.

CHAPTER 11

Security Design and Financing Innovations

11.1 Capital Structure and the Security Design Problem

In most previous chapters we analyze capital structure choice as a choice between debt and equity. However the financing decisions of entrepreneurs or managers are often not limited by these two choices. There are many different types of securities. Some of them like convertible bonds or shares have already been mentioned, e.g., in Chapter 9; some of them will be discussed later in this chapter. Often firms invent/design new types of contracts/securities. The problem of finding an optimal security is called a security design problem.[1] Formally, to answer the question of optimal securities one should usually consider a set of very general payoff functions (usually continuous functions of firm profit) that describe payments to the holders of securities and find the optimal function that is associated with an optimal security that the firm should use. Usually these problems are slightly more complicated technically than the traditional debt-equity choice. Although potentially optimal contracts can be very

[1] For a general review of security design literature see, e.g., Allen and Barbalau (2024).

Supplementary Information The online version contains supplementary material available at https://doi.org/10.1007/978-3-031-85459-0_11.

A. Miglo, *Capital Structure in the Modern World*,
https://doi.org/10.1007/978-3-031-85459-0_11

complicated, often the optimal contracts that arise are simple. In fact, for many researchers the objective of research in security design is not to find some complicated contracts but to prove why relatively simple contracts represent optimal securities when starting from very general assumptions. For example, Nachman and Noe (1994) analyze optimal security design in a one-period environment with asymmetric information where firms have private information. Brennan and Kraus (1987) show that in these conditions a perfect signaling by a good firm is usually impossible as we discussed in the previous chapter. As we saw in Chapter 3, Myers and Majluff (1984) suggested (in a traditional debt-equity choice setup) that a good firm should always rely on retained earnings to finance new projects to avoid an underpricing of securities issued by the firm externally. In its absence they will issue debt and only as a last resort will issue equity (so-called pecking order). Risky debt also suffers from asymmetric information problems (for example in the form of higher interest rates for firms) but not to the same degree as equity underpricing. This was proven in a more general (security design) setting by Nachman and Noe (1994). A similar result was obtained by Innes (1993).

Another important line of research in security design literature is based on moral hazard issues and uses a principal-agent setting (see, e.g., Innes, 1990; Dewatripont et al., 2003; Gottlieb & Moreira, 2022).

Similar to the traditional debt-equity choice literature, security design problems are usually characterized by one or more market imperfections. Given the technical difficulties of security design problems it is more challenging for researchers to analyze multiple imperfections in the same model.

11.2 Security Design and the Origin of Debt and Equity

To illustrate the Brennan and Kraus (1987) idea, consider a company that is raising funds for an investment project. The investment cost is B. There are two types of firms. A type j firm's earnings are denoted R_j, $R_j \geq 0$, $j = 1, 2$. R_1 is distributed according to the distribution function F and the density function f and R_2 is distributed according to the distribution function G and the density function g. A firm's type is not known to the public. x is the fraction of type 1 firms in the market.

The timing of events in this situation is as follows (Fig. 11.1).

Type 1's earnings first-order dominate type 2's earnings, i.e., $G(R) \geq F(R)$ for any R. Also type j issues a security that can be described as $s_j(R)$, i.e., when the firm's earnings are R, the security holder will get $s(R)$. Let $s(R)$ be non-decreasing, i.e., $s_1'(R) \geq 0$ for any R. This is a typical assumption in security design meaning that a higher firm profit should not lead to a lower payoff for any holder of firm securities. An efficient signaling equilibrium is when every type of firm receives their first-best value in equilibrium and no firm has any incentive to deviate from its equilibrium strategy or mimic another type.

Proposition 11.1 *If Project 1's cash flow distribution first-order dominates Project 2's cash flows and $s_j(R)$ is non-decreasing, an efficient signaling equilibrium does not exist.*

Proof The shareholders' payoff is $R - s(R)$ when a firm's earnings equal R. Suppose that an efficient signaling equilibrium exists. In this case each type gets its first-best value (expected earnings from the project minus the investment cost). So for type 1 it is $ER_1 - B$ and for type 2 it is $ER_2 - B$. Consider a type 2 firm mimicking a type 1. The difference between the shareholders' expected payoff in this case and their equilibrium payoff is

$$\begin{aligned}\Delta_T &= \int_0^\infty (R - s_1(R))g(R)dR - \int_0^\infty (R - s_2(R))g(R)dR \\ &= \int_0^\infty (s_2(R) - s_1(R))g(R)dR\end{aligned}$$

We also know that $\int_0^\infty s_1(R)f(R)dR = B$ and $\int_0^\infty s_2(R)g(R)dR = B$ meaning that expected payoff to investors covers the investment cost. We will show that $\Delta_T > 0$ or that $\int_0^\infty s_1(R)g(R)dR < \int_0^\infty s_1(R)f(R)dR = B$.

Consider $\int_0^\infty s_1(R)(f(R) - g(R))dR$. Let $v = s_1(R)$ and $du = (f(R) - g(R))dR$. Then integrating by parts gives us

$$\begin{aligned}\Delta_T &= s_1(R)(G(R) - F(R))|_0^\infty - \int_0^\infty s_1'(R)(F(R) - G(R))dR \\ &= \int_0^\infty s_1'(R)(G(R) - F(R))dR\end{aligned}$$

This is positive since $s_1'(R) \geq 0$ and $G(R) \geq F(R)$ for any R.

So a separating equilibrium does not exist.

As Proposition 11.1 argues, no signaling equilibrium exists. So the equilibrium is pooling. Which pooling is the best for type 1? Type 1 wants to minimize investors' expected earnings or

$$\int_0^\infty s_1(R) f(R) dR \tag{11.1}$$

subject to investors' budget constraint:

$$\int_0^\infty s_1(R)(xf(R) + (1-x)g(R))dR = B \tag{11.2}$$

Following Nachman and Noe (1994), the optimal pooling problem after integrating by parts (11.1) and (11.2) can be expressed as

$$min \int_0^\infty s_1'(R)(1 - F(R))dR$$

subject to

$$\int_0^\infty s_1'(R)(1 - xF(R) - (1-x)G(R))dR = B$$

and $1 \geq s_1'(R) \geq 0$.

The Lagrangian[2] to the above problem is

$$\mathcal{L} = \int_0^\infty s_1'(R)(1 - F(R) - \lambda(1 - xF(R) - (1-x)G(R))dR + \lambda B$$

$$== \int_0^\infty s_1'(R)(1 - xF(R) - (1-x)G(R))(H(R) - \lambda)dR + \lambda B \tag{11.3}$$

$$\text{where } H(R) = \frac{1 - F(R)}{1 - xF(R) - (1-x)G(R)} \tag{11.4}$$

Following Nachman and Noe (1994) if we assume that the distribution F conditionally stochastically dominates G,[3] then $\frac{1-F(R)}{1-G(R)}$ and

[2] Lagrangian function, used to solve constrained minimization problems in optimization theory. See, e.g., Hoffmann and Bradley (2004).

[3] See, e.g., Shaked and Shanthikumar (2007).

$\frac{1-F(R)}{1-xF(R)-(1-x)G(R)}$ are monotonically increasing in R (see also Fulghieri et al., 2020). Then (11.3) leads to the following proposition.

Proposition 11.2 $S_1(R)$ *is the solution if there exists* λ *such that.*

$$s_1'(R) = 1\,if\;H(R) < \lambda;\;[0,\,1]\,if\;H(R) = \lambda;\;0\,if\;H(R) > \lambda \tag{11.5}$$

This is because in (11.3) $H(R) - \lambda$ is monotone and $1 - xF(R) - (1 - x)G(R)$ is positive so when R is small and $H(R) - \lambda$ is negative, $s_1'(R)$ should be as large as possible, i.e., $s_1'(R) = 1$ and when R is large and $H(R) - \lambda$ is positive, $s_1'(R)$ should be as small as possible, i.e., $s_1'(R) = 0$. This security is debt (see Fig. 11.2).

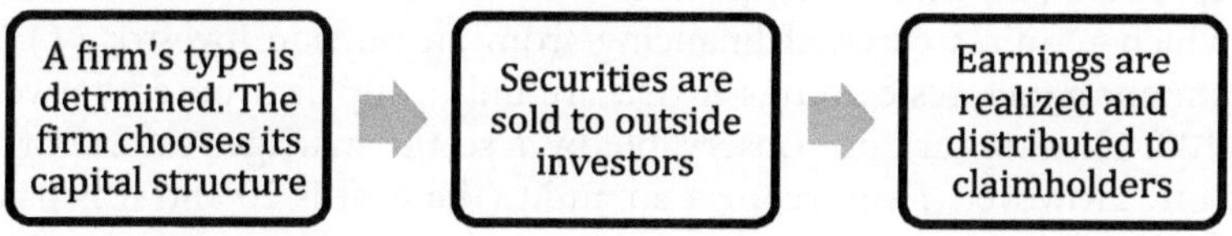

Fig. 11.1 Sequence of events

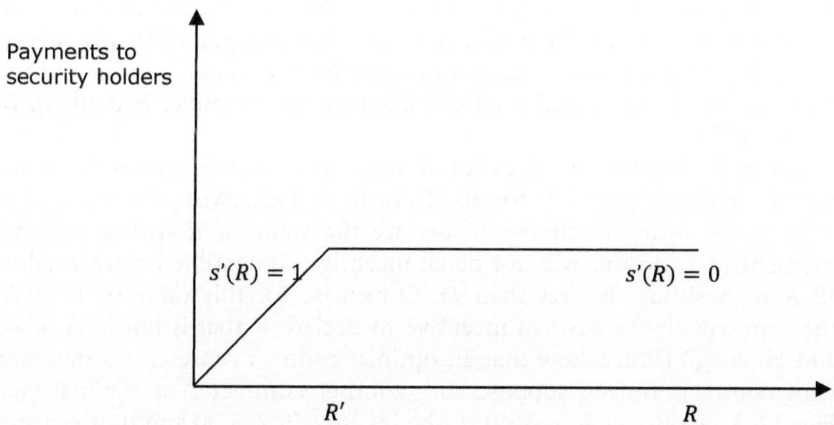

Fig. 11.2 Optimal contract (debt)

As was discussed in Chapter 8, debt also arises as an optimal contract in Gale and Hellwig (1985) who use the costly-state-verification approach pioneered by Townsend (1979). They show that when the state of the world is only observable by the entrepreneur and there is some monitoring cost, a standard debt contract is optimal. The investor receives a fixed amount and does not verify the state when the return is above a certain threshold. The investor receives the full return of the project (lower than the fixed amount above) and verifies the state when the return is below the threshold. This can be thought of as bankruptcy. Intuitively, it is optimal to minimize states where auditing cost is incurred. Paying the full amount to the investor when auditing happens helps reduce the amount paid when auditing does not happen (the face value of debt) and therefore reduces the probability of auditing. To see the idea in more detail, consider an example with a firm that is run by a manager/entrepreneur (E) who owns the firm. The firm has to make an investment 20, which requires external financing from an outside investor (I). The investment generates earnings R that are uniformly distributed between 0 and 100. Earnings are not observable by I so the manager can report any amount. However, I can request an audit (the cost is 20 and it is paid by the firm) of the firm. A financing contract between I and E determines the schudule of the investor's payments $P(R)$ as a function of R (earnings declared by E). The question is what is the optimal contract $P(R)$ that will maximize the firm's expected earnings under the condition that the investor is compensated for its investment. It was argued that the revelation principle implies that the truth should be told in equilibrium and the contract should be incentive-compatible (see, for example, Fudenberg & Tirole, 1991).

Let A be the set of values for R when the investor makes an audit. First note that $P(R) = D$ for all R not in A. Otherwise, for any R that is in A, the firm will choose to declare the value of R with a minimal payment to I. So this will not be an incentive-compatible contract. Also, all R in A should be less than D. Otherwise for this value of R in A, the firm will always have an incentive to declare R that is not in A. Gale and Hellwig (1985) show that an optimal contract represents a standard debt contract. Indeed suppose that another contract A is optimal (see Fig. 11.3). Contract A pays 40 to the investor if $R > 50$ and 0 otherwise. So the investor's expected return is $40*5/10 = 20$. The expected audit cost is $20*1/2 = 10$, where ½ is the probability of the audit (when $R <$ 50). The E' s expected return is $50 - 20 - 10 = 20$. Consider contract

B. It pays 25 if $R > 25$ and R otherwise. The investor's expected return is: $25*7.5/10 + 12.5*2.5/10 = 21.875$. The E's expected return is $50 - 21.875 - 5 = 24.125$. So contract B is better than contract A for the entrepreneur. It represents a standard debt contract (see Fig. 11.3). In fact this contract can even be improved a little by making sure the investor's payment is equal to 20.

Sometimes investors such as banks may be able to obtain information about a firm's quality or produce analytical information. Fulghieri and Lukin (2001) show that good firms want to partition their securities so that some of the claims are information sensitive. If the cost of becoming

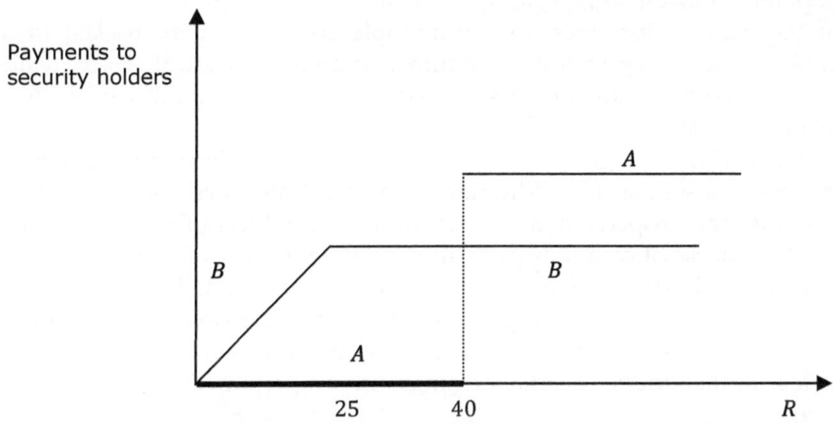

Fig. 11.3 Optimal contract under costly state verification

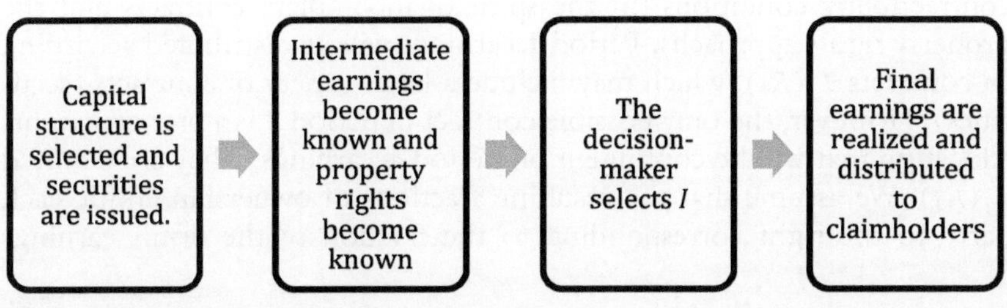

Fig. 11.4 Sequence of events

informed is low and the degree of asymmetric information is high, firms may prefer a more information sensitive security to promote information production by "specialized" outside investors. This explains the negative correlation between debt and firm value because firms with low profitability do not need to issue equity, which is sensitive to a firm's value. Fulghieri and Lukin also predict that younger firms with good growth opportunities are more likely to be equity financed. These firms can be especially interested in information production by outside investors.

Axelson (2007) also considers a model where potential investors may be privately informed about the value of the underlying assets of the firm. In the single asset case, debt is often an optimal security when the number of potential investors is small, while equity becomes optimal as the degree of competition increases. In the multiple asset case, debt backed by a pool of assets is optimal if the number of assets is relatively large, while equity backed by individual assets is optimal when the number of assets is relatively small.

Miglo (2009) suggests that in firms where moral hazard is an important issue, a simple rule ("the rule of marginal revenues") may exist that describes the property rights allocation of the holders of securities based on the analysis of cash flow patterns for different types of contracts (securities).[4] To illustrate the idea, consider a firm with assets-in-place that are expected to generate earnings in two periods. After observing the intermediate earnings R_1^0 and R_2^0, the firm's decision-maker makes a decision (select I) that affects the final earnings in both periods. After the decision is made, the firm's earnings in period 1 are $R^1 = R_1^0 - I$ and in period 2 they are $R_2 = R_2^0 + I + R(I)$. I may be interpreted as an amount of investment in a project. But in fact, I can be negative too. In this case it can be interpreted as borrowing or increasing sales with a discount.

A difference exists between period 1 and period 2 in terms of contractibility conditions (in the spirit of incomplete contracts and the property rights approach). Period 1 earnings will be distributed according to contracts $T_j(R_1)$, which may include a large variety of contracts (securities). However, the only possible contract in period 2 is a property rights allocation that will be contingent on period 1 earnings. They are denoted $T_j(R_1)$. We assume that the resulting fractions of ownership entitle each party to the right corresponding to the fraction of the firm's earnings

[4] See also Ayotte and Bolton (2011) for a related analysis that takes into account the minimization of enforcing costs of contracts.

period 2. $T_j(R_1)$ are monotonic. Only piece-wise linear contracts are considered since they are the most common type of contract observed in reality. Property rights should provide the decision-maker with the optimal incentive to choose s. The sequence of events is as follows (Fig. 11.4).

Optimal situations occur when property rights are distributed according to the current marginal revenues of existing securities. For instance, if the current marginal cash flow rights of the decision-maker are 10% (if the firm's value increases by \$1, the payoff to the agent will increase by 10c), his optimal fraction of ownership in the future business should also be 10%. This provides decision-makers with the optimal incentives to make decisions.

Proposition 11.3 *If contracts are piece-wise linear, I is sufficiently small and $T_j'(R_1^0) = \alpha_j(R_1^0)$, then the interests of each claimholder and the firm's value maximization are aligned.*

Let I^* be the optimal decision from the firm's point of view, i.e., $R(I)$ (the total change in the firm's earnings after the decision is made) is maximized when I^* is selected. Assuming that $R(I)$ is concave and differentiable, it implies $R'(I^*) = 0$. Suppose that claimholder j is the decision-maker. The payoff of j equals $P_j(I) = T_j(R_1^0 - I) + \alpha_j(R_1^0)(R_2^0 + I + R(I))$.

When I is sufficiently small, it equals (since T_j is piece-wise linear):

$$P_j(I) = T_j\left(R_1^0\right) - T_j{'}\left(R_1^0\right)I + \alpha_j\left(R_1^0\right)(R_2^0 + I + R(I)) \tag{11.6}$$

It implies: $P_j{'}(I) = -T_j{'}(R_1^0) + \alpha_j(R_1^0)(1 + R'(I))$. j will make optimal decision for the firm when $P_j{'}(I^*) = 0$. As was mentioned above $R'(I^*) = 0$. It implies that $P_j{'}(I^*) = 0$ if $T_j'(R_1^0) = \alpha_j(R_1^0)$.

The "Rule of marginal revenues" is consistent with standard securities. Suppose, for example, that there are two claimholders: A and B. B's contract is debt with a face value D and A's contract is levered equity: $T_2(R_1) = min\{R_1, D\}$ and $T_1(R_1) = max\{0, R_1 - D\}$ (see Fig. 11.5). If cash flow is greater than the face value of debt, then residual property rights belong to the equityholder ($T_1'(R_1) = 1$), and if cash flow is less than the face value of debt, the creditors own it ($T_2'(R_1) = 1$). Miglo (2009) also considers other contracts including three-part linear contracts and situations where earnings shifts are large.

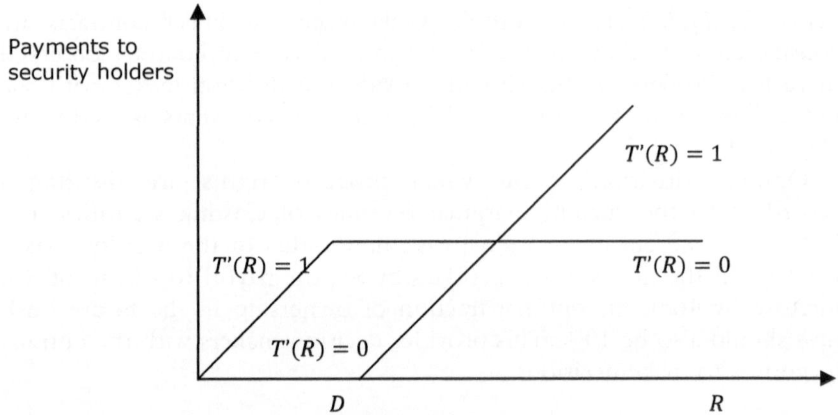

Fig. 11.5 The rule of marginal revenues under debt financing

11.3 Latest Advances in Security Design Research

In the previously mentioned papers, feasible contracts (securities) are characterized by monotonic payoff functions. Koufopoulos et al. (2019) consider a model of financing under asymmetric information by relaxing a traditional assumption regarding monotonic securities. They characterize the optimal contract when entrepreneurs can misreport their earnings by some amount. Straight debt is often suboptimal and never uniquely optimal. The optimal contract is non-monotonic and involves profit manipulation in equilibrium. It can be implemented either including performance-based bonuses, or via milestone payments (as in venture capital).

Malenko and Tsoy (2019) consider a security design model where an entrepreneur who is privately informed about the distribution of the project's cash flows, raises financing from an uninformed investor. The investor faces ambiguity (Knightian uncertainty)[5] about the distribution of cash flows. The investor demands robustness and evaluates each security by the worst-case scenario. They show that both standard outside

[5] An ambiguity is a situation of uncertain outcomes but in contrast to traditional uncertainty the probabilities of possible outcomes are not known (for more information about it see, e.g., Ghirardato et al. 2004).

equity and standard risky debt arise as equilibrium securities. They also argue that the equilibrium security differs depending on the degree of uncertainty and on whether private information concerns assets-in-place or the new project. If private information concerns the new project and uncertainty is sufficiently high, standard equity arises as the unique equilibrium security. When uncertainty is sufficiently small, the equilibrium typically features risky debt. In the intermediate case, both risky debt and standard equity arise in equilibrium. In contrast, if private information concerns assets-in-place, standard equity is never issued in equilibrium, irrespective of the level of uncertainty, and the equilibrium security is (usually) risky debt.

Fulghieri et al. (2020) study a security design problem under asymmetric information, in the spirit of Myers and Majluf (1984). They introduce a new condition on the right tail of the firm value. When asymmetric information has a small impact on the right-tail, risky debt is preferred for low capital needs, but convertible debt is optimal for larger capital needs. In addition, they argue that warrants are the optimal financing instruments when the firm has already pre-existing debt in its capital structure. Finally, they also provide conditions that generate reversals of the standard pecking order.

Yang and Zeng (2019) consider a model where investors can acquire information about the firm. The firm deliberately designs the security to induce investors to acquire the information that is least harmful to its interests. When investors have the bargaining power in security design or can only acquire information after financing, the optimal security is equity. When the firm has bargaining power, the optimal security depends on the importance of information for production and can be either debt or a combination of debt and equity. Inostroza and Tsoy (2022) show that when firms select security design that affects the structure of informational signals that they receive at the trading stage, the optimal security design is pure equity. Debt is optimal as the least informationally sensitive security only when additional restrictions on security or signal design are introduced.

In addition/in contrast to the literature mentioned above, in Miglo (2022) the payments to investors can be made in cash as well as using goods produced by the firm (payment-in-kind or PIK). The idea is that PIK can provide useful information to the entrepreneur when the demand for the product is uncertain. This in turn can help with optimally selecting production decisions. In general this research helps to provide explanations for new types of financing such as crowdfunding or token issues (we will provide more discussions about crowdfunding in Chapter 12).

11.4 Latest Financing Innovations: From Hybrid Securities to PIPE, SPAC, and VIE

This section takes a closer look at different types of innovative securities. Previously we mentioned that convertible securities for example convertible preferred stocks are popular among venture firms (Chapter 8). Convertible bonds were created a long time ago (we mentioned convertible debt in Chapter 4 when discussing opportunities to mitigate an asset substitution problem) but in recent years new types of convertible bonds were created.[6] A convertible bond is a regular corporate bond that has the added feature of being convertible into a fixed number of shares of common stock. Note also that a security that combines features/elements of two different kinds of financing (e.g., debt and equity) is often called a hybrid security (see, e.g., Kleidt, 2006). One of the relatively recent types of convertible bonds is a mandatory convertible (they were first issued in 1991). Mandatory convertibles will automatically be converted to stock at a specific time, unlike normal convertible securities, which the holder has the right to convert at any time. Securities with a mandatory conversion therefore have a similar level of risk as the underlying common stock. Firms may choose mandatory convertibles because ratings agencies may view them as equities. Between 2018 and 2021 there was a significant increase in mandatory convertible bond issuances partly to raise funds for mergers and acquisitions activities. Among theoretical research on mandatory convertibles note Chemmanur et al. (2014). They argue that the firm issues traditional debt and equity or traditional convertibles if the extent of asymmetric information facing it is large but the probability of being in financial distress is relatively small; it issues mandatory convertibles if it faces a smaller extent of asymmetric information but a greater probability of financial distress. The intuition is that when firms issue mandatory convertibles that are automatically converted into equity the firm can avoid the cost of financial distress, which can be especially beneficial if the extent of these costs is large.

[6] For some data see, e.g., Calamos (2020).

Next consider exchangeable convertible bonds and exchangeable convertible preferred stocks. The former are issued by one company but convertible into the stock of another company. Exchangeable securities may be an interesting strategy for firms that have acquired a large portfolio of another company's shares or those with spin-offs.[7] The market for these securities is usually larger in countries outside the United States, where firms are more likely to own other firms' shares. There are a couple of relatively recent lines of research related to exchangeable bonds namely the announcement effect of their issues on stock prices and also their role in privatization. These are potentially interesting lines of research with mixed evidence in some areas.[8] Exchangeable convertible preferred shares can be exchanged into convertible bonds. Firms may issue these securities when they are not be able to take on more debt without damaging their financial reputation or credit rating.[9]

Next consider a synthetic convertible. This security is usually created by using a credit instrument of a third party and not of the firm whose underlying stock performance determines its value and payoffs. There are two types of synthetic securities. The first is bank-issued structured notes. These notes are arranged by an investment bank and have the credit risk of a third party. They have the attributes of the convertible security, with one important difference: the credit risk is not that of the company whose common stock underlies the convertible and provides the convertibility feature but instead, that of a third party. During the financial crisis of 2008, the investment community learned that they can have significant counterparty risk in times of financial stress. Secondly, there are synthetic convertible units (SCUs). SCU is a convertible created by combining securities. A convertible bond can be thought of as the sum of its parts, that is, a straight bond combined with a long-term call option (the right to convert the bond into stock). See Fig. 11.6.

[7] A spin-off is when for example a firm (also called the parent company) distributes shares of a subsidiary to its shareholders, making the subsidiary a separate company. The firm usually keeps a large stake in the new company.

[8] See, e.g., Kaźmierczak and Marszałek (2013), Ammann et al. (2006) and Wang et al. (2019).

[9] For more information about exchangeable convertible bonds see, e.g., Chisholm (2010; ch. 18).

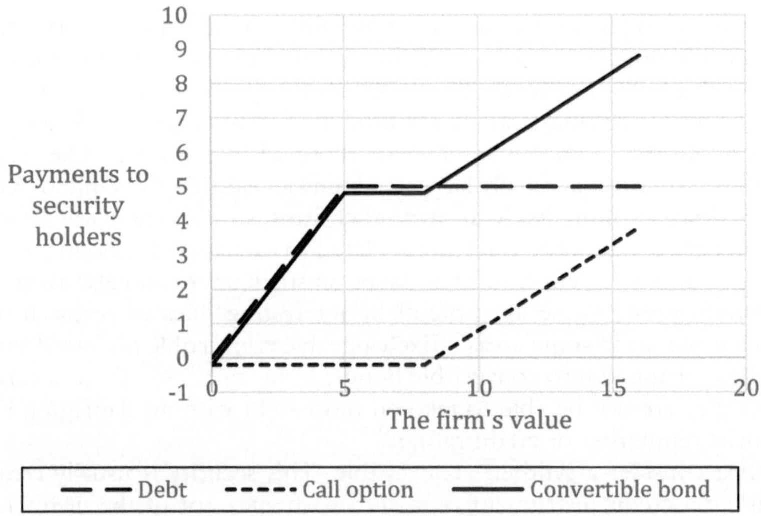

Fig. 11.6 Convertible bond

In Fig. 11.6 the long-dash-line is standard debt, the short-dash-line is the payoff function for a call option[10] and the solid line is the payoff function for a convertible bond that is a sum of the two previously described securities. A synthetic convertible can be constructed by combining these parts in such quantities that help to provide a combination of risk and reward that a manager seeks. This allows the manager to synthetically create a convertible security for a company that may not have any convertible or even non-convertible debt outstanding. The synthetic convertible is created when a credit instrument (that can be a Treasury bond, sovereign debt, or a straight corporate bond) is combined with a long-term call option, long-term equity anticipation securities (LEAPS[11]) or warrants. The ultimate objective for using SCUs is to reduce the interest rate on bonds using an appeal to a broader investment base with specific risk-return combination demands. On the other hand SCUs are quite

[10] As one can see on Fig. 11.6 if the firm value is less than 8 (roughly) the call option will not be exercised and otherwise it will be exercised so the payoff is similar to equity.

[11] LEAPS (Long-Term Equity Anticipation Securities) are options that have an expiration date greater than 1 year. See, e.g., https://www.investopedia.com/terms/l/leaps.asp.

complicated to use and may require the financial background necessary to understand a synthetic security. The growing popularity of these securities is manifested for example in the recent creation of an investment fund dealing with them.[12]

In 2020, new issues of convertible securities totaled $158.6 billion, surpassing the annual issuances of the previous 12 years. Historically, the convertible market has been strong in periods of economic growth especially after periods of stagnation or crisis. Recall that as discussed in Chapter 8, convertible securities are a popular tool of financing venture firms. During the 1980s and 1990s, the Japanese convertible market was quickly developing. It was a period of solid economic growth. In the 2010s (i.e., after 2007–2009 financial crisis), we saw an increase in contingent convertible bonds, particularly within the European financial sector.

Further convertible securities are often motivated by their role in mitigating the asset substitution problem, which can be important for firms with growth plans and significant debt. A growing equity market can provide an incentive for companies to include an option on their equity in their debt. When a high share price is expected firms can prefer to issue convertible securities over non-convertible debt, as corporations prefer to see their debt retired by conversion rather than through refinancing. Volatility can also influence convertible issuance. Investors may need more incentive to purchase securities with the potential for risk mitigation so they can be motivated by a convertible bond's fixed-income characteristics.

As we discussed previously equity issuing firms can face an asymmetric information problem that may affect the issuing price (as discussed in Chapter 3). Further, these firms may face agency problems associated with equity issues, e.g., free cash flow problems (Chapter 8), among others. IPO issuers may face another agency problem, e.g., underwriters may not have a strong incentive to maximize sale proceeds but instead can focus on reaching different arrangements with investors. Specifically, underwriters offer low-priced shares to favored investors, expecting to be repaid in other transactions (Ritter & Welch, 2002). Ljungqvist (2007) mentioned a second advantage of repeated interaction is that it allows underwriters to "bundle" offerings across time that can help them to get

[12] See, e.g., https://www.ft.com/content/ff17265d-2cf8-493c-8479-8e66267e9516.

lucrative contracts on IPOs in the future, i.e., they may tolerate buying some low-quality IPOs as long as the loss they suffer in any given IPO does not exceed the value benefits they expect from doing business with the underwriter. For relatively low-quality IPO firms, this situation can ex ante be helpful. It acts as insurance, allowing them to raise capital even when given a lukewarm market reception.

To deal with an IPO, underwriters can create special purpose acquisition companies (SPACs). The purpose is acquiring (or merging with) a private firm, hence making the private company public without dealing with a significant amount of bureaucracy, etc., associated with a traditional IPO. The firm negotiates with the issuer to determine the offer price and the number of shares sold and helps determine the share allocation among investors. The firm profits only if the deal is completed. The SPAC setting offers several advantages. First, a SPAC divides the process of going public into distinct phases. In the initial stage, the sponsor raises capital from investors. A SPAC starts as a newly formed firm, so there is limited scope for information asymmetry (about the target firm) compared to a traditional IPO that starts with an operating business. In the next phase the SPAC merges with a private business and introduces new institutional investors known as PIPE (private investment in public equity).[13]

The VIE (variable interest entity) model assumes that the holders of voting equity do not have traditional characteristics of control (and therefore that the entity is a VIE). It is the case if any of the following conditions exist: the entity is thinly capitalized (i.e., the equity is not sufficient to fund the entity's activities without additional subordinated financial support); the equity holders as a group have at least one of the following four characteristics: lack the power to direct activities that most significantly impact the entity's economic performance; possess nonsubstantive voting rights; lack the obligation to absorb the entity's expected losses; lack the right to receive the entity's expected residual returns. The VIE model requires the reporting entity to determine whether an entity is a VIE at the time of its creation (or on the reporting entity's first date of involvement with that entity), and to re-evaluate whether or not that entity is a VIE if certain events occur. VIE has become quite a popular topic in theory and in practice for the last 10–15 years.

[13] For more information about SPAC see, e.g., Shachmurove and Vulanovic (2019).

Gillis and Lowry (2014) give the example of Alibaba, one of the largest Chinese corporations, who decided to conduct their IPO outside of China because they were not able to find a comfortable way to deal with questions related to group control after IPO, in particular regarding dual-class shares.

Finally note the existence of equity/debt trusts or trust preferred stock that have a relatively short history compared to traditional securities. They were first issued in 1993 as mentioned in Engel et al. (1999). Engel et al. (1999) also mentions that these securities were created to be treated as preferred stock for financial statement purposes (i.e., to increase the capital/assets ratio for example) and as debt for tax purposes (i.e., payments on trust preferred stock are deductible by the issuer) and finds some evidence confirming these points.

Questions and Exercises

1. Consider the security design problem in the spirit of one in Proposition 11.3 but suppose that the assumption that I is sufficiently small is relaxed. What is the optimal contract/security in this case?
2. Consider an entrepreneurial firm that designs a financing campaign for the production of its innovative product or service. The production is denoted by q. The cost of production is $K = cq^2/2$. The firm has no initial resources available. To finance the production cost the firm needs to raise funds from an infinite number of potential investors. Investors are identical. The value of the product to investors equals v. The market price of the product after the project completion is also v. During the campaign, the firm raises an amount F. The firm is owned by an entrepreneur. After the completion of production the firm's amount of cash equals $C = F - K$ and the total value of the firm assets equals $X = F - K + vq$. In contrast to traditional financing/security design models where payments to investors are made in cash here the firm can use two kinds of payments: in cash or PIK. Another feature of the model is that the firm's main decision (q) is non-contractible.

The financing contract is $(F, q_0, P(X))$. Here q_0 is the number of items promised to be paid (delivered) to investors (in contrast to q, q_0

can be verifiable/contractible), and $P(X)$ is cash payment to investors. Everybody is risk-neutral and the risk-free interest rate is zero. Investors provide funds as long as their expected payoff covers investment costs. The entrepreneur offers a contract $(F, q_0, P(X))$ to investors. Investors can accept or reject the contract. If the latter is the case, payoff is zero for both entrepreneurs and investors. If the former is the case investors provide financing F and the entrepreneur selects q. After the production completion payments are made according to the contract.

(a) Prove that in a perfect market (i.e., when q is contractible) any contract is optimal such as $q = v/c$, $q_0 \leq v/c$, $F = v^2/2c$ and $P\big(v\big(v\big(\frac{v}{c} - q_0\big)\big) = v^2/2c$.

(b) Prove that under moral hazard any contract is optimal such as: $q_0 \leq v/c$, $F = v^2/2c$, $vq_0 + P(v(q - q_0)) = v^2/2c$ and $0 \leq P'(X) \leq 1, \forall X \geq 0$.

3. A convertible bond can be seen as a sum of straight debt and a call option.
4. VIE is a security that combines the features of warrants for tax purposes and the features of options for other administrative objectives.

References

Allen, F., & Barbalau, A. (2024). Security Design: A Review. *Journal of Financial Intermediation, 60*, 101113.

Ammann, M., Fehr, M., & Seiz, R. (2006). New Evidence on the Announcement Effect of Convertible and Exchangeable Bonds. *Journal of Multinational Financial Management, 16*(1), 43–63.

Axelson, U. (2007). Security Design with Investor Private Information. *The Journal of Finance, 62*(6), 2587–2632.

Ayotte, K., & Bolton, P. (2011). Optimal Property Rights in Financial Contracting. *The Review of Financial Studies, 24*(10), 3401–3433.

Brennan, M., & Kraus, A. (1987). Efficient Financing under Asymmetric Information. *The Journal of Finance, 42*(5), 1225–1243.

Calamos, J. (2020). *Convertible Securities: Structures, Valuation, Market Environment, and Asset Allocation.* https://www.calamos.com/globalassets/media/documents/market-insights/convertiblesecurities.pdf

Chemmanur, T., Nandy, D., Yan, A., & Jiao, J. (2014). A Theory of Mandatory Convertibles. *Journal of Banking & Finance, 42*, 352–370.

Chisholm, A. (2010). *Derivatives Demystified: A Step-by-step Guide to Forwards, Futures, Swaps and Options* (2nd ed.). Wiley.

Dewatripont, M., Legros, P., Matthews, S., & S. (2003). Moral Hazard and Capital Structure Dynamics. *Journal of European Economic Association, 1*(4), 890–930.

Engel, E., Erickson, M., & Maydew, E. (1999). *Debt-Equity Hybrid Securities*. Available at SSRN: https://ssrn.com/abstract=175868.

Fudenberg, D., & Tirole, J. (1991). *Game Theory*. MIT Press.

Fulghieri, P., & Lukin, D. (2001). Information Production, Dilution Costs, and Optimal Security Design. *Journal of Financial Economics, 61*, 3–41.

Fulghieri, P., García, D., & Hackbarth, D. (2020). Asymmetric Information and the Pecking (Dis)Order. *Review of Finance, 24*(5), 961–996.

Gale, D., & Hellwig, M. (1985). Incentive-Compatible Debt Contracts: The One-Period Problem. *Review of Economic Studies, 52*(4), 647–663.

Ghirardato, Paolo & Maccheroni, Fabio & Marinacci, Massimo. (2004). Differentiating Ambiguity and Ambiguity Attitude. *Journal of Economic Theory. 118*. 133–173. https://doi.org/10.1016/j.jet.2003.12.004

Gillis, P., & Lowry, M. (2014). Son of Enron: Investors Weigh the Risks of Chinese Variable Interest Entities. *Journal of Applied Corporate Finance, 26*(3), 61–66.

Gottlieb, D., & Moreira, H. (2022). Simple Contracts with Adverse Selection and Moral Hazard. *Theoretical Economics, 17*, 1357–1401.

Hoffmann, L. D., & Bradley, G. L. (2004). *Calculus for Business, Ecics, and the Social and Life Sciences* (8th ed.). McGraw Hill.

Innes, R. (1990). Limited Liability and Incentive Contracting with Ex-ante Action Choices. *Journal of Economic Theory, 52*, 45–67.

Innes, R. (1993). Financial Contracting under Risk Neutrality, Limited Liability and Ex Ante Asymmetric Information. *Economica, 60*(237), 27–40.

Inostroza, N., & Tsoy, A. (2022). Optimal Information and Security Design. *SSRN Working Paper 4093333*.

Kaźmierczak, D., & Marszałek, J. (2013). The Use of Exchangeable Bonds During the Privatization Process, *e-Finanse: Financial Internet Quarterly. University of Information Technology and Management, Institute of Financial Research and Analysis, 9*(4), 86–95.

Kleidt, B. (2006). *The Use of Hybrid Securities*. Springer.

Koufopoulos, K., Kozhan, R., & Trigilia, G. (2019). Optimal Security Design under Asymmetric Information and Profit Manipulation. *The Review of Corporate Finance Studies, 8*(1), 146–173.

Ljungqvist, A. (2007). IPO Underpricing. In Chapter 7 Editor(s): B. Espen Eckbo (Ed.), *In Handbooks in Finance, Handbook of Empirical Corporate Finance* (pp. 375–422). Elsevier.

Malenko, A., & Tsoy, A. (2019). Asymmetric Information and Security Design under Knightian Uncertainty. *Working Paper*. https://sticerd.lse.ac.uk/seminarpapers/et01112018.pdf.

Miglo, A. (2009). Property Rights and Earnings Manipulation. *International Research Journal of Finance and Economics, 31*, 116–128.

Miglo, A. (2022). Backers: Consumers or Investors? Crowdfunding vs. Traditional Financing as an Optimal Security Design Problem. In Mohammad Keyhani (Ed.) Ch. 12 in Handbook on *Digital Entrepreneurship* (Springer). University of Calgary, Clyde Hull Rochester Institute of Technology.

Myers, S. C., & Majluf, N. (1984). Corporate Financing and Investment Decisions when Firms have Information that Investors do not have. *Journal of Financial Economics, 13*, 187–222.

Nachman, D., & Noe, T. (1994). Optimal Design of Securities Under Asymmetric Information. *The Review of Financial Studies Spring, 7*(1), 1–44.

Shachmurove, Y., & Vulanovic, M. (2019). SPAC IPOs. In D. Cumming & S. Johan (Eds.), Ch. 19, *The Oxford Handbook of IPOs*, Oxford University Press.

Shaked, M., & Shanthikumar, J. G. (2007). *Stochastic Orders*. Springer.

Townsend, R. M. (1979). Optimal Contracts and Competitive Markets with Costly State Verification. *Journal of Economic Theory, 21*, 265–293.

Yang, M., & Zeng, Y. (2019). Financing Entrepreneurial Production: Security Design with Flexible Information Acquisition. *The Review of Financial Studies, 32*(3), 819–863.

Wang, L., Chen, L., & Chen, J. (2019). Announcement Effect and its Determinants of Exchangeable Bonds. *Finance Research Letters, 30*, 76–82.

CHAPTER 12

Capital Structure and FinTech Developments

12.1 FinTech, COVID-19 Crisis, and Their Impact on the Finance Industry

FinTech is short for Financial technologies, which is a quickly growing sector in finance. Two ideas contributed to its impressive developments in the beginning of the twenty-first century. The f is the immense developments in Internet-based technologies. The second, and probably more important, is the new view on the role of financial intermediaries (FI). Under the traditional approach clients of traditional FI (e.g., commercial banks) bring their funds to a bank who then accumulates them and makes decisions about how to use them, i.e., whether to provide loans to businesses or make other investments. Under the new approach investors and businesses deal directly with each other and the role of FIs mostly consist of facilitating this relationship, making it more convenient, more transparent, faster, less costly, and ultimately more efficient. Some experts argue that FinTech facilitates disintermediation in finance (see, e.g., Dhar & Stein, 2017).

Supplementary Information The online version contains supplementary material available at https://doi.org/10.1007/978-3-031-85459-0_12.

A. Miglo, *Capital Structure in the Modern World*,
https://doi.org/10.1007/978-3-031-85459-0_12

Broadly, the FinTech ecosystem can be divided into the following fields: (1) financing or capital-raising activities, which include crowdfunding and token issues; (2) credit or FinTech loans; (3) investments or investment management services, which include such new activities like roboadvising for example; (4) payments that include activities like the development of cryptocurrencies such as bitcoin for example; (5) others areas (regtech, insurtech, digital security, etc.). Capital structure problems are mostly related to the first group, i.e., newly developed FinTech-related strategies of raising funds, which are the focus of this chapter.

These new strategies have led to significant changes in the area of capital structure management since for example now firms (in particular innovative firms) have at their disposal new ways of raising funds, which in some cases cannot be easily classified as specific types of traditional debt and equity. That's why new models and new ideas related to capital structure management related to FinTech have been actively developing in the last 10–15 years.[1]

The COVID-19 crisis played a role in this development as well since during that period many businesses had no other choice but to switch to online methods of businesses including the finance sector which to a large extent contributed to a relative rebalancing away from the traditional sector and in favor of FinTech.

12.2 New Financing Opportunities Related to FinTech

New financing opportunities related to FinTech include crowdfunding and token issues. Crowdfunding is the practice of funding a start-up company or a project by raising funds from a large number of people ("crowd"). It is usually performed via the Internet using an online (crowdfunding) platform. Moritz and Block (2016), Cumming and Hornuf (2018), Estrin et al. (2018), Mochkabadi and Volkmann (2020), and Miglo (2022a) provide good reviews of the literature in this field.

There are four different types of crowdfunding: equity-based where investors will receive shares of the company; reward-based where investors are counting on some extra benefits from the company like future product

[1] For a general overview of FinTech industry basics see, e.g., Das (2019). Thakor (2020) focuses on the comparison of FinTech firms with traditional banking business.

discounts among other things; donation-based crowdfunding, where donations take place, which is good for nonprofits and social causes; debt-based crowdfunding where money comes in the form of loans.[2]

Equity-based crowdfunding and debt-based crowdfunding have many similarities with traditional debt and equity, however there are some significant differences as well. In the spirit of the FinTech features discussed earlier, crowdfunding campaigns usually let firms raise funds with less bureaucracy compared to the issues of traditional equity and debt. Further they can be done faster since the issuer can reach a large number of potential investors using an online platform. The downside though is usually problems with the secondary market. Although some forms of equity and debt, e.g., private equity may not have an active secondary market, traditional (public) shares or bonds often have an active secondary market after the primary issue. Reward-based crowdfunding is usually considered the most innovative type of crowdfunding which cannot be classified as traditional equity nor debt and is often recognized as one of the top emerging business/technology innovations.[3] It often includes significant interactions between firms and funders/customers in the form of product feedback. Backers are able to pay different levels of money to receive items such as a free youth membership to the Whalley Cricket Club plus two adults memberships with a £60 pledge.[4] The highest level in that case was a £400 pledge to receive a Sponsorship board paid for by MBSigns to display for four years on the perimeter of the pitch.

There are 2 types of crowdfunding campaigns. One is called the "all or nothing" type (AON). These type of campaigns have a set goal to raise and a set funding period. Once the funding period comes to an end the project owner usually only receives the funds if the project's goal was met or surpassed. In the case that the goal is not met, the investors (also called backers or funders in the case of crowdfunding) get their investments back. The other campaign type is known as the "keep it all" (KIA). This

[2] Note that real-estate crowdfunding seems to be on the rise (see, e.g., Shahrokhi and Parhizgari, 2020). Although it is hard to say theoretically what are the main differences between this type of crowdfunding and other types of crowdfunding.

[3] See, e.g., https://www.technologyreview.com/2012/04/25/186464/10-emerging-technologies/.

[4] https://www.crowdfunder.co.uk/whalley-cricket-club-crowd-funding.

type allows the entrepreneur to keep any and all funds raised during the funding period, regardless of whether the initial goal is met or not.

The United States is usually recognized as the most successful country in the world in terms of crowdfunding development. Two largest crowdfunding platforms (Kickstarter and Indiegogo) are US-based. They are both reward-based crowdfunding platforms. England is often recognized as a leading country in Europe in developing crowdfunding (Dushnitsky et al., 2016; Kukk & Laidroo, 2020; Rau, 2020). The size of crowdfunding in England in 2018 was USD 10.4 bln. (Wenzlaff et al., 2020) while the total volume of crowdfunding in Europe was about USD 18 bln and in a comparable European country such as Germany, for example, this number is significantly smaller (USD 1.4 bln). Further, some cities in England are sometimes branded as hubs of FinTech development (e.g., Manchester[5]).

Crowdfunding regulation is in general in relatively early stages of its development as compared to other types of financing. In the United Kingdom for example, the Financial Conduct Authority (FCA), the regulator responsible for all financial securities and investment products, also regulates crowdfunding. Some experts argue that it makes crowdfunding safer and more attractive for entrepreneurs and investors. Some analysts though consider the question of regulation degree as an interesting one since one of the ideas of crowdfunding is to avoid long bureaucratic processes related to traditional IPOs for example and therefore some experts argue that the degree and the character of regulation should be carefully thought through (see, e.g., Ellman & Hurkens, 2019b; Hornuf & Schwienbacher, 2017; Miglo, 2023).[6]

Assetz is an example of a company dealing with debt-based crowdfunding. It was launched in 2013 and since then developed a marketplace that has become a good platform for investors and businesses to invest and borrow. They have lent over £1bn to businesses and they have paid over £100 m of gross interest to their investors.[7] In both 2018 and 2019, Assetz Capital was recognized as one of the United Kingdom's top 100 fastest-growing technology companies in the Sunday Times Tech

[5] https://www.investinmanchester.com/sectors/financial-professional-and-business-services/fintech; see also Miglo (2021b).

[6] For more information about crowdfunding in the United Kingdom, see the UK Crowdfunding Association website or the Nesta UK Crowdfunding Directory.

[7] https://www.assetzcapital.co.uk/our-story.

Track 100. In 2020, Assetz Capital was also approved for accreditation as a lender under the Coronavirus Business Interruption Loan Scheme (CBILS) by the British Business Bank, the government backed loan scheme to help the economy through Covid-19.

Token issues for financing innovative companies include initial coin offerings (ICOs), security token offerings (STOs), and initial exchange offerings (IEOs). The issuance of new tokens is usually done in exchange for money or for a cryptocurrency such as Bitcoin.[8] The ICO phenomenon dates back to 2013. Since then, the number of projects has been growing quite impressively. In a typical ICO, an entrepreneur raises capital by pre-selling utility tokens which give their owners the right to use the company's product or service once it is developed. Under STO, a company sells tokenized traditional financial instruments, like, for example, equity where tokenholders receive rights on a firm's future profits. In contrast to utility tokens, security tokens are regulated. Similar to crowdfunding the regulation of token issues is still in relatively early stages. In the United States, for example, the Securities and Exchange Commission (SEC) applies the Howey test to determine whether an asset qualifies as a security. Essentially, investments are considered securities if money is invested, the investment is expected to yield a profit, the money is invested in a common enterprise and any profit comes from the efforts of a promoter or third party (Ante & Fiedler, 2020). Under IEO, a company sells tokens using the service of organized exchange for cryptocurrencies such as Binance, LBANK, and Coinbene.[9] The exchange is directly involved in the selection of projects, organization, and sale of tokens and becomes the key marketing partner of the project. IEOs had strong momentum in 2019 with largest Bitfinex IEO raising $US1 bln.[10]

One of the most recent developments in the area of tokens is NFTs (non-fungible tokens). While most tokens are fungible or exchangeable (every token is the same as every other token), NFTs are all unique. In this sense they are similar to a work of art or one-of-a-kind collectables.

[8] About Bitcoin see, e.g., Böhme et al. (2015).

[9] Myalo (2019).

[10] ICO and IEO report (2020). Also see Miglo (2022c).

NFTs can be associated with a particular asset (possibly a digital one or physical as well including image, art, music, or recording of important events, e.g., a sports event). Usually an NFT may provide licensing rights to use the asset for a specified purpose. An NFT can be traded and sold on digital markets.

12.3 Crowdfunding

One of the most popular ideas of crowdfunding is that firms can use them to learn information ("crowd wisdom") about the market. Learning means that a firm/entrepreneur improves its information about market demand during crowdfunding and uses it later.

The following model illustrates this point.[11] Consider a firm with an innovative product or service. The production is q and the cost of production is K per unit. The expected spot market price is p. The firm can also use a reward-based crowdfunding campaign (the product price during the campaign is p_c) where the firm promises to deliver the product to investors (also called backers or funders) who participate in the crowdfunding campaign. The firm should determine c and s, which are the crowdfunding pre-sales and spot sales, respectively: $q = c+s$. The cost of the crowdfunding campaign is B. The demand for the product is either 0 with probability 50% or A (as long as the price does not exceed P; if $p > P$ the demand is zero; we also assume $P > K$ meaning the firm's product is potentially profitable). Also A includes the demand from the crowdfunding campaign c and on the spot market s. For example if $A = 10$ and 3 investors participate in the crowdfunding campaign then the demand on the spot market is 7. Also, we assume that if the demand exists and the firm conducts a crowdfunding campaign, investors are indifferent between participating in the campaign or buying on the spot market (as long as they anticipate $p = p_c$) so we assume that in this case the demand for crowdfunding is determined randomly.

Without crowdfunding the firm produces the quantity of items q and then sells them for the price p. When selecting p, the firm maximizes its

[11] In the spirit of Miglo (2022a).

expected revenue from spot sales. It means that with probability 50% the demand exists and sales equal ps and otherwise there is no demand and sales equal 0 so the expected sales equal $0.5ps$. If $P > 2K$, the optimal price is P and the optimal quantity is A so the expected profit is

$$0.5AP - AK \tag{12.1}$$

Indeed it would make no sense to produce less than A and set p less than P since $P > 2K$. Otherwise the optimal $q = 0$. The price is irrelevant when demand does not exist. The problem with the "spot sales only" strategy is that the firm will sustain a relatively high production cost because it makes the production decision before knowing the demand.

With crowdfunding the firm gets to know the demand after the crowdfunding campaign because the firm can observe c, which reflects whether the demand exists (if $c > 0$) or not (if $c = 0$). c could be equal to 0 even if demand exists but the probability of this is infinitely small. If after crowdfunding the firm realizes that demand is A then the firm produces $s = A - c$ units and sells them for the price $p = P$ and if the firm realizes that demand is 0 then $s = 0$. When preparing its crowdfunding campaign, the firm's expected profit equals

$$0.5A(P - K) - B \tag{12.2}$$

The difference between (12.2) and (12.1) equals:

$$0.5AK - B \tag{12.3}$$

That is positive as long as B is sufficiently small (which is consistent with empirical evidence that crowdfunding campaigns are usually relatively less costly than say conducting an IPO), the firm's expected profit is higher with crowdfunding.

Proposition 12.1 *If* $P \geq 2K$ *then crowdfunding is optimal if* $0.5AK \geq B$ *and otherwise spot sales are optimal; 2) if* $P < 2K$, *crowdfunding is optimal.*

Proof Follows from above.

The following are the implications of Proposition 12.1.

(12.3) is positive only if B (the cost of crowdfunding campaign) is relatively small. This is intuitive since the firm is facing a trade-off between the benefit and the cost of learning market demand (crowd wisdom). If we assume that the cost of the campaign is positively correlated with the size of the campaign and also with some one-time investment costs (e.g., hiring a marketing manager), this result leads to the prediction that crowdfunding (reward-based crowdfunding) will be the preferred strategy for relatively small projects. Chemla and Tinn (2019) predict that smaller campaign size (they interpret it as a shorter campaign duration) is associated with a higher probability of crowdfunding success and as such is positively correlated with the attractiveness of crowdfunding, which is consistent with the spirit of the above point. This is also consistent with the empirical findings in Mollick (2014).

If A (i.e., the difference between the demand in a good state (demand exists) and bad state (demand does not exist) increases then the likelihood that (12.3) is positive increases. This point means that the likelihood of crowdfunding increases when uncertainty regarding market demand increases. For a related analysis see Strausz (2017), Schwienbacher (2018), Ellman and Hurkens (2019a), and Chemla and Tinn (2019).

Asymmetric information is also considered an important factor in crowdfunding. Consider the following model.[12] An entrepreneur has an idea of a new product/service. Before production can start a capital investment I is required. The expected quality of the future product after the project is completed is uncertain and can be high (with probability π) or low. There are two types of entrepreneurs. Type l is characterized by the parameter π_l, type h has parameter π_h where $\pi_l < \pi_h$. By definition, h has a higher expected product quality. π is the entrepreneur's private information while the public is aware of the distribution of π. Let μ be the proportion of type h entrepreneurs, $0 < \mu < 1$. Let $\pi_m = \mu\pi_h + (1 - \mu)\pi_l$ be the average probability of high-quality product among the entrepreneurs. The entrepreneur can finance the required investment by using traditional financing strategies (debt or equity) or crowdfunding.[13] If the firm uses equity financing, investors offer finance

[12] See Miglo (2024) for more details.

[13] Note that the model can be applied to different types of equity (e.g., venture capital, private equity, etc.) and debt (e.g., a bank loan, P2P lending, etc.). Equity-based/debt-based crowdfunding can be considered as type of equity/debt on a very general level as well.

in exchange for a fraction α of firm equity. If debt is selected the face value of debt is determined.

If the quality of the product is high, all consumers/potential backers value the good at v and if the quality of the product is low the value is 0. The total number of potential customers is normalized to unity without loss of generality. If crowdfunding is selected, the entrepreneur determines the crowdfunding price p. After investment is completed products are delivered to investors/backers. Backers can participate in the campaign or those who did not participate in the campaign can purchase the product on the spot market. Under debt or equity financing the firm raises funds from investors. After investment is completed, the product quality becomes known and the firm sells the product on the market for the price P. The firm (project) is owned by an entrepreneur who maximizes his expected earnings. Everybody is risk-neutral and the risk-free interest rate is zero. Note that risk neutrality implies that investors provide debt/equity financing as long as their expected earnings cover the investment costs. Also, it implies the risk-neutral probability estimation of expected product quality by backers participating in a crowdfunding campaign. Further, all potential consumers/backers can select to either participate in the crowdfunding campaign or wait and purchase the product on the spot market. They make their choices by maximizing their expected surpluses, i.e., the expected value of the product minus the price. In case if the expected surpluses are equal we assume that the fraction x of potential consumers will purchase the product on the spot market and respectively the fraction $1 - x$ will participate in crowdfunding.

To illustrate the main ideas consider the case $x = 0$.[14] There are two types of potential equilibria: a separating one where each type selects a different strategy and a pooling one where both types select the same strategy. Similarly to Chapter 11, if multiple equilibria exist then we use the minimal mispricing criterion (see, e.g., Nachman and Noe (1994)). We will first show that a separating equilibrium does not exist. For debt and equity, it is similar to signaling problems discussed previously (Chapters 3 and 7). So below we will show it for crowdfunding. Next we will consider a pooling equilibrium. Debt dominates equity by minimal mispricing as was argued in previous chapters so we will compare equity

[14] For more details including the case $x > 0$ see Miglo (2024).

and crowdfunding and will argue that pooling with equity dominates pooling with crowdfunding.

Proposition 12.2 *An efficient separating equilibrium where each type's profit is equal to its symmetric information case values does not exist.*

Proof Suppose an equilibrium exists where h selects crowdfunding. Then $p_h = \pi_h v$. The right-hand side shows the expected product value for a crowdfunding campaign participant. Since $x = 0$, and the expected value of the product is also $\pi_h v$ (because in a signaling equilibrium potential consumers interpret crowdfunding to be a high-quality signal) all consumers participate in crowdfunding. h makes profit $\pi_h v - I$. Also, suppose that l selects a different strategy and makes profit $\pi_l v - I$. l would then mimic h. Indeed if l mimics h its payoff is $\pi_h \text{v} - I > \pi_l v - I$. As was previously mentioned, for the case of equity it follows from traditional asymmetric information results (see, e.g., Chapter 7).

Now consider pooling.

Proposition 12.3 *Pooling with crowdfunding is less likely than pooling with equity.*

Proof Under pooling with equity $\alpha = \frac{I}{\pi_m v}$. Indeed in this case the investors' expected profit is $\frac{I}{\pi_m v}\pi_m v = I$. h's payoff is $\pi_h v\left(1 - \frac{I}{\pi_m v}\right)$. Under pooling with crowdfunding $p = \pi_m v$. h's payoff is $\pi_m v - I$. h's payoff under pooling with equity is greater than under pooling with crowdfunding. Indeed

$$\frac{(\pi_m v - I)(\pi_h v)}{\pi_m v} \geq \pi_m v - I$$

because $\pi_h > \pi_m$.

Intuitively if a firm uses crowdfunding all cash will be received by the firm in advance and since the fraction of equity sold (in the case of equity financing) is less than 1, a type *h* entrepreneur will do worse under reward-based crowdfunding than under equity financing (since under equity financing the entrepreneur sells only a fraction of the firm under asymmetric information at the pooling price across *h* and *l* types). Miglo (2024) considers different variations of this basic idea including a variation where asymmetric information is combined with other types of market imperfections and argues that the basic result largely holds.

Proposition 12.3 implies a pecking order. When an entrepreneur has a choice between debt, equity, and (reward-based) crowdfunding then under asymmetric information about the product quality a pecking order exists, i.e., pooling with debt is more likely than pooling with equity, which in turn is more likely than pooling with crowdfunding. The effect of asymmetric information has strong implications on an entrepreneur's choice. Similarly to the reasoning in, e.g., Myers (1984) one can assume that for some firms (especially for entrepreneurial firms and start-ups) the amount of available debt is limited (debt capacity) or debt has an additional cost (e.g., a condition of having a credit rating or credit history). Similarly when comparing crowdfunding with traditional equity one can assume that equity financing is limited/costly, e.g., the entrepreneur's own funds (internal equity) are absent/limited; "sweet" equity from relatives and friends is limited as well; venture capital can have some additional cost as well, etc.).

Empirical evidence seems to be consistent with some elements of the pecking order that include crowdfunding. For example, according to some sources the total volume of P2P lending/debt-based crowdfunding exceeds that of equity-based crowdfunding (see, e.g., Alternative Finance 2021 report https://www.jbs.cam.ac.uk/wp-content/uploads/2021/06/ccaf-2021-06-report-2nd-global-alternative-.nance-benchmarking-study-report.pdf; see also p2pmarketdata: https://p2pmarketdata.com/articles/crowdfunding-statistics-worldwide/). Also, Walthoff-Borm et al. (2018) find that firms use equity-based crowdfunding when they do not have sufficient internal funds (otherwise they would prefer internal funds, which mitigate any asymmetric information problems). Other papers that analyze crowdfunding under asymmetric information include Belleflamme et al. (2014), Miglo and Miglo (2019), Chakraborty and Swinney (2021), and Bolandifar et al. (2023).

Similar to the traditional debt-equity choice moral hazard issues can affect crowdfunding as well. Examples of research in this area include Strausz (2017), Chemla and Tinn (2019), Miglo and Miglo (2019), Ellman and Hurkens (2019b), Belavina et al. (2020), and Miglo (2022b).

12.4 Token Issues

Unlike crowdfunding, tokens have a secondary market. It can attract investors who are not necessarily interested in consuming the product. Consider a firm with an innovative product or service. The firm plans to make an investment I and then sell the product for two periods. The production is q_t and the value of the product is $v_t, t = 1, 2$. In each period, the demand by potential consumers is Q_t. For simplicity assume that the variable cost is negligibly small (e.g., the firm produces an online app). The firm is owned and run by an entrepreneur who is subject to moral hazard. In each period the firm can sell tokens or use crowdfunding. If the firm uses crowdfunding then it can raise a maximal amount $Q_1 v_1$ in period 1. If this amount exceeds I the firm will be able to complete the project and start production. The firm profit is $Q_1 v_1 + Q_2 v_2 - I$. Otherwise the firm would not be able to start the project and the profit is 0. If the firm uses tokens then in addition to potential consumers, "speculators" (i.e., investors who are not interested in consuming the firm product but in creating a capital gain by selling the product on the secondary market) can participate in the campaign. If $v_2 > v_1$ and the product value (and respectively the token price) is expected to be higher in period 2, speculators can buy tokens in period 1 and sell them in period 2 on the market for the value v_2. The firm will issue additional $N = (I - Q_1 v_1)/v_1$ tokens in period 1. As one can see in this case the total amount raised in period 1 should cover the investment cost: $(Q_1 + N)v_1 = I$. This strategy works if $Q_1 v_1 + Q_2 v_1 > I$. The firm profit is $(Q_1 + N)v_1 + (Q_2 - N)v_2 - I$.

Also, moral hazard issues can be applied in both crowdfunding areas and token issues. The following model illustrates this point. Consider a firm with an innovative product or service. The firm plans to make an investment I and then sell the product for two periods. The production is $q_t, t = 1, 2$. The cost per item equals c. In each period, the demand is $p_t = a - q_t$. The firm is owned and run by an entrepreneur who is subject to moral hazard. At the end of period 1, he is able to divert funds received during period 1. In this case the entrepreneur's profit equals aF, where F is the amount of funds raised during the ICO and a is the probability of not being caught (a parameter that reflects institutional strength).

Consider period 2. When selecting p_2, the firm maximizes its expected profit, which equals $(p_2 - c)q_2 = (p_2 - c)(a - p_2)$. The solution is:

$$p_2 = \frac{a+c}{2}$$

The firm's expected profit is

$$\frac{(a-c)^2}{4} \tag{12.4}$$

Without any moral hazard problems, in period 1, when selecting p_1, the firm maximizes its expected profit, which equals $(p_1 - c)q_2 - I = (p_1 - c)(a - p_2) - I$. The solution is:

$$p_1 = \frac{a+c}{2}$$

The firm's expected profit is

$$\frac{(a-c)^2}{4} - I \tag{12.5}$$

Total amount of funds raised during the ICO (period 1) equals:

$$F = p_1 q_1 = \frac{a+c}{2}\frac{a-c}{2}$$

With moral hazard, the entrepreneur faces the following choice. If he continues with the project, the profit over two periods equals the sum of (12.4) and (12.5):

$$\frac{(a-c)^2}{4} - I + \frac{(a-c)^2}{4} \tag{12.6}$$

If he diverts funds, the profit equals

$$\alpha F = \alpha \frac{a+c}{2}\frac{a-c}{2} \tag{12.7}$$

If the following holds

$$\frac{(a-c)^2}{4} - I + \frac{(a-c)^2}{4} < \alpha \frac{a+c}{2}\frac{a-c}{2} \tag{12.8}$$

then (12.7) is greater than (12.6), the entrepreneur has an incentive to divert funds. Funders will anticipate it and the campaign cannot be successful.

The above analysis implies the following. Consider the case with $I = 0$ and $\alpha = 1$. Then (12.8) holds if $c < a/3$. It demonstrates inefficiency. In an ideal world any project with $c < a$ should be undertaken. But in the second-best world only highly efficient projects may survive. In terms of threshold, if the company sets a threshold below the minimal acceptable by the market it will not be accepted. So a minimal threshold is: $F = p_1 q_1 = \frac{a+c}{2}\frac{a-c}{2}$. Note that it is negatively correlated with c implying that high-quality firms should have a higher threshold. The minimal acceptable threshold is $\frac{a+a/3}{2}\frac{a-a/3}{2} = \frac{a^2}{3}$. As follows from (12.8), if a increases (that can be associated with regulatory efficiency, transparency, etc.) the likelihood that (12.8) holds increases and it is more likely that tokens should be used. For more analysis of token issues that include moral hazard issues see, e.g., Chod and Lyandres (2021) Gan et al. (2020), and Miglo (2021a).

Among other ideas note the following. Similarly to crowdfunding the learning market demand idea is considered important for ICOs. Entrepreneurs learn information about market demand by observing the price of tokens issued during the ICO. See, among others, Miglo (2021a), Amsden and Schweizer (2018), and Catalini and Gans (2018).

Another line of research focuses on networks benefits of token issues. Some examples include[15] the following. Developer network effect means that if more people and firms are interested in developing tools that can improve a platform quality, then a greater number of these tools will make the platform more attractive to use. A marketing network effect means that the more people that use the platform, the more likely it is that new participants are willing to join because the product is more popular and thus more likely to be seen by new users. Network effects are analyzed for example in Li and Mann (2018), Sockin and Xiong (2020), Bakos and Halaburda (2019), Cong et al. (2021), and Miglo (2022a).

Questions and Exercises

1. Reward-based crowdfunding platforms are a place where firms can safely secure bank loans.

[15] See, e.g., https://blocksurvey.io/learn-tokenomics/token-network-effect.

2. John made the decision to finance the purchase of three new vans for his delivery service business with equity. Which of the following sources of financing did John use?
   a. personal savings
   b. commercial banks
   c. reward-based crowdfunding
   d. debt-based crowdfunding
   e. ICO
3. The following is not one of the factors that is usually considered important in crowdfunding that affects the entrepreneur's decisions and also the outcome of crowdfunding or token issues.
   a. Network/community benefits
   b. Learning market demand; validate your concept in a public forum
   c. Moral hazard
   d. Information between investors and entrepreneurs is usually symmetric.
   e. Market feedback
4. The pecking-order theory of capital structure as applied to crowdfunding suggests the following order of financing:
   a. equity-based crowdfunding, reward-based crowdfunding, debt-based crowdfunding
   b. debt-based crowdfunding, equity-based crowdfunding, reward-based crowdfunding
   c. debt-based crowdfunding, donation-based crowdfunding, equity-based crowdfunding
   d. debt-basedcrowdfunding, reward-based crowdfunding equity-based crowdfunding
5. When a firm uses debt-based crowdfunding its leverage ratio decreases.
6. A common similarity among all ICOs is the issuance of new token in exchange for money or for another cryptocurrency (such as Bitcoin).
7. Jessica, founder of a new firm Intelligent Bikes, expects to spend the next one-half year developing and testing prototypes for a new electric bicycle equipped with a mini-computer. Suppose now that

Jessica used an alternative source for funding these costs (e.g., an incubator support). Also, suppose that now Jessica wants to raise more funds to fund further developments and the product of her product. Also assume that Jessica wants to provide financial rewards to her future investments but wants to keep full control of his firm in the future. What types of funding strategies would you recommend/not recommend to Jessica?

8. An entrepreneurial firm owns an innovative project. The firm is organized with unlimited liability. An investment of 300 is required (it includes a fixed cost that is invested in tangible assets that fully depreciate by the time the firm completes the project; variable cost is negligibly small). The demand for the good is 70 items for the price of 10 if the demand is high (with probability 50%) and 10 items for the price of 1 if the demand is low. Also under crowdfunding the entrepreneur is subject to moral hazard (free cash flow problem). The entrepreneur can divert funds received during the crowdfunding campaign and not use them for the purposes announced during the campaign. Suppose that the probability of being caught in this case is 50% and all "stolen" funds are returned to the government. The firm is planning to use reward-based crowdfunding (AON) or traditional funding (a bank loan with the interest rate 10%). Under reward-based crowdfunding, the firm announces the crowdfunding price and the campaign target.

    a. Discuss the "learning market demand" idea.
    b. Discuss the moral hazard problems in crowdfunding.
    c. Suppose the demand is high for sure. Calculate the entrepreneur's profit if the firm uses bank financing.
    d. Continue to assume that the demand is high for sure and that the entrepreneur is totally honest and does not consider diverting funds. Calculate the entrepreneur's profit if the firm uses crowdfunding assuming that the firm announces a campaign target of 300, and collects 70 pre-orders/contributions of 10 each from 70 backers. Also assume that the platform charges a fee of 50.
    e. What strategy is optimal for the entrepreneur? Comment why.
    f. Now suppose the demand is uncertain and the entrepreneur is subject to a moral hazard problem. Also assume that the entrepreneur maximizes his/her expected profit and the value

of his own assets is 400 (which he/she does not plan to use for firm financing since it will be inconvenient to sell assets, etc.). Calculate profits under both strategies (bank loan and crowdfunding).

g. Discuss your result in the previous question.

9. IEO is a type of ICO when the token sales are usually handled by a renowned cryptoexchange.
10. One of the advantages of an ICO compared to traditional reward-based crowdfunding is that tokens have a secondary market.
11. (Excel) Create a table of 100 crowdfunding campaigns (AON) from the Kickstarter platform (using, e.g., kickstarter.com or external sources of data, e.g., https://webrobots.io/kickstarter-datasets/), which has information about the campaign targets and the ratio of funds raised (total amount raised/target). Graphically illustrate the connection between these two factors. Discuss.

References

Amsden, R., & Schweizer, D. (2018). *Are Blockchain Crowdsales the New "Gold Rush"? Success Determinants of Initial Coin Offerings* (Working paper). Online https://papers.ssrn.com/sol3/papers.cfm?abstract_id=3163849

Ante, L., & Fiedler, I. (2020). Cheap Signals in Security Token Offerings (STOs). *Quantitative Finance and Economics, 4*(4), 608–639.

Bakos, Y., & Halaburda, H. (2019). *The Role of Cryptographic Tokens and ICOs in Fostering Platform Adoption*, (CESifo Working Paper Series 7752). CESifo.

Belavina, E., Marinesi, S., & Tsoukalas, G. (2020). Rethinking Crowdfunding Platform Design: Mechanisms to Deter Misconduct and Improve Efficiency. *Management Science, 66*(11), 4980–4997.

Belleflamme, P., Lambert, T., & Schwienbacher, A. (2014). Crowdfunding: Tapping the Right Crowd. *Journal of Business Venturing: Entrepreneurship, Entrepreneurial Finance, Innovation and Regional Development, 29*(5), 585–609.

Böhme, R., Christin, N., Edelman, B., & Moore, T. (2015). Bitcoin: Economics, Technology, and Governance. *Journal of Economic Perspectives, 29*(2), 213–38.

Bolandifar, E., Chen, Z., Kouvelis, P., & Zhou, W. (2023). Quality Signaling Through Crowdfunding Pricing. *Manufacturing and Service Operations Management, 25*(2), 668–685.

Catalini, C., & Gans, J.S. (2018). *Initial Coin Offerings and the Value of Crypto Tokens* (NBER Working Paper, 24418).

Chakraborty, S., & Swinney, R. (2021). Signalling to the Crowd: Private Quality Information and Rewards-Based Crowdfunding. *Manufacturing and Service Operations Management, 23*(1), 155–169.

Chemla, G., & Tinn, K. (2019). Learning Through Crowdfunding. *Management Science, 66*(5), 1783–1801.

Chod, J., & Lyandres, E. (2021). A Theory of ICOs: Diversification, Agency, and Information Asymmetry. *Management Science, 67*(10), 5969–5989.

Cong, L., Li, Y., & Wang, N. (2021). Tokenomics: Dynamic Adoption and Valuation. *The Review of Financial Studies, 34*(3), 1105–1155.

Cumming, D., & Hornuf, L. (2018). *The Economics of Crowdfunding Startups.* Palgrave Macmillan. https://doi.org/10.1007/978-3-319-66119-3

Das, S. (2019). The Future of FinTech. *Financial Management, 48*(4), 981–1007.

Dhar, V., & Stein, R. M. (2017). FinTech Platforms and Strategy. *Communications of the ACM, 60*(10), 32–35.

Dushnitsky, G., Guerini, M., Piva, E., & Rossi-Lamastra, C. (2016). Crowdfunding in Europe: Determinants of Platform Creation across Countries. *California Management Review, 58*(2), 44–71.

Ellman, M., & Hurkens, S. (2019). Optimal Crowdfunding Design. *Journal of Economic Theory, 184*, 104939.

Ellman, M., & Hurkens, S. (2019). Fraud Tolerance in Optimal Crowdfunding. *Economics Letters, 181*, 11–16.

Estrin, S., Gozman, D., & Khavul, S. (2018). The Evolution and Adoption of Equity Crowdfunding: Entrepreneur and Investor Entry Into a New Market. *Small Business Economics, 51*(2), 425–439.

Gan, J., Tsoukalas, G., & Netessine, S. (2020). Initial Coin Offerings, Speculation, and Asset Tokenization. *Management Science, 67*(2), 914–931.

Hornuf, L., & Schwienbacher, A. (2017). Should Securities Regulation Promote Equity Crowdfunding? *Small Business Economics, 49*, 579–593.

ICO and IEO report. (2020). https://www.pwc.com/ee/et/publications/pub/Strategy&_ICO_STO_Study_Version_Spring_2020.pdf

Kukk, M.-L., & Laidroo, L. (2020). Institutional Drivers of Crowdfunding Volumes. *Journal of Risk and Financial Management, 13*(12), 326.

Li, J., & Mann, W. (2018). *Initial Coin Offering and Platform Building* (Working Paper), https://pdfs.semanticscholar.org/309e/f98741d5da2003df8317fd605e1ac83d6fb9.pdf

Miglo, A., & Miglo, V. (2019). Market Imperfections and Crowdfunding. *Small Business Economics Journal, 53*(1), 51–79.

Miglo, A. (2021a). STO vs. ICO: A Theory of Token Issues under Moral Hazard and Demand Uncertainty, *Journal of Risk and Financial Management* 14, 232.

Miglo, A. (2021b). *Comparing Crowdfunding Theory and Practice: The Case of Technology Firms in England* (Working paper), https://papers.ssrn.com/sol3/papers.cfm?abstract_id=3818387

Miglo, A. (2022). Theories of Crowdfunding and Token Issues: A Review. *Journal of Risk and Financial Management, 15*(5), 218.

Miglo, A. (2022). Crowdfunding and Bank Financing: Substitutes or Complements? *Small Business Economics, 59*, 1115–1142.

Miglo, A. (2022c). Choice Between IEO and ICO: Speed vs. Liquidity vs. Risk. *FinTech, 1*(3), 276–293.

Miglo, A. (2023). *A Theory of Crowdfunding Under Asymmetric Information and Discounting Cost*. Available at SSRN: https://ssrn.com/abstract=4659368.

Miglo, A. (2024). Crowdfunding, Asymmetric Information and Pecking Order. *Journal of Economic Studies*.

Mochkabadi, K., & Volkmann, C. (2020). Equity Crowdfunding: A Systematic Review of the Literature. *Small Business Economics, 54*, 75–118.

Mollick, E. R. (2014). The Dynamics of Crowdfunding: An Exploratory Study. *Journal of Business Venturing, 29*(1), 1–16.

Moritz, A., Block, J. (2016). Crowdfunding: A Literature Review and Research Directions. FGF Studies in Small Business and Entrepreneurship. In D. Brüntje & O. Gajda (ed.), *Crowdfunding in Europe* (1st ed., pp. 25–53). Springer.

Myalo, A. (2019). Comparative Analysis of ICO, DAOICO, IEO and STO. *Case Study, Finance Theory and Practice, 23*(6), 6–25.

Myers, S. C. (1984). The Capital Structure Puzzle. *The Journal of Finance, 39*(3), 574–592.

Nachman, D. C., & Noe, T. H. (1994). Optimal Design of Securities Under Asymmetric Information. *The Review of Financial Studies, 7*(1), 1–44.

Rau, P.R. (2020). *Law, Trust, and the Development of Crowdfunding*. Available at SSRN: https://ssrn.com/abstract=2989056

Schwienbacher, A. (2018). Entrepreneurial Risk-taking in Crowdfunding Campaigns. *Small Business Economics, 51*(4), 843–859.

Shahrokhi, M., & Parhizgari, A. M. (2020). Managerial Finance. *Patrington, 46*(6), 785–801.

Sockin, M., & Xiong, W. (2020). *A Model of Cryptocurrencies* (NBER Working Paper No. 26816) https://www.nber.org/papers/w26816

Strausz, R. (2017). Crowdfunding, Demand Uncertainty, And Moral Hazard - a Mechanism Design Approach. *American Economic Review, 107*(6), 1430–76.

Thakor, A. V. (2020). Fintech and Banking: What Do we Know? *Journal of Financial Intermediation, 41*, 100833.

Walthoff-Borm, X., Schwienbacher, A., & Vanacker, T. (2018). Equity Crowdfunding: First Resort or Last Resort? *Journal of Business Venturing, 33*(4), 513–533.

Wenzlaff, K., Odorović, A., Ziegler, T., Shneor, R. (2020). Crowdfunding in Europe: Between Fragmentation and Harmonization. In R. Shneor, L. Zhao, & B. T. Flåten (eds.), *Advances in Crowdfunding*. Palgrave Macmillan.

CHAPTER 13

Capital Structure Analysis: Some Examples

In this chapter we analyze the financing decisions and capital structures of Facebook and United Continental Holdings in 2016.[1] Facebook had low debt and United had relatively high debt. We argue that none of the existing capital structure theories can individually explain a firm's capital structure. However, they can be used together to describe patterns of observed behavior.

13.1 Social Media and Airline Industries

A social network's mission is to connect people who share common interests. Most networks are web-based. Among the most popular are American-based companies Facebook, Google + , LinkedIn, Instagram, Shialand, Reddit, Pinterest, Vine, Tumblr, and Twitter. Among other companies note Nexopia, Badoo Bebo, Vkontakte, Delphi, Skyrock,

[1] For capital structure analysis of Internet companies as of 2011 see, e.g., Lee et al. (2014). For capital structure analysis of some companies in the fertiliser industry for example see Khatik and Singh (2006). Also note that Facebook was technically transformed to Meta in 2021 although Facebook remains a common popular name and remains one of Meta's divisions. Also United Continental Holdings was changed to United Airline Holdings (UAH) in 2019. Also note that as of 2024 Meta still has a significantly lower debt/equity ratio than UAH.

A. Miglo, *Capital Structure in the Modern World*,
https://doi.org/10.1007/978-3-031-85459-0_13

StudiVZ, Tagged, Myspace, Cyworld, Mixi, NetEase, Renren, Friendster, Sina Weibo, and Wretch. Surveys reveal that 73% of US adults use social networking websites and that international markets are becoming increasingly important.[2]

Early social networks focused on bringing people together to interact with each other via the Internet. In the late 1990s, user profiles became a central feature of social networking websites, allowing users to find "friends" with similar interests. One of the first large social networking websites was Cyworld (South Korea). It also became one of the first companies to profit from the sale of virtual goods. Facebook, launched in 2004, became the largest social networking site in the world in early 2009.[3]

Usually social networks do not charge money for membership. Companies such as Myspace and Facebook sell online advertisement on their websites. Their business model is based on a large membership count so charging for membership would be counterproductive. Some researchers believe that most of the information that the networks accumulate, due to the nature of these networks, provides advantages with advertising strategies compared to regular businesses.[4] Social networks operate under an autonomous business model where networks' members serve dual roles as both suppliers and consumers of content. This is different from the traditional business model where the suppliers and consumers are distinct agents.

There has been rapid growth in the number of US patent applications that cover new technology related to social networking. The number of published applications has been growing rapidly since 2003. There are now over 3500 published applications and as many as 7000 applications may be currently on file including those that haven't been published yet.[5]

The airline industry is the business of transporting paying passengers and freight by air, typically by airplane or helicopter. The largest income in the airline industry comes from passenger services; hence the airlines

[2] http://news.biharprabha.com/2014/07/india-records-highest-social-networking-growth-study/ and Lunden (2013).

[3] *Kazeniac* (February 9, 2009).

[4] Tynan (July 30, 2007).

[5] *Nowotarski* (January 23, 2011).

are dependent on consumer and business confidence.[6] Flying, which is often included in a vacation, could be seen as a luxury good for private travelers.

An important aspect of passenger service is the business traveler, who most likely flies more frequently than, for example, the vacation (leisure) passenger. Airlines try to get the loyalty of business passengers by using, for example, frequent flyer programs. By earning more points, the benefits become larger and give the customer more incentive to fly. Business travelers are also more likely to purchase the upgraded services, which gives the airline a higher profit margin on their services. They are also often not very price sensitive: They make a lot of last minute orders and often do not have as many choices as private travelers. This results in a lower price elasticity of demand, so their demand would not fall that much in the event of an economic downturn in this sector.[7]

A significant factor in the development of the airline industry was the large-scale deregulation that started in the United States at the end of the 1970s and later spread into Europe and Asia. It affected the competitive environment in the industry by lowering entry barriers which led to accelerated competition in the deregulated regions. This introduced the need for cost efficiency and operating profitability management, and could be seen as the beginning of low-cost-carriers that began to successfully compete with incumbent well-established companies.

The airline industry is very procyclical and hence its success is strongly correlated with economic conditions. The deregulation has increased competition and affected growth and profitability. Profitability, even in the good years, is generally low: in the range of 2–3% net profit after interest and tax.[8] The net profit has been very volatile since the 1990s. One of the results of the financial crisis of 2007/2008 was record losses for the airline industry. The September 11, 2001 terror attack also had a negative impact on its profitability.[9].

[6] Avjobs, http://www.avjobs.com/history/airline-economics.asp.

[7] https://www.iata.org/whatwedo/Documents/economics/Intervistas_Elasticity_Study_2007.pdf.

[8] International Air Transport Association (IATA), Fact Sheet: World Industry Statistics, https://www.iata.org/pressroom/facts_figures/fact_sheets/Documents/fact-sheet-industry-facts.pdf.

[9] MIT Global Airline Industry Program, http://web.mit.edu/airlines/analysis/analysis_airline_industry.html

The increasing competition forced airlines to seek lower costs and higher productivity. This caused a high number of mergers, acquisitions, and internal growth to take advantage of economies of scale. The economic downturn and higher operating costs led to massive layoffs and cutbacks in the industry. These challenges led many large airlines (US Airways, United, Delta, and Northwest, among others) into Chapter 11 bankruptcy between 2001 and 2005. Under bankruptcy protection these airlines started cost reducing restructurings.

13.2 Methodology

We first analyze a company's capital structure with the help of a spreadsheet analysis, which is mostly based on the trade-off between the tax advantages of debt and the increased risk from debt financing.[10] We mostly use data from Yahoo! Finance and openly available data from companies' own websites. In addition to a traditional spreadsheet analysis an estimation of the value of financial flexibility will also be added.[11] As well as the share price underpricing estimation in case the firm issues new shares. In general, capital structure management in practice needs more analyses similar to the ones in this chapter (so-called case studies). It is an effective way to do research in areas that include several layers of analysis and different approaches and theories. Our book suggests that capital structure management represents such an area. There are a lot of competing theories of capital structure. Furthermore one of our main objectives is to find firms' optimal capital structure policies (as opposed to existing policies). Some of the theories are better formalized and are simpler to use in real-life situations (such as trade-off theory) while others are very complex (such as asymmetric information). A case study is a good research strategy because capital structure is a multidimensional topic (Singleton et al. [1993], Mertens [1998]). For an interesting review of case study research in corporate finance, see Stoner and Holland (2004).

[10] See Damodaran (2003), Fernandez (2015) and Lee et al. (2014) for examples of spreadsheet analysis regarding optimal capital structure.

[11] See, for example, A. Damodaran's note: http://people.stern.nyu.edu/adamodar/pdfiles/country/option.pdf.

13.3 Capital Structure Analysis

Facebook

Mark Zuckerberg and his Harvard roommates launched Facebook in 2004. Users can create a user profile, add other users as "friends," exchange messages, post status updates and photos, share videos and receive notifications when others update their profiles. Facebook had over 1.44 billion users in March 2015.[12] Facebook, Inc. held its initial public offering in February 2012 and began selling stock to the public three months later, reaching an original peak market capitalization of $104 billion. On July 13, 2015, Facebook became the fastest company on the Standard & Poor's 500 Index to reach a market cap of $250 billion.[13]

In June 2004, Facebook moved its headquarters to California. It received its first investment later that month from PayPal co-founder Peter Thiel.[14] In 2005, the company dropped "the" from its name after purchasing the domain name facebook.com for US$200,000. In May 2005, Accel partners invested $12.7 million in Facebook, and Jim Breyer added $1 million of his own money.[15] On October 24, 2007, Microsoft announced that it had purchased a 1.6% share of Facebook for $240 million, giving Facebook a total implied value of around $15 billion.[16] Microsoft's purchase included rights to place international advertisements on the social networking site. In October 2008, Facebook announced that it would set up its international headquarters in Dublin, Ireland.[17] Almost a year later, in September 2009, Facebook said that it had turned cash flow positive for the first time.[18]

[12] *"Facebook Reports First Quarter 2015 Results". April 22, 2015.* http://investor.fb.com/releasedetail.cfm?ReleaseID=908022. Retrieved January 23, 2016.

[13] Davis (July 13, 2015).

[14] "Why you should beware of Facebook". *The Age* (Melbourne). January 20, 2008. Retrieved January 23, 2016.

[15] Williams (October 1, 2007) and "Jim Breyer (via Accel Partners)". *CNBC*. May 22, 2012, http://www.cnbc.com/id/47387334. Retrieved January 23, 2016.

[16] *"Facebook and Microsoft Expand Strategic Alliance" (Press release). Microsoft. October 24, 2007.*

[17] *"Facebook to Establish International Headquarters in Dublin, Ireland" (Press release). Facebook. October 2, 2008.*

[18] *"Facebook 'cash flow positive,' signs 300 M users". CBC News (Toronto). September 16, 2009.*

Facebook filed its IPO documents with the Securities and Exchange Commission on February 1, 2012. The company applied for a $5 billion IPO, one of the biggest offerings in the history of technology. The IPO raised $16 billion, making it the third-largest in US history.[19] On May 22, 2012, the Yahoo! Finance website reported that Facebook's lead underwriters, Morgan Stanley, JP Morgan, and Goldman Sachs, cut their earnings forecasts for the company in the middle of the IPO process.[20]

On November 15, 2010, Facebook announced it had acquired the domain name fb.com from the American Farm Bureau Federation for an undisclosed amount. On January 11, 2011, the Farm Bureau disclosed $8.5 million in "domain sales income," making the acquisition of FB.com one of the ten highest domain sales in history.[21] Facebook has acquired more than 50 companies, including Instagram and WhatsApp. The acquisition of WhatsApp cost $19 billion: more than $40 per WhatsApp user. It also purchased the defunct company ConnectU in a court settlement and acquired intellectual property formerly held by rival Friendster. The majority of the companies acquired by Facebook are based in the United States; a large percentage of these companies are based in or around the San Francisco Bay Area. Facebook has also made investments in LuckyCal and Wildfire Interactive. Most of Facebook's acquisitions have been "talent acquisitions" and acquired products are often shut-down. Mr. Zuckerberg has stated: "…We have not once bought a company for the company. We buy companies to get excellent people… In order to have a really entrepreneurial culture one of the key things is to make sure we're recruiting the best people. One of the ways to do this is to focus on acquiring great companies with great founders."[22] The Instagram acquisition, announced on 2012-04-09, appears to be the first exception to this pattern.

[19] "Facebook Officially Files for $5 Billion IPO". KeyNoodle. February 1, 2012. Archived from the originalon October 18, 2013. Retrieved February 1, 2012; and Rusli and Eavis (May 17, 2012).

[20] Blodget (May 22, 2012).

[21] "FB.com acquired by Facebook". *NameMon News*. January 11, 2011.

[22] "Why Facebook buys startups". YouTube, https://www.youtube.com/watch?v=OlBDyItD0Ak.

Capital Structure

Facebook uses more equity financing than debt financing. Facebook changed its debt/assets ratio from 9.88% to 1.77% between 2011 and 2015 (see Tables 13.1 and 13.2). Facebook's cash flows and profits are so strong that they can finance the business with their retained earnings.

Trade-off theory states that capital structure is the result of a trade-off between the tax advantage of debt and the higher risk and bankruptcy costs resulting from debt financing. The spreadsheet analysis suggests that Facebook's optimal debt ratio was 30.0% in 2011 and 15% in 2015, which is higher than their actual debt/equity ratios those years.

Table 13.1 Results from Facebook Analysis 2011[23]

	Current Capital Structure	*Optimal Capital Structure*	*Change*
D/(D + E) Ratio	9.88%	30.00%	20.12%
Beta for the Stock	1.7	2.07	0.37
Cost of Equity	18.08%	21.45%	3.37%
Cost of Debt	2.30%	3.20%	0.90%
WACC	16.52%	15.98%	−0.55%
Firm Value (mln.)	31,565	32,643	1077
Value/share	26.34	27.34	1.00

Table 13.2 Results from Facebook Analysis 2015

	Current Capital Structure	*Optimal Capital Structure*	*Change*
D/(D + E) Ratio	1.77%	15.00%	13.23%
Beta for the Stock	0.93	1.038	0.11
Cost of Equity	11.09%	12.12%	1.03%
Cost of Debt	1.91%	2.80%	0.89%
WACC	10.92%	10.72%	−0.20%
Firm Value (mln.)	247,856	252,530	4673
Value/share	107.26	109.32	2.06

[23] See Damodaran (2003), Fernandez (2015) and Lee et al. (2014) for more details in methodology. Debt/equity ratios are measured in market values, WACC stands for cost of capital or weighted average cost of capital.

From the trade-off theory point of view, the low-debt ratio is hurting the company's profitability because it is underusing its debt tax shield. This situation is similar to a broader set of Internet companies (Lee et al., 2014). In recent years some companies have begun to realize that using tax shields can be beneficial. However, they usually use other ideas aside from the debt tax shield.[24]

The pecking-order theory implies that companies should use internal funds before using debt and equity and should use external debt before external equity. Facebook uses internal funds and equity but not much debt, which means that Facebook considered going for an IPO before debt, which contradicts the pecking-order theory. Second, this theory implies a negative correlation between debt and profitability, which is supported by Facebook's profitability and lack of debt. At the time of its IPO, Facebook had enough profits to keep its operation running but, rather than taking on more debt, it still decided to gather funds through equity. The latter will help create a market for firm shares including shares belonging to employees.

On one hand, the agency cost theory favors low debt implying a low bankruptcy cost and a high level of confidence for investors. This is consistent with Facebook's policies. On the other hand, the agency cost theory states that higher debt is good for a company because it can stimulate the manager to perform better. This part is not consistent with Facebook's case. In Facebook's case, the conflict between the shareholders and the managers is of little importance because the company is very profitable. In the long term, things may change. An important indicator of potential conflict between shareholders and managers is the fraction of shares owned by the managers. According to SEC filings, Mr. Zuckerberg, his co-founders, and his early investors control about 74% of the voting power through ownership of Class B stock, which gives them 10 votes per share. Shareholders who bought stock in the IPO were issued Class A stock, with just one vote per share. Zuckerberg personally controls about 55 percent of the voting power through his ownership of 422 million class B shares and voting agreements with other shareholders.[25]

[24] Darby III (May 15, 2007).

[25] Taylor (June 11, 2015).

At the same time the total number of shareholders is quite large. It appears that Facebook uses partial ownership in terms of involvement of employees in shareholdings as a tool to motivate personnel to perform efficiently instead of using external pressure by creditors. Although by issuing shares, Facebook might be sharing ownership with different groups of people, but it is avoiding the risk of letting the company be controlled by too few people. Womak (2012) mentioned that a part of the IPO proceeds would be used to cover taxes including a $3 billion bridge loan to fund taxes for employees who exercise restricted stock units.[26] The units can't be sold until about five months after the IPO.

A conflict between the creditors and shareholders is not likely to happen because Facebook has less concern for creditors' problems as it has less debt. According to the Facebook policy, the board of directors has an obligation to Monitor and Manage Potential Conflicts of Interest. The Board also ensures that there is no abuse of corporate assets or unlawful related party transactions. One of the reasons why Facebook wanted to go public rather than use debt could have been to avoid conflicts between the company and outsiders.

An equity issue can also be consistent with the spirit of their business model where members serve dual roles as both the suppliers and the consumers of content. This is similar to the crowdfunding idea that customer involvement provides incentives for them as suppliers. This can also be related to Facebook's overall corporate culture. The link between capital structure decisions and corporate culture looks like a promising area for future research, as mentioned in Chapter 6.

As the flexibility theory and life cycle theory propose, it is not beneficial for new firms to use debt financing; they rely more on equity to make their operations smooth at early stages of their existence, hence they are considered more flexible. Facebook's expansion and growth business approach requires a lot of funds. Their business model with a no-cost membership is based on a large number of customers, which creates a good environment for advertisement. Acquisitions are a big part of this strategy. The initial public offering in April of 2012 helped the company grow. Our calculations show that the value of flexibility is 0.86% of the asset's value, which is greater than the potential reduction in the cost of

[26] http://www.bloomberg.com/news/articles/2012-05-18/facebook-16-billion-ipo-seen-as-fuel-for-strategic-deals-tech.

Table 13.3 Results from United Analysis 2015

	Current Capital Structure	*Optimal Capital Structure*	*Change*
D/(D + E) Ratio	51.66%	45.00%	−6.66%
Beta for the Stock	0.79	0.707	−0.08
Cost of Equity	9.76%	8.97%	−0.78%
Cost of Debt	2.21%	1.91%	−0.30%
WACC	5.86%	5.79%	−0.07%
Firm Value (mln.)	45,329	45,810	481
Value/share	58.78	60.07	1.29

capital from moving to an optimal debt/equity ratio. This may explain why management does not want to increase the debt/equity ratio.

According to the life cycle theory of growing and mature firms, firms are more likely to have a higher leverage ratio, which results in low flexibility. It is the opposite in Facebook's case, as it does not use a lot of debt. The Debt/equity ratio for Facebook in 2012 was higher than it was in 2015.

The signaling theory states that from the investor's perspective, the market reaction of an issuance of debt is neutral and is negative of equity. In Facebook's case, the evidence is ambiguous. Negative reactions to equity issues were observed in April and May 2012 although the reasons for each might be different.

Market timing. The market timing hypothesis provides a good explanation for the timing of firms' IPOs. For example, nearly all companies issue equity through public offerings at opportune times, most notably during the "tech craze" or "dot-com bubble" of the late 1990s. One can see that firms underwent public offerings when the market recovered from the tech crash of 2000 or at other times when the management felt their stock was overvalued. Companies make stock repurchases at windows of opportunities when they believe their stock is undervalued. However, from a broader point of view, the market timing theory does not explain a firm's capital structure well besides the IPO decision (Table 13.3).

United Continental Holdings

As of 2016, United Continental Holdings, Inc. (UCH) is a publicly traded airline holding company headquartered in Chicago. UCH owns and operates United Airlines, Inc. The company is the successor of UAL Corporation, which agreed to change its name to United Continental Holdings in May 2010, when a merger agreement was reached between United Airlines and Continental Airlines. As a result of the merger, Continental shareholders received 1.05 shares of UAL stock for each Continental share, effectively meaning Continental was acquired by the UAL Corporation; at the time of closing, it was estimated that United shareholders owned 55% of the merged entity and Continental shareholders owned 45%.[27] Once completely combined, United became the world's largest airline, as measured by revenue passenger miles.[28]

UCH has major operations at Chicago–O'Hare, Denver, Guam, Houston–Intercontinental, Los Angeles, Newark (New Jersey), San Francisco, Tokyo–Narita, and Washington–Dulles. UCH's United Air Lines, Inc. controls several key air rights, including being one of only two American carriers authorized to serve Asia from Tokyo-Narita (the other being Delta Air Lines). Additionally, UCH's United is the largest US carrier to the People's Republic of China and maintains a large operation throughout Asia.

Both airlines took losses in the recession and expected the merger to generate savings of more than $1 billion a year.[29] Combined revenues were projected to be about $29 billion.[30] Unlike Facebook, revenues have not been significantly growing in UCH for the last 4 years. Employer-workers relationships are of significant importance.

Susan Carey (2012) describes the pilot strike at UCH in 2012.[31] Pilots at United Continental Holdings Inc. were frustrated that nearly two years of negotiations at the merged airline had failed to yield a joint contract, concluded a strike vote in July 2012 with 99% of the voters approving

[27] *"United Continental Holdings, Inc. - Investor Relations – News". Ir.unitedcontinentalholdings.com.*

[28] *"United, Continental create world's biggest airlin". The Sydney Morning Herald. May 4, 2010,* http://www.smh.com.au/business/world-business/united-and-continental-create-worlds-biggest-airline-20100503-u426.html. Retrieved January 23, 2016.

[29] *"United and Continental Airlines to merge". BBC News. May 3, 2010,* http://www.bbc.com/news/10095080. Retrieved January 23, 2016.

[30] *"United, Continental create world's biggest airline". The Sydney Morning Herald. May 4, 2010,* http://www.smh.com.au/business/world-business/united-and-continental-create-worlds-biggest-airline-20100503-u426.html. Retrieved January 23, 2016.

[31] Carey (July 17, 2012).

a plan to withdraw their services, if allowed by federal mediators. Pilots wanted raises and other improved terms, and insisted that the merger synergies United Continental sought could not be fully obtained without a joint pilot contract.

In 2014/2015 the situation improved significantly because of the low fuel oil/fuel prices. It is interesting that the company decided to use their good situation and excess cash on improving their financial situation rather than on aggressive expansion plans.[32] As a part of it, UHC seems content to spend most of its free cash flow on share buybacks. Given that it has the lowest market cap of the three big legacy carriers, this focus on buybacks may be wise. United plans to complete a $1 billion buyback program announced last year, and it recently announced a new $3 billion share repurchase authorization.

Capital Structure

United uses a much higher debt ratio than Facebook. In 2015 it was about 51% (see Table 10.3).

Trade-off theory based spreadsheet analysis suggests that United's optimal debt ratio was 45.0% in 2015, which is lower than what their actual debt ratio was that year. Unlike Facebook, UCH assets are mostly tangible, which helps explain why their debt ratio is higher.

The pecking-order theory implies that the company should use internal funds before using debt and equity and should use external debt before external equity. It seems that it is consistent with United's strategy since it does not issue new shares publicly and when the cash situation improves (for example 2015) UHC plans to buy its shares back. It is not clear, however, why shares were not purchased back using borrowing during the times when the cash flow was not as high as in 2015?! The answer can be provided by a spreadsheet analysis or trade-off theory since raising debt in bad times can be quite expensive.

On one hand, the agency cost of debt theory (asset substitution, debt overhang) favors keeping low debt. This is not consistent with United's policies. On the other hand, the agency cost theory states that higher debt is good for a company because it can stimulate the manager to perform

[32] Levine-Weinberg (October 13, 2015).

better. This part is consistent with the United case. Compared to Facebook, the conflict between the shareholders and managers has greater importance as the company is struggling financially and the insiders do not own as much equity as in Facebook's case (see Table 10.4). At the same time the total number of shareholders is quite large. A conflict between the creditors and shareholders is likely to happen because United is more concerned with the creditors as it has more debt (Table 13.4).

As the flexibility theory and life cycle theory propose it is more natural for UHC to use debt financing than it is for Facebook. UHC can be considered a mature business with a well-established reputation, principles, and traditions. Also, their expansion and growth plans are not comparable with those of Facebook. Our calculations show that the value of flexibility is 0.043% of the assets value, which is smaller than in the case of Facebook.

The signaling theory states that from the investors' perspective, the market reaction is neutral on the issuance of debt and negative on equity. It may also explain why UCH does not issue shares publicly.

The 2010 strike suggests that labur relationships are important. As we mentioned in Chapter 8, a higher debt level can improve a firm's bargaining position. It can also help negotiate for government support. A higher debt level can also signal a higher output in an oligiopolistic market as was discussed in Chapter 4.

UCH's production strategy can also play a part in explaining their capital structure decisions. Some young firms with a low cost-low quality approach may use low debt as mentioned in Chapter 7. For established firms, however, a high debt may signal a commitment to a larger output.

The following is a summary of our analysis. Facebook uses a low-debt/equity ratio. It is a profitable company and uses internal earnings and funds for most of its projects. It is only partly consistent with the POT since the company issued a large IPO and did not make a large loan or bonds issue. Also, the company does not use the debt tax shield

Table 13.4 Information UHC ownership

Equity	*United*
# of Institution Owners	549
% Owned by Institutions and Funds	86%
% Owned by Insiders and 5% Owners	6%

Source yahoofinance

prescribed by trade-off theory and spreadsheet analysis. Factors that may explain these patterns are need for flexibility, unique business model and corporate culture, and low degree of separation between ownership and management (debt is not needed as a discipline device).

UCH's capital structure seems to be more consistent with the major theories. The difference between the current debt/equity ratio and the optimal one prescribed by the spreadsheet analysis is relatively small. The company seems to benefit from the debt tax shield but does not extend debt unwisely. It follows the POT in that it primarily uses internal cash when available for capital spendings and debt secondarily, public issues of shares are not common. Other ideas can help explain capital structure. Separation between ownership and management is greater than in the case of Facebook so the role of debt, as a discipline device, is more important. There is a new idea that having debt as a commitment in bargaining with unions and the government is a reason for high debt. Some agency costs of debt, such as debt overhang and asset substitution, may be underestimated by management.

An additional idea is for both companies (especially UCH) to use international financing more efficiently. Corporations can raise international debt in different currencies. The currency differential does not just diversify risk, it helps lower interest rates because the international market is limitless. If a corporation conducts business in a foreign country and gets revenues in foreign currencies, then debt nominated in foreign currencies creates new opportunities. If earnings are hedged against the foreign currency's depreciation, then the company can profit when the foreign currency depreciates, as it reduces the real value of the debt.

References

Blodget, H. (2012, May 22). *Facebook Bankers Secretly Cut Facebook's Revenue Estimates in Middle of IPO Roadshow, Yahoo! Finance*. Yahoo!, Inc., http://finance.yahoo.com/blogs/daily-ticker/facebook-bankers-secretly-cut-facebook-revenue-estimates-middle-133648905.html

Carey, S. (2012, July 17). Pilots at United Continental Approve a Strike. *The Wall Street Journal*, http://www.wsj.com/articles/SB10001424052702303612804577533062188787068

Damodaran, A. (2003). *Corporate Finance: Theory and Practice*. Wiley Series in Finance.

Darby, J.B. III, (2007, May 15). International Tax Planning: Double Irish More than Doubles the Tax Saving, *Practical US/International Tax Strategies, 11*(9), http://www.gtlaw.com/portalresource/lookup/wosid/contentpilot-core-2301-5813/pdfCopy.name=/darby07g.pdf?view=attachment.

Davis, M. (2015, July 13). Facebook Close Sets Speed Record for $250 Billion Market Cap. *Bloomberg.com*, http://www.bloomberg.com/news/articles/2015-07-13/facebook-s-close-sets-speed-record-for-250-billion-market-value

Fernandez, P. (2015). *Optimal Capital Structure: Problems with the Harvard and Damodaran Approaches.* Available at SSRN: http://ssrn.com/abstract=270833

Kazeniac, A. (2009, February 9). Social Networks: Facebook Takes Over Top Spot, Twitter Climbs. *Blog.compete.com*, https://blog.compete.com/2009/02/09/facebook-myspace-twitter-social-network/

Khatik, S. K., & Singh, P. K. (2006). Capital Structure Analysis of the Fertiliser Industry: A Case Study of IFFCO and Indo Gulf Corporation Ltd., India. *International Journal of Financial Services Management*. 1. https://doi.org/10.1504/IJFSM.2006.009624.

Lee, Z., Liang, S., & Miglo, A. (2014). Capital Structure of Internet Companies: Case Study. *Journal of Internet Commerce, 13*(3–4), 253–281.

Levine-Weinberg, A. (2015, October 13). United Continental Stock Is Flying Higher on Strong Guidance. *The Motley Fool*, http://www.fool.com/investing/general/2015/10/13/united-continental-stock-is-flying-higher-on-stron.aspx

Lunden, I. (2013, December 30). 73% Of U.S. Adults Use Social Networks, Pinterest Passes Twitter In Popularity, Facebook Stays On Top. *TechCrunch*, http://techcrunch.com/2013/12/30/pew-social-networking/

Mertens, D. (1998). *Research Methods in Education and Psychology: Integrating Diversity with Quantitative & Qualitative Approaches*. Sage Publications.

Nowotarski, M. (2011, January 23). Don't Steal My Avatar! Challenges of Social Network Patents. *IP Watchdog*, http://www.ipwatchdog.com/2011/01/23/dont-steal-my-avatar-challenges-of-social-networking-patents/id=14531/

Rusli, E., & Eavis, P. (2012, May 17). Facebook Raises $16 Billion in I.P.O. *The New York Times*, http://dealbook.nytimes.com/2012/05/17/facebook-raises-16-billion-in-i-p-o/?_r=0.

Singleton, R., Straits, B., & Straits, M. (1993). *Approaches to Social Research*. Oxford University Press.

Stoner, G. & Holland, J. (2004). Chapter 3 - Using Case Studies in Finance Research. Editor(s): Christopher Humphrey, Bill Lee. *The Real Life Guide to Accounting Research*. Elsevier. 37–56. ISBN 9780080439723.

Tynan, D. (2007, June 30). As Applications Blossom, Facebook Is Open for Business. *Wired*. http://www.wired.com/2007/07/facebook-platform/

Williams, C. (2007, October 1). Facebook Wins Manx Battle for facebook.com. *The Register* (London). http://www.theregister.co.uk/2007/10/01/facebook_domain_dispute/

CHAPTER 14

Capital Structure Theory Applications in Non-traditional Areas

14.1 Signaling in Academic Partnerships

Scientific articles are either single-written or written by a team of researchers. In most cases a formal agreement between parties does not exist. However in the latter case the co-authors can usually fully enjoy all benefits of the published article and in the former case authors usually have some help from other academics (mentioned for example in a typically long list of acknowledgments that exists in many articles) but the benefits are quite different in this case.[1] The co-authorship resembles equity financing in a sense that the ownership (of an article) is split between different people and the single work has some common features with debt because the ownership of the article remains with one person. So can one apply some ideas from capital structure theory when considering a researcher's choice of for example whether to invite another academic as a co-author or to just ask for comments?!

[1] See, e.g., Lazebnik et al. (2023) for an analysis of co-authorships. Also see, e.g., Borry et al. (2006) for an analysis of trands in the number of co-authroships vs. single-written papers.

Supplementary Information The online version contains supplementary material available at https://doi.org/10.1007/978-3-031-85459-0_14.

A. Miglo, *Capital Structure in the Modern World*,
https://doi.org/10.1007/978-3-031-85459-0_14

Consider the following model. A researcher (R) has an idea of a new project/article. Before the project can start external help (e.g., from a reputable academic (A)) is required. The expected quality of the future article v (measured, e.g., by the number of expected citations; the impact on the likelihood of R's promotion at a university, etc.) after the project is completed is uncertain.[2] There are two types of researchers. Type l is characterized by the parameter v_l, type h has parameter v_h where $v_l < v_h$. By definition, h has a higher expected project quality. v is the researcher's private information while the public is aware of the distribution of v. Let μ be the proportion of type h researchers, $0 < \mu < 1$. R can get the required external help by asking A for comments (c) or asking him/her to be a co-author (e). A, who provided these comments expects that the author of the article will return the favor in the future by for example providing his own comments when needed. Suppose that the quality of the returned favor is proportional to v (a higher expected quality of articles implies a higher expected quality of future comments) i.e., it equals av where a is the coefficient of the value of comments related to articles, $a < 1$. In the case of co-authorship the article quality can increase as compared to the case when A just provides comments. So we assume that in the former case A can select the amount of hours I that he/she will dedicate to the project. Also assume that the final value of the article equals $V = v + xI$, i.e., it increases with the number of hours A spends to help R. Also under joint co-authorship, the benefits to R are smaller than the benefit in the case of single authorship (for example universities and journals often consider relative contribution of each researcher). For simplicity we assume that benefits to R equal to benefits to A in the case of joint co-authorship and equals $0.5V$. Further assume that R maximizes his expected payoff. Everybody is risk-neutral and the risk-free interest rate is zero. Note that risk neutrality implies that A contributes to the article as long as his/her expected earnings cover the costs.

[2] By the value we mean the value to its producers/authors. The social value is usually hard to determine since it may include some indefinite period of time benefits (think about Pythagoras theorem or smth).

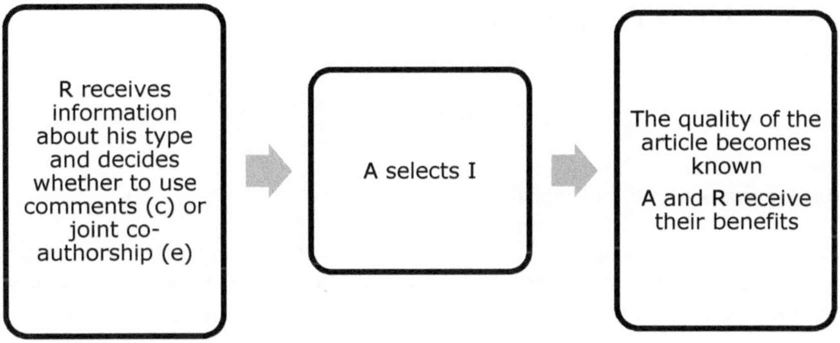

Fig. 14.1 The sequence of events

The sequence of events is illustrated in Fig. 14.1. We assume that the researcher receives information about his type in period 0.

Under strategy c, A would dedicate the amount of hours based on the following:

$$I = av \tag{14.1}$$

Under co-authorship the similar condition is $0.5(v + xI) = I$ or $I = \frac{0.5v}{1-0.5x}$. Further assume that returning a favor (future comments by academics) has a negligibly small cost for R at the moment R writes the article and is not taken into consideration by R when making his article strategy. Then under strategy e the payoff of R is $0.5\left(v + x\frac{0.5v}{1-0.5x}\right)$ and under c it is $v(1-a)$. So under symmetric information about v, the optimal strategy choice depends on the relative values of a and x. For example, if $x = 1$ then e is definitely better than c since the benefit under e equals v while the benefit under c is less than v. Alternatively if for example 1-a is greater than 0.5 and x is negligibly small, e.g., x = 0 then c is better. To see the role of asymmetric information, suppose that under symmetric information both payoffs are equal. Note that the payoff under co-authorship is more flat in v so intuitively co-authorship will be preferred (similar to intuitions discussed previously in the book regarding the choice between traditional debt and equity).

Proposition 14.1 *Suppose that: 1) the researcher's type is private information; 2)*

$$v(1-a) = 0.5\left(v + x\frac{0.5V}{1-0.5x}\right) \tag{14.2}$$

then comments is the optimal strategy.

Proof First a signaling equilibrium does not exist because the low-quality type of researcher will mimic the high-quality type. Consider pooling. Under pooling with comments, the high-quality researcher payoff is

$$v_h(1-a) \tag{14.3}$$

Under co-authorship the external academic budget constraint is: $0.5(\mu v_h + (1-\mu)v_l + xI) = I$ or

$$I = \frac{0.5(\mu v_h + (1-\mu)v_l)}{1-0.5x}$$

and the high-quality researcher payoff is

$$0.5(v_h + x\frac{0.5(\mu v_h + (1-\mu)v_l)}{1-0.5x}) \tag{14.4}$$

From (14.2) we have:

$$a = 1 - \frac{0.5}{1-0.5x}$$

The difference between (14.4) and (14.2) is $0.5\left(v_h + x\frac{0.5(\mu v_h+(1-\mu)v_l)}{1-0.5x}\right) - v_h\left(1 - \frac{0.5}{1-0.5x}\right) = \frac{0.25x((\mu v_h+(1-\mu)v_l - v_h)}{1-0.5x}$. This is negative because $v_l < v_h$.

So strategy c dominates e by the mispricing criterion we used in previous chapters. This may explain the puzzle mentioned previously of why some researchers prefer comments not co-authorship. Further research can incorporate other imperfections in the model similar to the ones used in capital structure theory including different types of moral hazards, life cycle ideas, incomplete contracts, behavioral finance, etc.

14.2 Capital Structure Theory and Government Finance

The theory of optimal financing for the government is more and more influenced by microeconomic theory. For example, the sovereign debt theory uses the reputation model or incomplete contract approach whereby the legal enforcement of debt is too costly, inefficient, or even impossible, and therefore the debtor must be self-interested in debt reimbursement.[3] However, other microeconomic foundations developed within the financial theory on the corporate level and in particular capital structure theory seem to not be used often at the governmental level.[4] During my PhD studies I started to work on a project that studies the similarities between money for government and equities for corporations (see Miglo, 2020). Also recently Bolton and Huang (2018) called the problem of government financing the capital structure of a nation. Indeed the three main sources of corporate financing are: internal funds, equity, and debt. The three main sources of financing for government expenditures are: taxes, seigniorage, and debt. Both government debt and corporate debt usually include a principal and interest where the latter is usually calculated using an interest rate. The inability to pay debt (either corporate or issued by a government) back usually leads to the borrower's default or bankruptcy. Both corporate internal funds and taxes collected by the government depend on the efficiency of the firm in the first case and that of the government in the second case. There are many similarities between shares issued by corporations and money printed by governments. For example, both money and corporate shares are residual claims whereas debt is not. Also note that the amount of outstanding shares as well as money in circulation depends on the issuer's decision (corporation for shares and government for money). Finally, the real value of shares depends on a firm's success and the real value of money depends on the efficiency of the economy.

Suppose that a government considers a public project and denotes the total expenditures for this project as G. The country's GDP after the project completion is Y. For simplicity assume that there is 1 product in

[3] See Cole and Kehoe (1998), Cole et al. (1995), Diamond (1989), and Eaton and Gersovitz (1981), among others.

[4] See Wedig et al. (1996) for similar ideas regarding the comparison of private and state enterprises financing.

the economy and denote its price by p. To finance the project the government can use debt D or it can issue money. Let ΔM be the nominal quantity of money issued (we also assume that initially the quantity of money in the economy is M_0 and government's debt is 0) and let e denote the real value of 1 unit of money in period 0. The government budget constraint is then:

$$D + \Delta M e = G \tag{14.5}$$

Let F be the face value of debt. The sequence of events is present in Fig. 14.2.

If $Y \geq F$ the debt is repaid in total. If $Y < F$, debtholders receive Y. Hence the debtholder's payoff is equal to

$$E_1 = \min\{Y, F\} \tag{14.6}$$

The real consumption in period 1 in

$$C = \max\{Y - F, 0\} \tag{14.7}$$

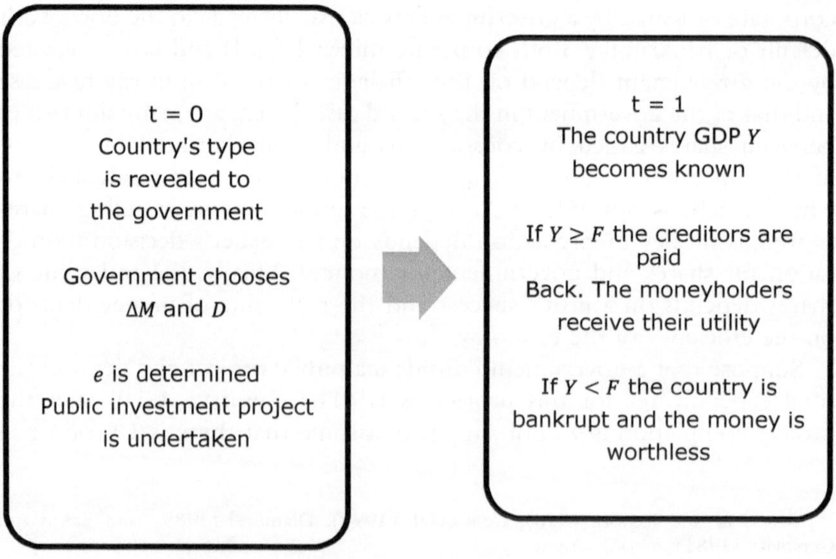

Fig. 14.2 The sequence of events

To purchase period 1 consumption the consumers use their nominal money stock $(M_0 + \Delta M)$. The consumers' budget constraint is:

$$M_0 + \Delta M \geq pC \tag{14.8}$$

where p is the price level. Since money is worthless after period 1 the constraint (14.8) is binding in equilibrium. Since the consumers are risk-neutral, the real value (in real consumption units) of one unit of money in period 1 (E_2) is equal to $\frac{1}{p}$ and Eqs. (14.7) and (14.8) imply that this equals

$$E_2 = \frac{1}{p} = \frac{C}{M_0 + \Delta M} = \frac{\max\{Y - F, 0\}}{M_0 + \Delta M} \tag{14.9}$$

These formulas are equivalent to the corporate capital structure case. Indeed consider a firm that looks for financing for an investment B, which produces a cash flow R. Denote the initial number of shares outstanding by N. In order to finance the project the firm may issue equity (let ΔN be the number of shares issued) or debt (D) with a face value D'. *As was discussed in Chapter 11 (see, e.g., Fig. 11.2), if a financial contract is debt (with face value D') then the contract holder's earnings are given by*

$$W_D = \min\{R, D\prime\} \tag{14.10}$$

Further *shares are securities with the following earnings:*

$$W_S = \frac{R'}{N'} \tag{14.11}$$

where R' means the firm's net profit (after repayment of debt if necessary) and $N' = N + \Delta N$ means the total number of shares after the issue. (14.10) and the following identity $\min\{R, D\prime\} + \max\{0, R - D'\} = R$ implies that (14.11) is equivalent to the following:

$$W_S = \frac{\max\{R - D\prime, 0\}}{N + \Delta N} \tag{14.12}$$

(14.6) and (14.9) are equivalent to (14.10) and (14.12). Money to governments is similar to what equity is to corporations, and the seigniorage-sovereign debt choice can be analyzed as the equity-debt choice at a corporate level. We can also see why in this economy people keep money. This is because in the case when real GDP (in real units) is high then prices are low and money holders can fully benefit from this deflation as compared to the debtholders' earnings, which are limited in real units by F.

Miglo (2020) further argues that the Ricardian equivalence is equivalent to Modigliani and Miller and that the trade-off theory can also be applied at the government level to some extent, etc. Recall from Chapter 2 that trade-off theory suggests that capital structure reflects a trade-off between the tax benefits of debt and the expected costs of bankruptcy. Expected bankruptcy costs depend on the probability of bankruptcy and the magnitude of bankruptcy costs. Similarly to the corporation, the probability of government default increases with the amount of debt. With regard to the magnitude of bankruptcy, costs note that on a corporate level they depend on such factors as the tangibility of a firm's assets, the industry in which a firm is operating (see, e.g., Branch, 2002), etc. Since most external government loans are not easily enforceable, direct costs of bankruptcy may represent costs associated with the actual settlement of bankruptcy procedures which, unlike the cases at the corporate level, may include political conflicts and perhaps even wars. Some researchers argue that excessive external debt leads to a higher risk of unrest and civil war (Goldmann, 2012). The concept of bankruptcy cost implies that countries with tangible assets (governments invested in industries with tangible assets) should borrow more. In general safer countries, countries with more political stability, etc., should borrow more. This is consistent with, for example, Aisen and Veiga (2011). Also countries with high military power like, for example, Russia (who have presumably high direct bankruptcy costs from the lenders' point of view) should borrow less. There is no direct implication of the tax idea for the government since governments do not pay taxes and government debt does not have any tax advantages. Indirectly, it may be related to the marginal costs and benefits of taxes in other forms. The decrease in the purchasing power of money after a money issue can be seen as an inflation tax (see, among others, Kiguel and Nuemyer (1989), Poterba and Rotemberg (1990)).

Further if asymmetric information exists (regarding for example Y in the above model) then the following results can be obtained similar to the pecking-order theory. First *debt dominates seigniorage*. This result is consistent with empirical evidence. For most countries seigniorage as a percentage of GDP is a relatively small ratio (see, e.g., Polański &

Szadkowski, 2020). Also similarly to the underpricing phenomenon after issuing shares (see Chapter 7) *seigniorage reduces the real value of money*. This result is also consistent with empirical evidence. For example, Haslaq (1998) states that a large body of empirical evidence suggests that the rate of money creation is closely correlated with inflation. Hence, faster money creation costs society by eroding the purchasing power of money already in circulation, which is the inflation tax. Good illustrations are well known historical examples of hyperinflation related to large volumes of printed money: European countries at the end of WWI and in the 1920s, Argentina in the 1980s, etc. Finally asymmetric information would imply a *pecking order of government finance*. Countries should use taxes as much as possible for financing and avoid external financing because tax collection is not subject to asymmetric information problems unlike borrowing or printing money. This seems to be consistent with the observation that taxes usually cover about 70–90% of government spending[5] (similarly at the corporate level internal funds cover about 60–70% of investments[6]), followed by debt and seigniorage. Miglo (2020) also discusses opportunities for other capital structure theories in the case of government capital structure.

14.3 Capital Structure and the Choice of Organizational Form

This section analyzes the simultaneous choice of capital structure and organizational form under asymmetric information. Many/all businesses face this choice yet not many articles address this problem. These two decisions are often closely connected (e.g., when a new firm creates a business plan and applies for a start-up loan or when a private firm decides to go public and make an IPO, etc.). In theory though, their analysis is usually done separately.

[5] If for example one compares average numbers about government expenditures as percentage of GDP (about 40%) and taxes to GDP ratio (about 34%). See, for example, https://www.oecd.org/content/dam/oecd/en/topics/policy-sub-issues/global-tax-revenues/revenue-statistics-canada.pdf and https://www.oecd-ilibrary.org/docserver/595b4d0b-en.pdf?expires=1733152893&id=id&accname=guest&checksum=9445FCF6C8DAA0118B4E5F0B338B9037.

[6] See, for example, Brealey et al. (2016).

Consider a firm with an investment idea/project. The project costs B and generates earnings X with probability p and 0 otherwise. The firm is owned by an entrepreneur. The value of the entrepreneur's personal assets is W. The risk-free interest rate is normalized to zero. The bank provides loans as long as the expected earnings cover their cost. Assume that each entrepreneur has 2 possible sources of financing (debt D and equity E, D + E = B) and also 2 possible organizational choices (limited liability L and unlimited liability U). So there are 4 possible strategies in terms of pairs capital structure/organizational form. Let a be the fraction of equity offered to investors (a = E/B). If U is selected, the project is not successful and the firm is bankrupt, the entrepreneur will be forced to sell his personal assets to cover the debt.

The entrepreneur's expected utility in case of L equals

$$W_L = (1 - a_L)p(X - F_L) \tag{14.13}$$

where F_L is the face value of debt for a firm with limited liability and a_L is the fraction of equity offered to investors under L.

Consider a firm with unlimited liability. The entrepreneur's profit if the project is undertaken equals the expected profit from the project minus the payment to the debtholders minus the loss of personal assets. We have

$$W_U = (1 - a_U)(p(X - F_U)) - (1 - p)\min\{W, F_U)) \tag{14.14}$$

where F_U is the face value of debt and a_U is the fraction of equity offered to investors under U. (14.14) means that if the project is successful (probability p) there is no personal assets loss and the entrepreneur's payoff is $(1 - a_U)(X - F_U))$. Otherwise the entrepreneur loses some of his personal assets (there are two cases depending on whether W exceed his debt or not as we discuss below).

If information about X is symmetric and there are no moral hazard problems and other imperfections, e.g., taxes, etc., then the choice is irrelevant (similar to Modigliani–Miller proposition). Indeed in this case $F_L = D/p$ and $a_L = \frac{B-D}{pX-B}$. Then (14.13) implies $W_L = pX - B$. Under U there are two cases. First if $W \geq B$ then the entrepreneur's expected utility equals $W_U = pX - B$ as implied by (14.14).[7] Indeed since the entrepreneur's wealth is large enough, debt is risk-free for lenders in

[7] Technically as discussed in Miglo (2023) there are several cases depending on the degree of symmetry between different equityholders regarding their personal assets. For

the case of unlimited liability. This means that the face value of debt equals $F_U = B$, where F_U is the face value of debt for a firm with unlimited liability and also $a_U = \frac{B-D}{pX-B}$. The second case is $W < B$. In this case $F_U = (D-(1-p)W)/p$ and $a_U = \frac{B-D}{pX-B}$. Then (14.14) implies $W_U = pX - B$. So under any strategy the entrepreneur's payoff is $pX - B$. Now suppose that information about X is asymmetric. A possible result is that for example if $W > B$, the optimal strategy is unlimited liability with debt since it completely mitigates the asymmetric information problem (in the spirit of Bester, 1987). Indeed in this case $F_U = B$ and the entrepreneur's profit is $pX - B$. Miglo (2023) and Miglo and Brodziak (2019) analyze different imperfections and the optimal pairings of capital structure and organizational form. Among related research note the following. Horvath and Woywode (2005) analyze an entrepreneur's choice between a limited liability firm and an unlimited liability firm when debt financing is used. They argue that the benefit of limited liability appears as a concave function of investment volume and the investors' wealth. Guinnane and Schneebacher (2020) focus on historical aspects of the organizational form choice problem.

14.4 Capital Structure and the Choice of Optimal Taxes and Bankruptcy System

In this section we discuss the optimal capital structure when the tax rate is endogenized and when some other factors that are usually considered given in traditional capital structure models are also endogenized. This contributes to explaining the corporate tax rate as well as to generate capital structure predictions.

Consider a model where the government selects the corporate tax rate. The government faces an infinite number of identical firms. A firm can be described as follows. It has an investment project that costs B and generates earnings X with probability p and 0 otherwise. The firm faces a constant tax rate t on its corporate income. If the earnings are insufficient to cover the promised debt payment, D, (for simplicity D represents interests only and the principal is equal to 0) there is a deadweight loss

simplicity we assume that W > B means that the joint personal assets of all equity holders exceed F and also that they share all benefits and losses proportionally to their fractions of equity.

of $cD^2/2$ that is used up in the process. This loss can include direct bankruptcy costs such as fees paid to lawyers and indirect bankruptcy costs such as losses due to a general lack of confidence in the firm. If earnings are large, equityholders receive $(R - D) * (1 - t)$. Otherwise, they receive nothing. Also the project has a positive NPV, i.e.,

$$pX > B \tag{14.15}$$

The government first selects t. After observing t, the firm makes its capital structure decision. The government is interested in maximizing the firm expected output (profit) W.[8] We solve the model backward. First consider the firm capital structure choice for a given t. The firm's value V equals

$$V = (1 - e)\left(p(X - F)(1 - t) - (1 - p)cD^2/2\right)$$

where e is the fraction of the firm sold to new equityholders. Also $F = D/p$. Also we assume that the bankruptcy costs are borne by equityholders. Further, the new equityholders constraint is $e\left(p(X - F)(1 - t) - (1 - p)cD^2/2\right) = E$. So

$$V = p(X - D/p)(1 - t) - (1 - p)cD^2/2) - B + D$$

Optimal debt is:

$$D = \frac{t}{(1 - p)c} \tag{14.16}$$

Now consider the government choice of t.

$$G = p\left(X - \frac{D}{p}\right)(1 - t) - (1 - p)cD^2/2) - B + D$$

[8] One can extend the model by making different assumptions about the government objective function, e.g., by assuming that it is a weighted sum of W and the amount of collected taxes or that the government objective is to maximize W under condition that net taxes are greater than some minimal amount, etc. If the former is the case and if the weight of W in the objective function is high enough then qualitatively the solution should not be significantly different.

Or taking into account (14.16):

$$G = p\left(X - \frac{t}{c(1-p)p}\right)(1-t) - (1-p)c\left(\frac{t}{(1-p)c}\right)^2/2 - B + \frac{t}{(1-p)c}$$

Then dG/dt = = $-pX + \frac{t}{(1-p)c}$. If $\frac{t}{(1-p)c} < B$ (that can be the case when B or c are sufficiently large for example) this is negative because of (14.15) and (14.16).

So optimal $\boldsymbol{t} = 0$ and optimal $\boldsymbol{D}$ for the firm is $\boldsymbol{D} = 0$. Several points are behind these ideas. First note that one line of research is connected to the inclusion of personal taxes in traditional models and respectively using the term effective tax rate advantage of debt rather than the traditional corporate tax rate.[9] In this line it is usually argued that financing with debt may bear some tax-related costs for shareholders compared to financing with equity that may have some tax advantages, e.g., capital gain taxation with lower tax rates, etc. Some papers argue that the real effective debt tax rate is often relatively small in practice (nearly zero) (see, e.g., Blouin et al., 2010).[10] This observation became even more relevant in recent years in, e.g., the United States where the corporate tax rate was significantly reduced in 2017 (see, e.g., Auerbach, 2018) mitigating the tax advantage of debt even further. Among related papers note Chen and Frank (2022). In this paper the firm can optimally select the number of shares issued. The paper analyzes the effect of taxes (both corporate and personal) on firm production decisions. Other related literature includes debate about the corporate income tax. Traditional "folk" opinion is that the corporate tax is the price corporations pay for the right of limited liability (Meade, 1978). However, the quantitative determination of these benefits is a different issue. Musgrave and Musgrave (1980) and Rosen (2004) noticed that it is hard to link the real amount of benefits corporations receive from limited liability and the magnitude of corporate taxation. A quantitative determination of the optimal tax should

[9] See, e.g., Graham (2013).

[10] See also Hennessy and Chemla (2022) regarding difficulties in estimating the effect of changes in different parameters including tax rate on optimal levels of debt in existing literature taking into account differences in approaches from an econometrician and from a CFO point of view

then quantify the shareholders' advantage of limited liability, which in turn depends on other benefits and costs that shareholders of corporations face. A part of these costs are costs endured during bankruptcy. So when quantifying benefits of the corporate tax it is logical to balance them against potential bankruptcy costs.

So far we have been discussing the endogenity of tax rates in the trade-off model of capital structure. Similarly one can also endogenize bankruptcy system (i.e., allow the government to select a bankruptcy system), which may affect the magnitude of bankruptcy costs. There has been literature comparing the efficiency of different bankruptcy rules but the discussion is far from over as countries are still having radical bankruptcy reforms, i.e., the Dodd–Frank Act in the United States in 2011 and the European reform in 2019, the reform in Italy in 2005 (Aghion et al., 1994; Cornelli & Felli, 1997; Davydenko & Franks, 2008; McGowan and Andrews, 2016). Further one can simultaneously consider the optimal choice of corporate tax rate and bankruptcy system. Indeed an uncoordinated choice of bankruptcy system and corporate tax rate can lead to extreme capital structure biases by businesses such as extremely high or extremely low debt for example. Even if the extreme capital structure choice is not the case, the government might want to benefit from providing incentives to firms to select investment and capital structure policy that will maximize the government objective function.

Among related papers note Acharya et al. (2011) that investigates the impact of bankruptcy codes on firms' capital structure choices in the presence of corporate taxes. It develops a theoretical model to identify how firm characteristics may interact with the bankruptcy code in determining optimal capital structures. The authors argue that the difference in leverage choices under a relatively equity-friendly bankruptcy code (such as the United States') and one that is relatively more debt-friendly (such as the United Kingdom's) should be a decreasing function of the anticipated liquidation value of the firm's assets.[11]

[11] See also Krasa et al. (2008) and Blazy et al. (2013).

Questions and Exercises

1. Consider the model from Sect. 14.1 assuming that the benefits to R and A from co-authoring an article are equal to V and not 0.5 V as in the text. Find the optimal strategy under symmetric information about v.
2. Consider the model from Sect. 14.4 assuming that a = 0.5.

References

Acharya, V. V., Sundaram, R. K., & John, K. (2011). Cross-country Variations in capital Structures: The Role of Bankruptcy Codes. *Journal of Financial Intermediation, 20*(1), 25–54.

Aghion, P., Hart, O., & Moore, J. (1994). The Economics of Bankruptcy Reform Book: The Transition in Eastern Europe. In O. Blanchard & K. Froot & J. Sachs (eds.), *Restructuring* (Vol. 2, pp. 215–244). University of Chicago Press.

Aisen, A., & Veiga, F. (2011). *How Does Political Instability Affect Economic Growth?* (IMF Working Paper).

Auerbach, A. J. (2018). Measuring the Effects of Corporate Tax Cuts. *Journal of Economic Perspectives, 32*(4), 97–120.

Bester, H. (1987). The Role of Collateral in Credit Markets with Imperfect Information. *European Economic Review, 31*(4), 887–899.

Blazy, R., Deffains, B., Umbhauer, G., & Weill, L. (2013). Severe or Gentle Bankruptcy Law: Which Impact on Investing and Financing Decisions? *Economic Modelling, 34*, 129–144.

Bolton, P., & Huang, H. (2018). The Capital Structure of Nations. *Review of Finance, 22*(1), 45–82.

Borry, P., Schotsmans, P., & Dierickx, K. (2006). Author, Contributor or Just a Signer? A Quantitative Analysis of Authorship Trends in the Field of Bioethics. *Bioethics, 20*, 213–220.

Branch, B. (2002). The Costs of Bankruptcy: A Review. *International Review of Financial Analysis, 11*(1), 39–57.

Brealey, R., Myers, S., & Allen, F. (2016) *Principles of Corporate Finance.* McGraw-Hill

Blouin, J., Core, J. E., & Guay, W. (2010). Have the Tax Benefits of Debt Been Overestimated? *Journal of Financial Economics, 98*(2), 195–213.

Chen, H., & Frank, M. (2022). The Effect of Taxation on Corporate Financing and Investment. *The Review of Corporate Finance Studies, 11*(1), 47–87.

Cole, H., Dow, J., & English, W. (1995). Default, Settlement and signalling: Lending Resumption in a Reputational Model of Sovereign Debt. *International Economic Review, 36*, 365–385.

Cole, H., & Kehoe, P. (1998). Model of Sovereign Debt: Partial versus General Reputations. *International Economic Review, 39*, 55–70.

Cornelli, F., & Felli, L. (1997). Ex-ante Efficiency of Bankruptcy Procedures. *European Economic Review, 41*(3–5), 475–485.

Davydenko, S., & Franks, J. (2008). Do Bankruptcy Codes Matter? A Study of Defaults in France, Germany, and the U.K. *Journal of Finance, 63*(2), 565–608.

Diamond, D. (1989). Reputation Acquisition in Debt Markets. *Journal of Political Economy, 97*, 828–862.

Eaton, J., & Gersovitz, M. (1981). Debt with Potential Repudiation: Theoretical and Empirical Analysis. *The Review of Economic Studies, 48*(2), 289–309.

Goldmann, M. (2012). Sovereign Debt Crises as Threats to the Peace: Restructuring Under Chapter VII of the UN Charter? *Goettingen Journal of International Law, 4*, 153–175.

Graham, J. R. (2013). Do taxes Affect Corporate Decisions? A Review. *Handbook of the Economics of Finance SET* (Vols. 2A & 2B, p. 123). Corporate Finance and Asset Pricing.

Guinnane, T. W., & Schneebacher, J. (2020). Enterprise form: Theory and History. *Explorations in Economic History, 76*(C).

Haslag, J. (1998). Seigniorage Revenue and Monetary Policy: Some Preliminary Evidence. *Economic and Financial Policy Review, Federal Reserve Bank of Dallas, Q, III*, 10–20.

Hennessy, C. A., & Chemla, G. (2022). Signaling, Instrumentation, and CFO Decision-Making. *Journal of Financial Economics, 144*(3), 849–863.

Horvath, M. T. K., & Woywode, M. J. (2005). Entrepreneurs and the Choice of Limited Liability. *Journal of Institutional Theoretical Economics, 161*, 681–707.

Kiguel, M., & Neumeyer, P. (1989). *Inflation and seigniorage in Argentina* (Policy Research Working Paper Series No. 289). The World Bank.

Krasa, S., Sharma, T., & Villamil, A. P. (2008). Bankruptcy and Firm Finance. *Economic Theory, 36*(2), 239–266.

Kraus, A., & Litzenberger, R. H. (1973). A State-preference Model of Optimal Financial Leverage. *Journal of Finance, 28*, 911–922.

Lazebnik, T., Beck, S., & Shami, L. (2023). Academic co-authorship is a Risky Game. *Scientometrics, 128*, 6495–6507.

McGowan, M.A., & Andrews, D. (2016). *Insolvency Regimes And Productivity Growth: A Framework For Analysis* (OECD Economics Department Working Papers, No. 1309). OECD Publishing. https://doi.org/10.1787/5jlv2jqhxgq6-en

Meade, J. E. (1978). *The Structure and Reform of Direct Taxation, Report of a Committee* chaired by Professor J. E. Meade. George Allen & Unwin.

Miglo, A. (2020). Pecking-Order Theory for Government Finance. *Current Politics and Economics of the United States, Canada, and Mexico, 22*(1), 1–37.

Miglo, A. (2023). *Simultaneous Choice of Organizational Form and Capital Structure*. Available at SSRN: https://ssrn.com/abstract=4671120

Miglo, A., & Brodziak, M. (2019). *Taxes, Debt, Investments and the Choice of Business Form with Overconfident and Pessimistic Entrepreneurs*. Available at SSRN: https://ssrn.com/abstract=3408732

Musgrave, R., Musgrave, P. (1980). *Public Finance in Theory and Practice*. McGraw-Tokyo.

Polański, Z., & Szadkowski, M. (2020). *Seigniorage and Central Banks' Financial Results in Times of Unconventional Monetary Policy* (NBP Working Papers 331). Narodowy Bank Polski.

Poterba, J., & Rotemberg, J. (1990). Inflation and Taxation with Optimizing Governments. *Journal of Money, Credit and Banking, 22*(1), 1–18.

Rosen, H. (2004). *Public Finance* (7th ed.). McGraw-Hill/.

Wedig, G., Hassan, M., & Morrisey, M. (1996). Tax-Exempt Debt and the Capital Structure of Nonprofit Organisations: An Application to Hospitals. *The Journal of Finance, LI, 4*, 1247–1283.

CHAPTER 15

Ending Thoughts

The first part of this book focused on the major theories of capital structure: trade-off theory, pecking-order theory, asset substitution, credit rationing, debt overhang, the role of behavioral finance, and incomplete contracts in capital structure theory. According to most empirical research, none of these theories are able to fully explain real-life decisions made by companies. However, in most research related to capital structure, these basic ideas are used either as reference points or intermediate tools that help develop further ideas. The future of capital structure theory is still uncertain in my opinion. Will any theory(ies) emerge as a clear "winner" (in terms of its ability to explain the reality) or will they all combine into one "big" theory? Will any of these basic ideas be completely forgotten because the market imperfections used as a basis will no longer be relevant in practice, or because empirical research consistently rejects the results of a theory? In my opinion all of these possibilities are still on the table. It seems that unlike other areas of finance, researchers of capital structure are still far from bridging the gap between its theory and practical reality. Grahan and Harvey (2001) is a good reference point.

Part 2 discussed different topics of capital structure. As was mentioned earlier, the objective of the book was not to cover as many topics of capital structure as possible but rather to review the major theoretical concepts and provide basic tools to understand the complicated area of capital

A. Miglo, *Capital Structure in the Modern World*,
https://doi.org/10.1007/978-3-031-85459-0_15

structure. Many advanced theories of capital structure discussed in this book are still growing areas of research. I think that some areas are very promising including the links between capital structure and corporate/ national culture, dynamic versions of trade-off theory and pecking-order or signaling theories, interactions between capital structure choices and bargaining strategies (with unions, suppliers, or governments), capital structure of small and start-up companies, links between capital structure choices and market timing, theoretical foundations of flexibility, life cycle ideas of capital structure, and capital structure management of financial institutions and its role in preventing financial crises. One of the most prominent lines of research is related to the development of FinTech and the aspects of capital structure management related to it. In the last 10–15 years new ways of financing have been created which are neither traditional debt nor equity, e.g., crowdfunding or token issues in particular reward-based crowdfunding and utility tokens (ICO), non-fungible tokens, etc.

Educators should spend more time teaching capital structure given that the topic has seen tremendous growth in recent years. Students are very excited when they hear the word entrepreneurial finance (young talent plus money combination!) and are very excited about such professions like investment banker and corporate treasurer. All of it is directly related to capital structure knowledge. But not only are they excited. I have noticed that in recent years students have stopped being afraid of capital structure topics and courses and have begun to speak professionally, and with interest, about capital structure-related topics! So I think that new courses specifically dedicated to capital structure theory and management and new programs preparing specialists in the area of capital structure analysis and management could be created at universities. Another reason for the existence of the large gap between the theory and practice of capital structure is that educators focus mostly on the positive aspects of the theory and its applications and not on its normative aspects. As a result, students may be aware of existing models but are not able to apply them in real life when they become managers. I feel that this is especially true for asymmetric information and agency cost theories, which are without a doubt the most technically complicated. Educators need to find a way to explain the practical applications of these theories.

Finally I am personally a big fan of further integration of universities and the financial sector. Practitioners should be given the opportunity to teach more courses and professors should allocate more time to practical work. Nobel Prize winner Josef Stiglitz is a good example. Theories have become more and more complicated so if the gap between theory and practice is not being constantly reduced, severe consequences will follow. The challenges of this approach are to find practitioners who have deep theoretical knowledge or to find professors who are able to work in managerial positions. Both combinations are pretty rare from my experience. Where we stand now, it is hard to imagine that in the near future a large volume of (constantly growing exponentially) complicated mathematical research will be able to seriously penetrate into the practical sector with satisfactory speed and intensity.

My book is intended primarily for those who feel very excited about the financial sector both theoretically and practically. I tried to make most of my points in a theoretically rigorous fashion and bridge the deep theoretical concepts with the practical examples and cases. If you my dear reader feel this way I will be very satisfied. And good luck with your exciting journey in the world of finance and capital structure!

Index

A. Miglo, *Capital Structure in the Modern World*,
https://doi.org/10.1007/978-3-031-85459-0